The Lights of El Milagro

The Lights of El Milagro

Kevin W. Riley, Ed.D.

2008

The Lights of El Milagro

ACKNOWLEDGEMENTS   xiii

INTRODUCTION   xv

• *El Milagro* • *Mexican Gas* • *Boston Tea Party* • *The Graduate*
• *Gunpowder* • *Post Cards* • *Wings*

PART I: MUELLER'S REVOLT   I

CHAPTER ONE: **Catching in a Crowd**   3

• *Tattoos* • *Catching in a Crowd* • *OMBAC* • *Giving 'em the Pilgrims*
• *The Pilot* • *Serra's Otters* • *Crips and Bloods* • *Eagle's Nest*
• *No Brakes* • *Pirates* • *Buffalo Soldiers* • *A Rat in the Stalls*
• *Monarch* • *Golden Bell* • *Icarus* • *Busters*

CHAPTER TWO: **Our Children Will Change the
World...Or They Won't**   29

• *Firestorm* • *Disneyland* • *Equalizer* • *Satellites* • *Houston*
• *Forgiveness* • *First Teacher* • *Long Shadows* • *Academies*
• *Michelangelo* • *A Child Named Oprah* • *Bull's-Eye*

CHAPTER THREE: **The Covenant**   49

• *The Launch* • *The Franchise* • *Vouchers* • *Shanker*
• *Number 64* • *Nuclear Fire* • *Road Map* • *Speed of Light*
• *Philadelphia* • *Libi Gil* • *Orchard* • *Call the Question*
• *Imagine They Blossom*

CHAPTER FOUR: **A Blinding Fog**   75

• *The Road without You* • *Union World View* • *Migden*
• *A Premonition* • *No Fear* • *Wild West* • *Fog* • *"Stay above It"*
• *Teamster Goons* • *The Judge from Sacramento* • *Jackson Parham*

• *Toxic Mess* • *Simple Math* • *Seventeen Months* • *Huevos*
• *The Conference Call* • *A Few Clarifying Questions*
• *Hopper's Letter* • *Hey Idiots* • *Capoeira*

CHAPTER FIVE: **The Whispers of Heretics**   103

• *Revolution* • *Change 101* • *Jennifer's Project*
• *Advanced Change 301* • *Layers* • *La Jardin de Paz*

CHAPTER SIX: **We Are Our Wheels**   123

• *Wheels* • *Systems*

PART II: **THE SEVEN SYSTEMS**   127

CHAPTER SEVEN: **The Mission Light**   129

• *Monsoon* • *Knowing Your Stuff* • *Ozzie & Harriet* • *Vertigo*
• *Quinceañera* • *Fresh Paint* • *Skyline* • *Frogs* • *Ninjas*
• *Moving Day* • *No Doubt* • *Tijuana Lights* • *Long Shot*
• *Overnight* • *The Prize*

CHAPTER EIGHT: **Rainmakers**   155

• *Exodus* • *Forty Teachers* • *Skeptics* • *Job Fair*
• *Bus Tokens* • *The Gift of Commitment*
• *How Warriors Pray* • *Leaking Boats* • *The Gift of Talent*
• *Toros* • *Bend It* • *Wizard* • *The Gift of Innovation*
• *The Gift of Collaboration* • *Apollo 13*
• *The Gift of Intrinsic Motivation*
• *Corporate Tillman* • *Evaluations* • *El Patio* • *Tejano*
• *The Gift of Resiliency* • *The Gift of Compassion*
• *A Love Poem for My Students* • *Amen*

CHAPTER NINE: **Dancing With Our Own Shadows**   183

• *Gettysburg* • *A Golden Era* • *Calling the Shots* • *The Real Power*
• *Six Committees* • *The Council* • *Lessons from Jefe*
• *Sword from Stone*

CHAPTER TEN: **The Gospel**   205

• *The Pyramids* • *True North* • *The Base* • *Opening Day*
• *Feng Shui* • *Teacher Leaders* • *Pedagogy* • *Freeze Dried*
• *Too Many Standards* • *Challenger* • *Black Belt*
• *Breaking Bread* • *Yogi on Homework* • *The Game*

CHAPTER ELEVEN: **How We Know We're Winning**   231

• *Williamsport* • *Bass Ackwards* • *The Hall* • *Kaizen*
• *Texas Dust* • *Bench Press* • *Bootstraps*
• *The Law of Unintended Consequences* • *Voodoo* • *New Tools*
• *Blue Binders* • *Hunter S. Thompson* • *MAPS*
• *NFL Geeks* • *Little Eyes* • *Shake on It* • *Finish Line*
• *Every Day in America* • *Head Cold* • *Maps to the Holy Grail*

CHAPTER TWELVE: **Hope for Cristina**   275

• *Cristina* • *The Four Horsemen* • *Cristina's Gift*
• *The Quadrant System* • *Santos, Santos* • *Children Rising*
• *Bendiciones*

CHAPTER THIRTEEN: **La Casa de Leon**   297

• *Victoria De Leon* • *La Paz* • *Nopales* • *USC* • *Store Bought*
• *Monday Morning* • *3,000 Photographs* • *Chorizo*
• *Ride Along* • *The Lion*

CHAPTER FOURTEEN: **The Soul of El Milagro**   319

• *The Center* • *Stonehenge* • *Moroni* • *Harmony*
• *The Grand Old Opry* • *Puerto Nuevo*

EPILOGUE   329

• *Guacamole*

ABOUT THE AUTHOR   331

"The future which we hold in trust for our own children will be shaped by our fairness to other people's children."
—Marian Wright Edelman

Acknowledgements

We write by our own lights. That's all I know.

And so I wish to thank the morning when the last stubborn pocket of darkness gives way to dawn. I wish to thank the sunrise over the desert too. And that moment when the sun drops off the flat edge of the ocean horizon and everyone stops on the boardwalk at South Mission to watch. Like fireworks. And we swear we can see a green flash.

I wish to thank the sliver of light that comes from stars; the wild white albedo of our reflective moon; and the promise that comes to us from deep space—that every beam of light is proof of a mighty God.

And I wish to thank my lights:

Anne, Kira and Keenan—thank you for inspiring me to complete what I had started. That's who we are together. We demand excellence, but lovingly abide the slow evolution of whatever genius that guides us. I hope this book will inspire you too.

Mom and Dad—wherever you are now in the incomprehensible vastness of a place we call heaven...thank you for every sacrifice you made so that I might one day be a light to others.

Patrick and Michael...we inspire each other in the strangest ways. Fight the darkness.

Kilty. Endless walks. No need for words.

Sal and Verlyn whose gentle encouragement kept this project alive. "When is your book going to be done? Well keep it going. Tell your story."

Rich Walker...you encouraged me to seek clarity: "Your book isn't just about a charter school. It is about a revolution! That's what gets my attention."

Jackson Parham, Maureen Deluca, Don and Joyce Mizock, Tim Evatt, Dennis Doyle, Gail Cato and Jane Flaherty: thank you for the time you each took to read sections of this work and to provide constructive criticism.

Thank you Libi Gil and Lowell Billings and the Governing Board of the Chula Vista Elementary School District—Pamela Smith, Patrick Judd, Bertha Lopez, Larry Cunningham, David Bejarano and now-Mayor Cheryl Cox. You consistently ask the two most important questions that district leaders can ask their charters: "Are you really doing everything that your charter autonomy—and the charter law—allows you to do for our students?" and "How can we support you in growing your school?" Were it not for your courageous leadership, neither this book nor El Milagro would exist.

To the Wizard, Ryan Santos, Ivonne Adrianzen-Watson and Conchita Yescas. You have challenged me and demanded that, above all, I lead with conviction, fairness, and creativity.

To the teachers of Mueller Charter School, who have paid for every innovation, every success, every quantitative gain in student achievement with their own sweat and tears and late-night, silent prayers. Sometimes your star shines so brightly, it feels as though greatness is pre-ordained. This book is a celebration of your collective energy.

Our teachers: Melinda Jones • Jenise Karcher • Kari Lohse • Karen and Jack Quinlan • Stacy Orenstein • Judith Estrada • Blanca Stingl-Hernandez • Julie Urda • Luisa Dasis • Michelle Saflar • Nancy Raffaele • Michele Albin • Sol Gonzalez • John Knox • Armando Vidales • Katie Fiske • Nicole Thomas • Cindy Estrada • Carolyn Ortiz • Graciela Lopez • Sandra Torre • Johanna Wagner • Nancy Holmes • Jami Troyer • Carolina Dumas • Carissa Page • Georgianne Rivera • Joel Michel • Gina Bebe-Lybarger • Susanne Sherk • Aimee Cisneros • Omar Burruel • Ricky Medina • Aimee Velazquez • Gina Drew • Heather Naddour • Gretchen Donais • Dawn Wold • Tanya Olivas • Claudia Urdanivea • Tony Arias • Myra Jimenez • Marisol Robledo • Mandie Lopez • Francisco Hermosillo • Jesus Gonzalez • Cindy Hu • Monica Carr • and Bertha Cortes-Gonzalez.

And Eva, Maria, Diana, Olga, George, Brian and Jose. And all of our support staff and aides and amazing charter helpers. Muchisimas gracias por todo.

I wish to thank the others that have passed our way and in their time, made us better too. They are like shadows now. Ghosts. Greg Valero, Jennifer Cook, Angelica Galaviz, Molly Shea, Linda Ramirez, Laurie Davies, Merle Daniels, Ken Collard, Ron and Maje, Patti Collins, Frank DeLuca, Irma Mudge. And there are many more.

And finally—I wish to thank the children of Mueller Charter School who have made each one of us a better educator and thus a better human being. And that is the power of their light. The rest is owed to El Milagro.

Introduction

A revolution is coming—a revolution which will be peaceful if we are wise enough; compassionate if we care enough; successful if we are fortunate enough...

—*John F. Kennedy*

EL MILAGRO

If I had my way, I would change the name of Robert L. Mueller Charter School to "El Milagro."

Since 90% of our students are Latino, Robert L. Mueller is not a name that resonates with them anyway. I have no idea what the "L" stands for, but I'm sure it would not bring any clarity to Mr. Mueller. At least not for our kids.

All I know is that Robert L. Mueller was a board member in Chula Vista, California, about fifty years ago. He wanted to build schools in this sleepy Southern California community back when it was tomato fields and dust and had an unobstructed view of the Pacific Ocean. Mueller lobbied for good schools and so, as an unsolicited reward, they named one after him. I once saw him in one of those brittle, sepia-toned, city hall photographs. He is a dead ringer for...well, Colonel Sanders. And though our students may enjoy KFC on the weekend, it is truly the only possible relevance they could find in our school name.

But then again, after fifty years of sixth-grade graduates, changing the school name to El Milagro is not a battle worth fighting. Not that we are afraid to fight. It is something we are good at. But we are also good at picking our battles.

So we go on as Robert L. Mueller Somebody Charter School.

But make no mistake about it. We are El Milagro: *The Miracle*. And we have plenty to teach.

We are not a 90-90-90 school. Not even close. We are not a blue ribbon school...a nationally distinguished school, a first prize school, a fly-the-banner school, a *select* school, a No Child Left Behind school, or a Governor's Choice School. According to the state test results, we are not even the highest-performing school in our own modestly performing school district.

We are El Milagro—not because of the false confidence engendered from our steadily climbing test scores—but because of the deep, deep change created when courageous people willingly challenge every assumption and strategy to turn an institution as old and dead as Robert L. Mueller himself completely upside down. We created a magical place to teach and learn. Neither paralyzed nor intimidated by a nation's demand for academic excellence, we have insisted on all children's capacity for achieving their full life potential. Now. El Milagro.

In time, test results will take care of themselves. For now, we make real change.

People who are willing to sacrifice win revolutions. Revolutionaries will fight until the fight is over. They are resilient. They are forward thinking.

MEXICAN GAS

The decades have raced by Mueller's old school. Some of the original neighbors remain. They have grown old with streets and trees and community institutions. Their children and then their grandchildren sat in these desks and played flag football on the very same playground.

Decades of children—generations of children—have filed past. They are all ghosts now. They number in the tens of thousands. Sometimes, before a new year is set to begin, I stand out on the open and empty playground and anticipate the laughter, the screaming, the rough play of still another group...and I can see them all at once. It is eerie.

Due west, just past the high cinder-block walls of Mueller Charter School, Interstate 5 rushes by. You can't go anywhere on this campus without hearing the freeway hissing and groaning. The sound becomes hypnotic—tire squeals or sirens or the deep metallic gear grinding of large trucks trying to keep the frenetic California freeway pace. Sometimes there are smells that chase the salt air: the power plant's chemical cloud or the distinctive Mexican gas that churns in the breeze like a bad cigar.

I wonder why old man Mueller wanted to build this school right next to the freeway. Maybe he didn't anticipate how heavy the traffic would be fifty years into the future. He didn't realize that this was the major gateway to the Mexican border just a few miles away. He didn't realize that the choking, unrelenting race up on that freeway would envelope this school in a constant state of fascinating and competing sound. He didn't allow for the evolution of SUVs and Hummers and freight trucks the size of aircraft carriers. He didn't know the hallowed walls would bear witness to drug and immigrant trafficking, to say nothing of the trafficking of souls along I-5 corridor north and south in lines so thick that the cars sometimes stand end to end for hours waiting to inch a few feet forward.

Builders must have used the same template for Mueller Charter School that they used for every other '50s- and '60s-era school in Southern California. Rows of buildings sit side by side like dusty shoe boxes. Classroom doors open out into the fresh and predictably temperate air. No need for closed hallways...just tiny greenbelts and end-of-the-row drinking fountains. Structures have come and gone. The buildings' age reads like tree rings as the cyclical color schemes layer and peel, layer and peel. In some ways, the patchwork of new buildings speaks to the continued vitality of the place. Enrollment grows, and grows. And grows.

And such is the development of Chula Vista itself—America's seventh fastest-growing community. Travel east on H Street now and you'll see golf courses, strip malls, shopping centers, and suburban housing tracts rolling endlessly off the horizon's furled ledge. The Olympic Training Center is located in Chula Vista. So is the Coors Amphitheater, Donovan Correctional Facility, multiple university extension campuses, a major community college, thousands and thousands of small and large businesses, and the Border Patrol headquarters. They are negotiating to bring the San Diego Chargers here and maybe some day an international airport. And there are now forty-three elementary schools, all of which, like Mueller, are part of the Chula Vista Elementary School District.

As the building boom moved eastward, so did the most expensive homes and the investment of taxpayer dollars. Gated communities, manicured parks, community swimming pools, and state-of-the-art amenities contrast with the dense population of poor families found here on the western end of I Street.

Chula Vista has always been a destination for Latino families migrating from Mexico and Central America to live in America. The steady migration of Latinos eventually reached a tipping point and triggered white flight. Moving vans carted away panicked families with all of their histories and heirlooms and xenophobia, packed now like old furniture in wooden crates. As a result, there is that much more room for poorer families, transient families, and for more children learning English as the entrée to an American education.

As the years have passed and the great Western Diaspora has unfolded, the Mueller community has fallen into disrepair and even squalor. Rows of '60s-era trailer homes border the campus on the northern and eastern sides. Some look like you could still hook them up to your old Studebaker and make the sentimental drive up Highway 101 as they did in the good old days after the big war.

On our campus' western boundary are the freeway "sound wall" and a giant culvert that sits like a moat to protect the campus from invading hordes. As a barrier to aggression it doesn't work. At night, local teenagers get high in the ditch and come up to spray paint the freeway-facing sound walls with enough graffiti to keep Frazee Paint in business for another fifty years.

In 1998, the good citizens of Chula Vista passed a bond to refurbish its older schools. Mueller Charter School was one of the beneficiaries of the voters' generosity; $6 million later, we were renovated, modernized, and wired for the twenty-first century. The neighbors hardly recognized the place.

The modernization sent a clear message to the Mueller Charter School community that their children mattered and that they deserved the very best. It was the beginning of our revolution. The seeds of El Milagro.

New buildings accommodated a rapidly growing enrollment, and a marquis was erected in front of the school that said, "Mueller Charter School...the only school in America named after a fried chicken restaurateur."

Well, not exactly.

But the campus was renovated nonetheless.

BOSTON TEA PARTY

Mueller's Revolt has been a long time coming and it has been simmering for nearly a decade. It is a revolt against *standard practice...* and *traditional thinking*...and *the status quo*...and *"this is the way we do things around here"*.

It is a revolt against the public's low expectations for children who are not products and beneficiaries of white privilege. There is nothing "soft" about that brand of bigotry. The truth, in the form of data, may very well reinforce and justify those low expectations. So this is also a revolt against that data and the great divide. It is a revolt against truth itself if that means we have to accept the assumption that our children are somehow less capable of greatness than any other children.

This is a revolt against outside influences, benevolent or otherwise, in whatever form they come. It is a revolt to secure our autonomy. A declaration of our independence from well-meaning school boards and from district office direction. It is a revolt against legislators passing laws for kids before they bother to learn their names. It is a revolt against unions that have no faith in the ability of teachers to manage their own destiny.

Mueller's revolt is serious business.

This is a blood coup. There are thick slicks of fresh tea swirling like a red tide in the Boston harbor. The fragile wooden crates bob and splinter and take on more seawater than they can absorb. So they sink. And in their destruction there is a very clear message for the king: "This is a revolt. We win these."

THE GRADUATE

It seems like every week another alumnus of Mueller Charter School stops by. Sometimes it is a college student dropping her little sister off and reminding us that—in spite of the public schools she attended—she is now poised to earn her MA in international business in just a few months. Sometimes it is an electrician, or a UPS driver, or some poor bastard who now lives in Connecticut and is out West on business. Sometimes it's an old lady, elderly enough to be my grandmother, coming by to say she is a Mueller grad too. That's okay, of course. There was a history long before Colonel Sanders-Mueller woke up one day and pictured his school rising like a great sentinel to elementary education.

They come by to visit their old elementary school and to remind us all that we are deeply invested in our institutions. We visit the house we grew up in, our old church, our old school. It is a sacred trust.

"Wow, this place has really changed. But I used to play tetherball right over there."

Anyone who looks hard enough can see the ghosts.

GUNPOWDER

I wrote this book in the hopes that you or somebody might read it.

Perhaps you are like me. You know we can create schools that are far more worthy of our children. Perhaps you too are tired of the complaints and criticism and helpless hand-wringing as if we don't know how to improve them. Perhaps you want to ignite a revolution of your own. If so, you have come to the right place. But be forewarned. There is nothing harder to change than an institution designed to never change.

I know something about school revolutions because I've launched a few. In fact, I have been launching one form of revolt or another in education for thirty years now. I was born a few months before the landmark decision in *Brown v. Board of Education*. It ignited a revolution too. Some babies breathed in lead paint back in the 1950's...I must have breathed in the gunpowder.

During my high school and college years, a succession of explosions in education law sent school leaders frantically searching for the cover of legal counsel. Soon enough those explosions were heard in special education, Title IX and gender equity, revised desegregation orders, school finance, and bilingual education. Each judicial decree detonated in the midst of a crowded field and the shrapnel sprayed everywhere. Our ears rang for decades. The message was clear: "The purpose of public education in America is to ensure that all children are provided the opportunity and support to reach their full academic potential."

A revolt was on against mass education; against the factory school, against painting our children's future by the numbers, against one-size-fits-all.

But public education barely changed.

During my career as an educator in California, we have experienced the "taxpayer revolt," *A Nation at Risk*, an explosion of technology, white flight, Prop 229, vouchers and charters and even home schools. I have experienced the extremes of the open classroom and the scripted lesson. I have seen the influence of Jaime Escalante and Madeline Hunter and Jonathan Kozol and Jawanza Kunjufu, Michael Nesbitt and Marva Collins.

But still our public schools have barely changed.

Throughout those thirty years, I have pushed back against the status quo because I always knew we could be different and we could be better than we were. I've often asked: What's wrong here? What the hell is wrong with our schools? Why do some kids just never seem to succeed in this system? They get only one "kindergarten-through-twelfth-grade experience" in their lifetime and the results will stay with them forever. Why can't we make it count? For every one of them?

Our schools do not reflect our nation's love of excellence, let alone our superiority in medical research, space travel, military strategy, art and architecture, organizational development, baseball, personal computing, or capitalist enterprise. They don't reflect the elegant perfection of our Constitution. So what is the problem? Racism? Bias? Indifference? Intolerance? Or is it a lack of competence, or expectations, or imagination? Or a lack of will? Perhaps it is the nature of our institutions themselves—mired in bureaucracy, protected by mighty forces of history, politics, culture, and law.

It doesn't have to be that way. There is a least one alternative.

We call it El Milagro and it too is a by-product of the revolt.

This movement is not about securing more funding...but rather, using our funds more strategically.

It's not intended to insulate us against external accountability systems, but rather, to foster the internal discipline required to hold ourselves accountable.

It is not designed to promote some magic teaching method, but to perfect a professional culture for which every professional is responsible.

It's not to diminish the teachers' unions and all that they have done for our profession. It's to develop an efficient school organization that is completely autonomous and self-sufficient; one that is impervious to the influence of external political forces.

There are solutions in El Milagro. Plenty of them. Solutions that are meaningful, replicable, effective, proven. And revolutionary. I have included them in this book:

Chapter One is about the lessons of leadership and the alternative path I took to be a charter school leader. I never wanted to be Mr. Green Jeans. I wanted to be Che Guevara.

Chapter Two is about the extraordinary potential that is in every child and what schools must do to unleash that potential. It is about our amazing children. The title of this chapter is intentional. Wake up. *"Our Children Will Change the World!"* Or they won't.

Chapter Three is a primer on charter schools and where they came from and how, by accident or intuition, the seeds of the revolution were thrown.

Chapter Four describes the chaotic, litigious, and distracting divorce that occurred between the local teachers' union and Mueller Charter School. It was truly "a blinding fog". Like a marriage gone bad, the adults were quarreling and the children paid.

Chapter Five is about organizational change, without which you cannot launch a revolution.

Chapter Six introduces the concept of transformational change.

Part II describes the seven systems that have carried Mueller Charter School and powered a transformation. They include:

Chapter Seven: The charter mission;

Chapter Eight: The people;

Chapter Nine: Our unique governance model;

Chapter Ten: The instructional strategies that have led to significant gains in teaching and learning;

Chapter Eleven: The methods for measuring those gains;

Chapter Twelve: The amazingly effective Resiliency Quadrant System—our own process for monitoring the social and emotional well-being of virtually every student simultaneously and continuously; and

Chapter Thirteen: The magic of home visits and the many roles our parents play.

And finally, **Chapter Fourteen** addresses a subject that schools don't think about often enough: the spiritual nature of our work. It too is a driving force of El Milagro.

POST CARDS

You can read these chapters any way you choose. They appear in their logical sequence and are intended to be read from beginning to end. But they are each comprised of multiple, independent essays that need no order at all. Feel free to skip around, drop in on chapters randomly or in a sequence that is your own. Read them like short stories or a box of letters you have collected from a friend. Or maybe postcards—war correspondence from the front lines where the demands are too great to apologize for the nature of our mission.

We are, after all, a *work in progress* at a time when our industry abides only models of extraordinary accomplishment.

We are still deep inside the journey. This is not a chronicle of the finished march. There are no victory parades or press releases or congratulatory calls from the White House. At least not yet. So we offer only postcards. Hand-written, scribbled in earnest and as fragmented as the uncertain task of leading change itself.

Can you smell the gunpowder in these pages? Lift this book up off your lap and shake it in the air—the gelignite will drop out in tiny specks that you can see only if the revolution matters to your kids too. In any event, here it is. We're all part of the revolution now.

I'll tell you the story of El Milagro. You do the rest.

WINGS

So by now you know that this book is not really about Mr. Mueller at all—nor his fried chicken restaurant chain, nor his old school. It's about El Milagro, the seven transformational changes, and a school that exists in a state of constant evolution. We are El Milagro until we get it right.

And it's about those rare schools that drive themselves—not out of fear or blind compliance—but out of a belief that whatever it is we are currently doing for kids, could be a whole lot better.

Schools are people. We lead and we follow. We teach and we learn. We invent and we brace ourselves for all that we might be for others. We leave our legacy.

In rare and wondrous moments, even the most odd and diverse instruments come together in a *Mr. Holland's Opus* kind of way. So open up our doors. Bienvenido. The music is sweet, the chicken wings...hot off the grill.

To my wife Anne, and to our two children—Keenan and Kira—so that we can each define our lives by our service to others.

PART I

MUELLER'S REVOLT

CHAPTER ONE

Catching in a Crowd

Sometimes it's easier to ride a horse in the direction that it's going.

—Native American Proverb

TATTOOS

We wear our life experiences like tattoos. They are permanent shapes and scars that define us. We cannot hide them under our sleeves or long pant trousers. They simultaneously intimidate, amuse, and stir the imagination. Like ancient cave drawings, they are the symbols that tell our story. They are our stories.

"Where'd you get that one?"

"At the Black Rose in Tucson. It's a tattoo parlor on 8th Avenue."

"Hmmm. A clown with teardrops...nice."

You can remove tattoos with a laser but it hurts more than when you got them and the scarring is worse. Our life experiences, on the other hand, are not so easy to remove. And even if you could slice them away with a red-and-white-hot laser light, what would be the point?

For anyone who has ever led a group of people—from Moses to Patton, Kennedy or Custer, Lombardi or Eisner—their leadership was ordained in the glorious shadows of their life experiences. Their hubris and humility balanced in the scope of all the moments that they lived to lead.

My journey to El Milagro wound through lessons from which I learned or did not; wound through experiences from which I grew or did not; spun through stories from which I matured or did not.

I am my stories. Here are my tattoos.

CATCHING IN A CROWD

Tattoo #1 says: Find your metaphor for courage.

Castle Park High School, my alma mater, opened in 1964. It sits on a broad mesa in the southern end of Chula Vista, a few miles away from Mueller Charter School. On fall Friday nights, the football stadium lights ignite in a ring of sacred candles. The forty-some years have yielded champion athletes and football stars who went on to great careers in colleges and in the NFL. But mostly, hard-working blue-collar kids go there. They are rich in their ethnic and cultural mix. Too often, if they have any success at all, in anything, they will have exceeded the loftiest of expectations.

Sometimes, when I drive past that old school, I can't believe how familiar it looks, and yet how much it has changed. In the daylight, when the stadium lights are off, it is run-down and tired. It needs to be painted. But, like Mueller Charter School, the ghosts are vivid. I graduated from Castle Park in 1972 with only one ambition, and that was to play in the NFL. I didn't have a fallback idea but I guess it doesn't matter.

Sometimes we lead. Sometimes we are led.

For whatever reason, I was good at catching footballs. I caught them at Castle Park High School and Northern Arizona University and eventually San Diego State. I wasn't very big but I ran good routes and worked very hard at what did. I caught a lot of footballs a lot of different ways—standing, jumping, running, flipping. And I caught them in the middle of some big-ass guys who just wanted to crush my rib cage to separate me from the ball and my ambitions. They call that "catching in a crowd".

Catching in a crowd is a good life metaphor for courage. It means you are going to play hard regardless of the consequences that threaten you. I learned that no matter how hard I got tackled, as long as I caught the football, it never seemed to hurt. *Keep your eye on the ball...run hard across the middle...ignore the slobbering fat guys...focus...catch the ball...tuck it away...endure the collision...pick up your teeth...run back to the huddle and do it again.*

If you catch the ball enough times, you will eventually wear down the opposition. Eventually, you will win. At least most of the time.

In the end, the NFL was never meant to be. I couldn't make a living catching footballs. But I could never have been an advocate for children without catching in a crowd.

OMBAC

Tattoo #2 says: Break the rules!!! (If it inspires learning)

From those days at Castle Park High School, it took only twenty-eight years, six colleges, four degrees, seven school districts, and nine teaching assignments to get to El Milagro. On the journey, doors close and doors open and we just have to walk through the right ones. One of my football coaches at Castle Park High School was Bing Dawson, who was also the captain of a local rugby team called Old Mission Beach Athletic Club or OMBAC. Bing Dawson invited me to come out and learn how to play this amazing game. He figured that if I ran fast enough to play football at San Diego State and I wasn't afraid to run through the middle of major college linebackers to catch footballs—maybe I would be okay carrying a rugby ball too. And so I did.

Then he invited me to return to Castle Park High School as an assistant football coach to work with the wide receivers and tell them about catching in a crowd. And to start my teaching career.

Bing Dawson was as big as a cement truck. No one ever said "no" to him, and I didn't either. I started playing rugby and found a new obsession. And during the time that I was growing in my rugby skills, OMBAC was growing too. Soon we started to win games. Then we won league championships. Then we won tournaments of all kinds. Then we beat teams from all over California. Then we traveled to New Zealand, the epicenter of international rugby. And while we regularly got our asses kicked by the superior technical skills of New Zealand players, we learned the game much better. Over the next few years, OMBAC toured Great Britain, Australia, Fiji, South Africa, Argentina, Canada, and took on teams from anywhere in the world.

Since those formative years, OMBAC has quietly become an American sports empire of sorts. They have won the United States National Championship—the Super Bowl of Rugby—twelve times. All under the leadership of their captain who became king...Bing Dawson.

I learned a lot about teaching from coaching. I was blessed to be around outstanding educators at the beginning of my career. Though I wasn't particularly coachable, I was well coached. I learned important values like ethics and professionalism. I learned the similarities between how we won football games on Friday night at Castle Park High, and how to achieve excellence in English class during the week. I learned how to use data, to make adjustments, to build on what we're good at and to transform weaknesses into strengths. I learned to bend the rules…if I followed them at all.

And I learned that everything happens for a reason.

GIVING 'EM THE PILGRIMS

My first full-time teaching job had nothing to do with teaching high school English or coaching football. It was a two-room schoolhouse on top of Palomar Mountain, on a tiny campus within the shadows of the world's largest telescope. From here, human beings have been peering into heaven for fifty years, looking for God, new planets, or evidence of extraterrestrial life—whichever comes first. At night the moon shines off the big dome with a planetary-like albedo. It is not hard to imagine that when extraterrestrial life-forms touch down on Earth, they visit here first. It is not hard to imagine, in this beautiful mountain place, that as eagerly as we peek into the universe seeking God, He's been right here all along.

The children I taught all lived on the mountain. Their parents were astronomers, or ranchers, or just social misfits growing pot and living off the land. I never had more than sixteen students at one time.

I was hired in January over the phone, sight unseen, without ever having so much as an interview. The superintendent was just happy that a live human with a valid teaching credential and no apparent criminal record was willing to drive all the way up Palomar Mountain to teach every day. He hired me even though a full debilitating cast entombed my right leg.

Two weeks before I called about the job opening at Palomar Mountain School, I broke my tibia in a fluke rugby accident. As if the game isn't physical enough, I was tackled out of bounds and ran into a tree that was growing alongside our home pitch called Robb Field. Without rugby for the rest of the season, I had nothing left to do but read the want ads and find full-time work. It was a causal relationship.

On my first day on the job, the superintendent drove me to the school site to introduce me to everyone. It was a nice gesture since I was so nervous. Besides, with my leg in a cast, I couldn't maneuver a car all that well, let alone drive up the side of a mountain.

On the way up to the school, I asked the superintendent about the curriculum.

"So, Mr. Orahood, can you tell me about the curriculum?"

"Oh, I don't know," he said, chomping on the black and shredded corner of his stale cigar. "Give 'em a little math…a little science. Have 'em read a little bit. Their parents will like that. Oh, and, of course, give 'em some history."

"Give 'em some history?"

"Right. Give 'em the freakin' Pilgrims."

It was 1981. There were no standards or expectations or high-stakes tests. Like most teachers, I was on my own. I experimented with concepts like curriculum integration, thematic teaching, and multiple intelligences without any idea that those were all legitimate, research-based instructional strategies. I created my own resources and tried to engage children in ways that ignited their drive to achieve. I gave them the Pilgrims and lots of other stuff, too. I survived on instincts for four awesome years and then moved to a school a little closer to home.

THE PILOT

Sometimes you realize that you can't keep teaching on a mountain. So I transferred to Muirlands Junior High School. There was an elegant contrast between Palomar Mountain School and Muirlands. One moment I was snuggled in the creepy, leaf-cracking, bug-whispering silence of a remote San Diego mountain, and in the next instant, I was standing amidst the affluence and pace associated with teaching and learning in a community called La Jolla. I made the midyear transition from teaching 16 students in a self-contained classroom to meeting 150 kids a day in five periods of traditional middle-school English in the San Diego Unified School District.

There were plenty of rules to ignore at Muirlands Junior High School. All that mattered to me was that my students learned. And so they did. I tossed the textbooks and the department guidelines and the union contract and the faculty handbook. I didn't need them at Palomar Mountain School and I didn't need them to teach children to write poetry. Poetry is, after all, a violation of all the conventions of grammar and language. *"...i should have been a pair of ragged claws..."*

Urban kids like TS Eliot as much as mountain kids do.

One day the principal called me to her office. While I was waiting outside the door, the vice principal passed by and left me with some sage advice. He warned me that the principal was going to offer me the opportunity to teach the *Hispanic Reading Pilot*.

"What the hell is the Hispanic Reading Pilot?" I asked.

"She wants to identify the lowest 25% of the children at Muirlands and provide a high-tech remediation program."

"Really? How high tech?"

"Look, it really doesn't matter. Trust me on this, Kevin, this program is the principal's baby...and she wants you to do it...but it is a guaranteed career killer!"

"Wow. A career killer. How come?"

"Because it is doomed to fail. Those children aren't going to learn. Not with you. Not with computers. Not with anything. It's gonna be all the Latino and African-American kids that are bussed in from Southeast San Diego through the district's VEEP Program."

"Isn't VEEP the voluntary integration program? The bussing?"

"Yeah, and it's a mess. Those kids don't want to be here."

"Well, they seem to ride the bus for a long time for a group of kids that don't want to be here."

"Listen. They are Latino, man. Hell, I'm Latino. I know these people. They ain't gonna learn."

I nodded politely just about the time the door flew open and the principal, Ms. Kaupp, invited me into her office.

"So, Kevin," said Ms. Kaupp, "I see Mr. Ortiz has been talking to you about the Hispanic Reading Pilot. Are you interested in taking on this challenge? Totally up to you."

"Can I use whatever strategies and materials I choose?"

"Of course. I don't care what you do as long as you get results."

"Can you get me some more computers?"

"I'll not only get you some more computers, I'll pass some grants your way too."

"Can you leave me in at least one section of English for the gifted kids?"

"You got it."

"Done. I'll take those classes."

Mr. Ortiz, the vice principal, looked perplexed. He was even a little insulted that I didn't take his patronizing advice.

No matter. I acquired twenty-five computers, and borrowed materials from the GATE program that were, by law, to be used only in classrooms for children who were ordained as *gifted and talented*. I dumped all of the district texts, relied on a wide range of reading materials and activities, and used the computers as writing tools. But most importantly, I taught the Hispanic Reading Pilot exactly like I taught the GATE classes. Same activities...same expectations. And to everyone's surprise but my own, those students made phenomenal gains in all aspects of their education; most notably in their writing.

In the end, I think the notion of *expectations* is what we really piloted. A belief in children. A willingness to advocate and to throw away the stuff that wasn't really helping them. I also learned an interesting lesson in school culture. The more successful the program was—the more Ms. Kaupp sung the praises of my students—and the more the other teachers looked at me like the hyenas in The Lion King. I wondered if teachers always eat their young.

SERRA'S OTTERS

Tattoo #3 would say: Leadership is building 'family'.

The old mission in San Diego is California's first and oldest church. It was originally built in what is now Presidio Park, right where Interstate 5 and Interstate 8 intersect in Mission Valley. The indigenous people who first lived in the neighborhood chose not to trust the warrior-soldiers arriving on tall horses and dressed to kill. They realized that they'd better encourage them to leave, so they shot flaming arrows through the roof of their mission and vandalized the food stores.

After a while, in spite of a great view of Interstate 8, Father Serra and the early settlers thought it best to move a few miles east and rebuild the mission on prime riverside real estate. Within a few centuries, they would be able to drive a golf ball from Father Serra's front window and have it land in the parking lot of Qualcomm Stadium, home to the San Diego Chargers. But, for now, they were content to establish their mission and go about the business of converting Native Americans to Christianity.

Father Serra went on to establish twenty-one missions in California, forever providing our state's fourth graders and their parents with a perennial favorite homework assignment—reconstructing a scale model of one of the old California missions.

Any California fourth-grader will also tell you that if it weren't for the sea otters, there never would have been a string of missions stretched across the rural landscape in a giant rosary of churches and barracks and military compounds from Qualcomm Stadium to Carmel.

In a classic cause-and-effect relationship, the sea otters triggered massive movements of marching empires bent on preserving the California coastline for their own. Because of the sea otters, Russians sailed to Monterey Bay in fleets of hunters and traders looking to harvest the docile otters' winter coats. Meanwhile, inspired by the news that the Russians were enjoying the exclusive shops and restaurants of the little romantic hideaway called Carmel-by-the-Sea, the Spanish army marched from Mexico City to Big Sur to send the Russians home.

Father Serra was inspired too. He was determined to build one mission for every army outpost; one mission in walking distance from the one before.

By the time the Spanish army and Father Serra arrived in Monterey, the Russians were long gone. But the missions stayed. Including the San Diego Mission de Alcala. The sea otters had left their indelible paw prints on the history and culture and wondrous landscape of the Golden State.

For most fourth-graders, the story ends there in a built-to-scale diorama of plastic palm trees and horses big enough to crush the mission roofs. But it doesn't end there for me.

I met Anne at the late mass at the San Diego Mission de Alcala one Sunday evening in 1986. On the way to Communion, we synchronized our paths to somehow wind up together in quiet reunion next to the baptismal font. We realized later that whatever we were thinking was probably not what you are supposed to be thinking when you are on your way to Communion. But Father Serra was nonjudgmental. He never condemned the Russians for their preoccupation with sea otters or for racing back to Moscow before they could completely acquaint themselves with the literature of John Steinbeck writing from Monterey's Cannery Row. And he blessed us too. The next year we were married at the old mission and later baptized both our babies there in the shade of the bougainvillea.

Thus our lives too are inspired by the sea otters. We owe them for their role in 200 years of California history, and for the old mission Father Serra consecrated...the genesis of my amazing family.

CRIPS AND BLOODS

Tattoo #4 says: The toughest kids are our best teachers.

I took everything I had learned from the Hispanic Reading Pilot to my next opportunity: serving as a staff development facilitator in the Race and Human Relations Program.

I was one of twenty classroom teachers on loan to the court-ordered integration program in the San Diego City School District. It existed to help teachers and administrators develop child-centered strategies that transcend race and ethnicity and promote equity in opportunities, treatment, and academic results. We were advocates for children... particularly those whom the school system had not historically serve so well.

Doug Harrell, one of my Race and Human Relations colleagues, had grown up on the streets of Pittsburgh and lived a tough life as a kid. Like me, his ticket out was his athleticism, and he paid for his college degree by playing basketball. Together, we started to develop some unique approaches to teaching other educators about one of the most misunderstood group of children in our school system: the kids in gangs.

Street gangs were spiraling out of control by the early '90s. Everyone wanted answers and information. We noticed that after the police department conducted staff development workshops for teachers on the subject of street gangs, more and more students were identified, misidentified, and treated with hostile contempt because they exhibited one sign or another that was supposedly a dead giveaway to their gang complicity. And, of course, children of color were most often the recipients of this treatment because when the gang workshops were presented they focused on African-American and Latino gangs. This was ironic because two other street gang empires find their origins in the beautiful climate offered by San Diego: the White Aryan Resistance and the white gangs trafficking in crystal methamphetamine. So even if we were going to start typecasting our children for their potential criminal involvement in schools, it seemed like we should be including skinheads and bikers and trailer-park-tweaker cartels that were also sucking high school kids into their ideology.

The police officers and local gang experts probably didn't mean to have children singled out for unfair treatment as a consequence of their presentations. But the topic of street gangs was big business on the educators' conference circuits. You could always count on a big audience if you advertised a session that included a cop and a "former gang member" who were going to teach the telltale signs of participation in juvenile gangs. And once they finished instructing the audience on the style of hats, NFL teams, colors, bandanas, shoestrings and hand signs that each gang features, teachers went back to their classrooms and saw gang members everywhere! It was the power of suggestion and misguided expectations. And children paid.

As resource teachers with the Race and Human Relations Program, Doug Harrell and I were able to teach people a more child-centered view, a way to intervene lovingly and respectfully, *additively*, so as not to push children out into the community prematurely. In spite of what the prevailing wisdom may have been, gang participation was not preordained for anybody. But kids didn't need their teachers to jump them in.

Ellie Topo was a participant in one of my workshops on "Understanding Children in Street Gangs." She was a shadow administrator in the Solana Beach School District. She was not the superintendent of record...but she was definitely in charge. She was a grant writer with thirty years of service to her tiny district. A big fish in a little pond. She brought in lots of money and had tremendous influence there. She served on the campaigns of board members and propped up the superintendent who was limping his way into retirement. Ellie Topo appreciated my passion for children and that is how I became principal at Skyline School.

Skyline School was in the very white and very affluent community of Solana Beach. It was a long way from the battles and lessons of the Race and Human Relations Program. I had been conditioned to fight and challenge and force people to look at themselves in the mirror. But in Solana Beach, none of that was necessary. The community was liberal and laid back and preoccupied with more pressing political issues like the outrageous proposal to build a train station down on Highway 101 or where companies wanted to install their cell phone receptors.

Suddenly I was the principal in one of the most prestigious elementary schools in all of San Diego County. They had great facilities, endless resources, a hugely supportive school board and fund raising foundation, active and appreciative families, and phenomenal teachers, all in affluent beach community. Every year their kids excelled on any kind of test you wanted to give them.

I wanted to launch a revolution at Skyline, but I was in the wrong place at the wrong time. There wasn't a fight. My militancy and inexperience were a dangerous combination for me and for everyone around me. I learned the tough lessons of organizational leadership the hard way. Even though we were able to create lasting innovations and massive change within the school and even in the district, it didn't ultimately have much impact on the children themselves. They kicked ass before I came; they have kicked ass since the day I left.

While I was at Skyline School we had a huge performing arts center built on the campus and it has housed many community events and children's performances ever since. It has stood as a kind of metaphor to my leadership there. You can still drive by and see the building, but like my legacy at Skyline School, it is somewhat empty. Were it not for my naiveté about what real leadership means, were it not for my inability to understand or care about others within the structure of an organization, were it not for my inability to understand the politics even of elementary schools—I might still be there. Building buildings.

Building a legacy. Leading where I wasn't needed. Teaching children who were learning in spite of all of us.

One day while I was fueling a very large and ominous cloud that was about to blow me out the backdoor like a Gulfport hurricane, a trusted colleague came to me and said, "Kevin, you have the potential to be an amazing principal someday. But it won't happen here. And it won't happen anywhere unless you quit thinking like a teacher."

"What do you mean? How do I think like a teacher?"

"I can't answer that. You have to discover the answer on your own. Someday you will look back and remember this conversation. I hope you will have learned by then. I hope for the sake of our children you will learn from your mistakes here."

"Mistakes? What mistakes? My school is awesome. Have you seen our new performing arts center? Have you heard about all of our innovative programs? They are coming from far and wide to see us teach!"

Then like the ghost of every dream we dream while awake on our feet...she disappeared.

Not long after that, so did I.

EAGLE'S NEST

Tattoo #5 says: Stand up and lead!

I'm scared of heights. The high ropes course that was a part of the ten-day leadership training at UCLA took that into account when they included the Eagle's Nest as one of the exercises that my group of public school principals was challenged to complete.

We were a group of fifty, mostly middle-aged California administrators, standing on the ground and squinting up through the morning sun to see the top of the forty-foot-high Eagle's Nest. We had taken buses to Pasadena that morning, to a ropes course set up in the canyons next to the Rose Bowl.

There were different ropes course "challenges"—some to be completed as a team and some as an individual. The idea was to lean into your discomfort and attempt the challenges that you didn't think you could do...either because you weren't fit enough, or strong enough...or because you didn't like swinging from ropes forty feet off the ground.

I tried a little of everything, but the breakthrough event was the Eagle's Nest.

The objective was to climb up the side of a telephone pole and step up on top of it. Each of us was strapped into a harness and helmet and tied to a rope with an experienced climber belaying at the other end. But the prospects of standing on top of a forty-foot-high telephone pole in the middle of Arroyo Seco on a summery Saturday morning didn't seem any easier just because there was a safety harness.

Two principals attempted the challenge before me. The first guy climbed confidently up the side, took one look at the subtleties of balancing atop an eighteen-inch-diameter telephone pole...and slid right back down. His eyes white-glazed, the size of donuts. He couldn't disguise his fear as he fled, unassuaged by the promise of safety measures.

The second principal climbed clumsily but determined. He had clearly spent a lot of time working on attributes other than his fitness, but he was game. As he reached the last rung, he pulled himself up, placed one foot on the flat nest top, and then paused...waiting for that last big push from somewhere deep inside that would have him standing upright. And he paused....and paused....and paused. The push never came.

Later it occurred to me that we had witnessed in these two climbers some very common reactions to the extreme challenges of school leadership. They were just doing what many principals do. The first followed the right path, made his way to the ultimate moment of personal challenge, and given the choice of testing his own courage with all eyes around him watching- or retreating...he retreated. The second followed the same path, placed one foot up to do the courageous thing, and literally froze in a five-minute state of paralysis. Were it not for the expert climber coaxing him down he might still be standing there, like some scared and shaking statue, straddling that frightening breach that separates quiet mediocrity and courageous accomplishment.

He had our support as we shouted encouragement from below. "Push up. We are with you! Take one more step! Don't quit! You can do this!"

If only his students could see him now. If only his teachers could see him—when he implores them to push ahead, to never doubt their own abilities or their collective courage. They might say to him too: "You stand up, Mr. Brucker! An organization can't rise above its leader. As you go...we go!"

My last visual memory was Davis Brucker being unceremoniously lowered by the buckles, swaying back and forth as the weight of his unspectacular effort joined gravity for the trip back to earth. I remember how pathetic he looked in that jelly-blue safety helmet, his arms dangling like a stuffed rag doll, his feet peddling as he groped in the descent for the ground he couldn't reach fast enough. And I remember how the harness cinched tight around his body weight, pulling at his crotch, revealing that he really did have testicles, even if he chose not to call on them for this exercise.

I resolved in my heart of hearts, and in that moment, that I would not be beaten like Davis Brucker.

So when the helmet was handed to me, I focused my eyes on the pole and ignored the heights and perils around me. I bolted to the top. I placed my right foot on the flat surface...and then the left...and I elevated to my full height. In one exhilarating instant, both feet on the top of the Eagle's Nest, I raised my arms in triumph like a scene from Rocky.

"YEEEOOOOOOOWWWWWWWW..." I hollered. My excitement was unrestrained. "SO YOU CAN JUST KISS MY ASS, ELLIE TOPO!!!"

All the other principals applauded from down below because I was the first to make it to the top. It gave them hope because now they knew it could be done. There were no tricks involved. You just had to have the will.

There is no climbing down from the heights of the Eagle's Nest. But getting down isn't the problem anyway. It's that final push up through fear and the shadows of failure that preceded. It's standing on the Eagle's Nest, where you have no business standing. It's watching your predecessors fail in droves. It's hollering in triumph and scaring the living crap out of the eagle himself. I could imagine him thinking: "Why is that freakin' idiot standing in the middle of my nest and making all that noise? And anyway, who the hell is Ellie Topo?"

To get down from the pole, you literally have to jump off. There is an old grey garden glove hanging about five feet away. It looks like it is suspended in midair...because it is. You spring out off your forty-foot high perch, high-five the glove, and the ropes and cams will catch you and guide you steadily to the ground. Normally, I wouldn't do something crazy like that. But I was already standing on top of a telephone pole that I had climbed on a dare.

So I jumped. "On belay!" And sure enough, the ropes lowered me like a toy piano...gently, gently to the ground.

The Principal's Institute at UCLA was a career-altering experience. Beginning with the ropes course, I learned a lot of things about myself and about my place as a principal in California. I learned about the fears and hopes of other principals from all over our state. I learned to reflect more deeply, to listen and learn, and to appreciate what a potent metaphor the Eagle's Nest would be for my entire career. Like catching in a crowd.

I learned that if I was going to achieve anything on behalf of children, I would have to do what others before me had failed to do: climb up on the Eagle's Nest and shout to the heavens.

NO BRAKES

Tattoo# 6: "First...Keep Kids Safe."

I had been a principal at Skyline School for two years, when, on an otherwise sunny Friday afternoon in October, I aged a full decade. All at once. I lived the principal's worst fear...the father's nightmare.

At the close of an otherwise unremarkable school day, children were slowly scattering in all directions as they do at every school in America. Some walk alone. Others walk in pairs or packs. Some climb on their bikes while others drop skateboards, like Skyline's most famous alumnus Tony Hawk, and grind along the curb. Some pile into their parent's cars, wherever the pre-arranged pickup spot might be. It is chaotic, yet somehow part of the rhythmic flow that transforms school—from a noisy, high-energy hive of human activity to a row of bundled buildings, settling now into a long and eerie weekend solitude.

I'd had a premonition about the dangerous flow of children into our parking lot. I had noticed that at the end of the school day, even the most committed PTA board members become maniacs in the parking lot, driving like impatient Catholics after morning mass. Parents seemed to see only their own children. They had little regard for rules or common courtesy required to support the safe flow of traffic. So we started to regulate the front of the school more carefully. We kept kids out of the parking lot altogether, and required them to get into cars at designated pickup spots along the curbs. I started to assign teachers to after-school supervision. I never missed a day in the parking lot myself. By late October, we had seven adults, every day, strategically located all around the school.

I didn't tell people I had a premonition. I just wanted them to be careful. I had some good excuses anyway. The construction of our new performing arts center brought lots of different kinds of people and vehicles to our campus. In addition, the ex-husband of one of the teachers was stalking her. He was a tweaker who had slowly lost his marbles somewhere along one methamphetamine binge or another... and she was convinced he was going to shoot up the school. So we hired undercover security guards to pose as construction workers and provide constant supervision of the grounds and parking lot.

We could have had the entire National Guard out this Friday afternoon, but that would not have saved Jimmy Cain.

Within seven minutes of the dismissal bell, Jimmy Cain had gathered his backpack, walked to his bike, unlocked it, and climbed on. He passed two teacher-supervisors, both of whom asked him to get off and walk his bike while on the school grounds. But he kept coasting. Down the steep hill that leads from Skyline's frenetic Friday afternoon parking lot, to Lomas Santa Fe Drive below. And now Jimmy Cain picked up speed.

Meanwhile, I stood in the middle of our gridlocked parking lot assisting the traffic flow. In the instant that I was leaning through the passenger window of a silver Astro van and reminding children to put on their seat belts, Jimmy Cain was dodging pedestrians and losing control of his bicycle that had no brakes. A half block to the east, the signal turned green and the Friday Lomas Santa Fe traffic bubbled past in multiple lanes, picking up freeway speeds.

Then in one terrifying instant Jimmy Cain slingshot out as if in some synchronized apogee perfectly engineered to collide with an oncoming city bus. And when they collided, Jimmy Cain's life changed forever, and so did mine.

Some boys raced up the hill for help.

"Dr. Riley!!! Jimmy Cain got hit by a bus...he is bleeding in the street!"

I ran down the hill, passed the line of impatient parents in SUV's too big to maneuver through elementary school parking lots. I was at his side within thirty seconds. Somehow, in my horror, I could still think clearly. I had asked our office staff to wait for confirmation before dialing 911. Maybe the boys were exaggerating. Maybe Jimmy Cain was already standing up, brushing the dirt off his pant legs and assessing the damage to his spokes and handlebars: *Oh, shit. My mom's gonna kill me for scratching the paint off my bike!* Maybe Jimmy Cain will get off with a stern warning about riding his bike off the school grounds. With no brakes. I thought, in a microsecond of blind optimism, *I'm gonna kick Jimmy Cain's little butt when I get my hands on him....*

But I didn't need to kick his butt. The bus already did. I confirmed through the walkie-talkie that indeed Jimmy Cain would require an ambulance, and that we should immediately begin trying to contact his mom.

I knelt by his side, along with an off-duty nurse who happened to be passing by. A puddle of deep red blood was growing under his head. His breathing was shallow. His bike had exploded on impact...and wrapped around him now like a canary cage. I chose not to move it, not to upset the delicate twisted sculpture that somehow served as his thoracic jacket. My instincts instead, were to lean upside down into the canary cage, and breathe for him. And so I did. And we whispered to him...and prayed...until the paramedics came.

Jimmy Cain survived, but he had suffered a traumatic head injury. He spent several weeks in a coma. My wife and I visited him every day—talking, praying, and visiting with his mom. And we were visiting the day he retreated from the safe cocoon of his silent coma. The doctor pricked his fingers and toes with a pin and assessed his reaction. Then, to our surprise, he climbed up onto the hospital bed, leaned over in his face, and shouted, "Wake Up! Jimmy Cain....wake up. If you can hear me....move your fingers!"

And when Jimmy Cain moved his fingers it was an astounding moment. He was Lazarus. He rose up out of death's deep cave, sleepy-eyed. They had removed the bike but the scars and tracks were far from healed. And he was unwrapped like a Christmas present, with anticipation. When a human brain is concussed by a city bus, there is no telling what changes will occur. It could be a loss of speech, a change in personality, sudden onset of seizures, or the development of some rare or unusual talent.

For Jimmy Cain, the changes were many—and none of them were any good. Nor sadly, were they temporary. He is an adult now, with severe speech loss, occasional seizures, and limited ability to walk and move.

I have not had another serious accident happen to a student since Jimmy Cain was crushed by a bus on Lomas Santa Fe on that October afternoon. While I have my many organizational goals and agendas from year to year, he has been my constant reminder that the safety of children is the most important responsibility that school leaders have. To this day, if I am at my school at the end the day—I am in the parking lot making sure that children are safe on their way home. To this day, I am panicked by the sounds of sirens between 2:30 and 3:00, when 1000 children from El Milagro scatter into the streets and that unrelenting traffic.

There is a postscript:

Jimmy Cain's father sued the city of Solana Beach and the school district and the school for $17 million. I was named in the suit but I couldn't blame Jimmy for this. Sometimes it's just business. Anyway, the suit was thrown out and Jimmy's father's only reward was that the city made the front of Skyline School much safer for children.

Meanwhile:

- The tweaker never came to terrorize his wife at Skyline School;
- The performing arts center was eventually completed and Jimmy Cain made an appearance the night of our grand opening;
- The construction workers and security guards all moved on, including our favorite—a happy, upbeat college kid from Africa. A few weeks after Jimmy Cain was fitted for a canary cage, he got a job that he thought would be much safer than standing in an elementary school parking lot dodging crazy parent drivers and watching for tweakers. So he gave his notice and thanked us for our embracing hospitality. We applauded him and wished him well. That very same night, following the spirited send-off from the good people at Skyline School and the subsequent celebration for his transition to a new job— he was killed in a stupid dispute over a parking space at his apartment complex...
- ...His name was Lucky.

PIRATES

Tattoo#7: If you are not getting fired...you are not trying hard enough!

There were lots of changes made at Skyline School, other than the building of a facility for the creative and performing arts. There was tremendous energy, a young staff, and a bright future. In many ways, we were a prototype *charter* school, separating ourselves in every way from all other schools in the area. We developed a multiage program that became known as Global Education. We organized the curriculum thematically around the study of global systems: cultural, sociological, legal, environmental, political. We also developed a two-way bilingual program, and secured a $700,000 federal grant to implement it. We developed a program for the creative and performing arts, for technology education and for physical education. We had long waiting lists to get in—not only for students but for prospective teachers too!

I insulated the staff from a meddlesome district office and we quickly became known—not as an innovative school—but as the rebel school. The nuance of both descriptions was not lost on any of us. In fact, it made us bolder. On special occasions, we even flew the black, pirate, skull and crossbones on the flagpole in place of our "Nationally Distinguished School" banner. Ellie Topo didn't think it was too funny, though. She hadn't brought me to the district to be a rebel and to move Skyline School further out of her sphere of influence. Furthermore, she felt that since she was responsible for bringing me here I was forever in her debt. I owed her.

As a new principal, I was good at creating programs and shaping policies. I was good at marketing our teachers' work. I was good at unconventional, creative, innovative thinking.

But I was horrible at district politics. I did not pick the right battles, I didn't learn when to back off, I didn't hold my tongue. I fought the power structure on behalf of students and my teachers. And in the Solana Beach School District the power structure was Ellie Topo. In January of my fifth year at Skyline School, we lost our superintendent, Bruce Givner, to brain cancer. He was immediately replaced in a unanimous decision by our school board by none other than Ellie Topo.

The next day I started to search for a new job.

BUFFALO SOLDIERS

Tattoo #8: If you keep doing the same things you have always done, you will get the same results.

Rancho Del Campo High School is housed, in of all places, an old army camp in the mountains, sixty-five miles due east of Solana Beach and Skyline School. It used to be home to the Buffalo Soldiers, members of the famed regiments that featured African-American soldiers on horseback, shedding the same red blood as white soldiers—but without the same respect and appreciation from the racist nation they fought for. Evidently, they figured out that if you stuck the Buffalo Soldiers far enough out in the San Diego mountains they would be out of sight and out of mind. That is, until you needed them to go execute another border campaign or fight a war to keep the nation safe.

When I reported for duty at the old barracks, it was not to ride atop a horse with the proud regiment of the 10th Cavalry. I'd never do as a Buffalo Soldier.

I reported as the new school principal, with enough baggage to fill a cargo plane and with my tail stuck squarely between my legs. But I had come to the right place this time because the students were looking for someone who was not afraid to advocate for them and speak the truth in meetings. They wanted a fighter. They walked on holy ground, and they knew it.

The kids were soldiers too. In fact, Rancho Del Campo was for young boys between the ages of fourteen and eighteen who had been arrested and placed in the custody of the juvenile justice system. They were incarcerated there. They were mostly broken and afraid. They had been convicted of everything from drug possession to carjackings, violent assault, and even murder. They had become the gang members that Doug Harrell and I had tried to prevent the teachers in San Diego Unified School District from creating. All those teachers and administrators thought we were crazy to suggest that if you treat kids like criminals they will become your expectations. But they did.

The best I could say about their surroundings at Rancho Del Campo High School was that it did not look like your typical prison. There were no bars or sniper towers. In fact, if kids wanted to leave they could. Of course, they were in the most hostile terrain of the Southwest. Desert rattlers, rednecks with guns, and 120-degree summer heat surrounded them. They could walk sixty-five miles back home or hitch a ride in their prison gear. Or they could cross the border into Mexico, which was only a mile or so to the south.

Or they could stay and do their time, learn what they could, make amends, reflect on where their young lives had taken them thus far, and resolve to do better. So could I.

I didn't have a lot of experience with juvenile offenders but I did bring a track record of effective and innovative programs and, of course, the newfound desire to work *with* people for changes that everyone could appreciate and see. More than anything, I asked a lot of questions.

"Why do you call the students by their last names? Their names are sweet music to them. You take away their identity by calling them by their last names. You 'institutionalize' them. You might as well just call them by their prison numbers."

"Why do you make kids read these old, outdated, boring textbooks? Why this dry old-euro-centric history book? The Buffalo Soldiers are all around us. Take the kids outside and listen to the ghosts."

"Why are this child's eyes all red? Did you notice he was squinting? He can't see!"

"Young man, when was the last time you had a complete,

comprehensive eye exam? No, not that wall chart thing at your elementary school....a complete exam in the office of an optometrist...? Never?"

"Hmmm. Why am I not surprised?"

"Did you know that children get arrested because of the crimes they commit? And that they often commit crimes because they have lost hope and have no sense of future...and they lose hope because school went poorly for them from about third grade on? And did you know that many of the children who struggle in school are just as bright and gifted as the children at Skyline School? And did you know that the thing that trips them up more than anything is their inability to read? And did you know that children often struggle with reading—not because they can't read—but because their eyes feel like they are on fire when they have to focus their pupils on a printed page? And did you know their eyes burn because they need to be retrained...and that often the difficulty could be corrected by simply wearing glasses? And did you know they don't have glasses because they haven't been properly diagnosed...and that even if they wanted to get their children properly diagnosed, many poor parents do not have medical insurance and thus couldn't get it done anyway? And did you notice how many children at Skyline School have glasses and braces on their teeth compared to the children at Rancho Del Campo High School and any other school that is attended by children from poorer families?"

"And did you know that the one person most likely to recognize a child in need of glasses is his teacher?"

"And why do you have such obviously low expectations for your students? Why do you accept this crappy work when we both know he could do better if he really wanted to? And don't you know...the great teachers have always inspired and motivated children to want to do better work?"

"And why are you uncomfortable when I visit your classroom? I am not here to observe you anyway. I am here to see your students. As a matter of fact, I will be here several times a week...is that okay?"

"Why do kids stare at me like I am *the man*? You think it's this freakin' tie? How about I lose the thing and relax a little?"

"Have you all ever heard of the Hispanic Reading Pilot?"

"Have you ever heard of the Buffalo Soldiers?"

A RAT IN THE STALLS

Six months after coming to Rancho Del Campo High School, the director of the Juvenile Court and Community Schools Program, my boss, announced that he was retiring. It was a stunning disappointment. He was the opposite of Ellie Topo. He left me alone and let me do what I needed to do. Besides he was sixty-five miles away and he was managing programs scattered all over San Diego County.

During the job search for his replacement, I had the crazy idea that I should apply. I had only been in the JCCS system for six months and I had spent that time quietly getting to know my surroundings. I was laying low and trying not to attract attention...like a rat in the stalls of the cavalry ponies. Evidently, it didn't work. I was somehow selected to be the new director. Now I was really in over my head.

As the Court School director, I was now responsible for children that traditional schools could not or would not serve—children who were incarcerated or returning from prison; children who were awaiting trial in juvenile hall; children who had been expelled; foster children; children in detox or in drug rehab centers; pregnant minors; homeless children; children who had been abandoned, neglected, or abused; and those who became wards of the court after their parents had been arrested or killed. We served 3,000 kids a day on some eighty-five campuses that covered an area roughly the size of Connecticut.

To call these children "at risk" would be an egregious understatement. These were children in profound life crisis. Yet in that system, I found children who desperately wanted to do the right thing. They recognized the value of school, they wanted an education, and many were remarkably resilient.

MONARCH

Tattoo #9: Some battles are worth fighting.

There was no shortage of critics or crybabies in the Juvenile Court and Community Schools. It seemed like we were creating a new project or program every day. Innovative schools were starting to pop up everywhere, like Starbucks franchises. Some were outstanding but a lot of them weren't. They were small start-up schools that were often created to serve the most fragile and unwanted kids in the county. Kids that were easy to politicize. Easy to exploit.

One of those projects was the school for homeless children in downtown San Diego. It was called *The Place*.

I had questioned the location of *The Place* from the day I first visited there. Why is it here on Market Street? Why does it have to be in this condemned building in a depressed and crime-ridden neighborhood?

Why does it have to be here, where old drunk guys piss in the doorway every night and crack addicts sleep in the alley? Why is it so freakin' dark? Is this the best we can do for homeless children? Oh, you mean they are not all homeless children? Well, nevertheless, why is *The Place* such a pile of shit and how did it warrant any kind of national attention, let alone the teacher of the year spotlight?

And no doubt about it, *The Place* got lots of attention. It was established by a teacher that became Former President Bill Clinton's National Teacher of the Year when he was looking for ways to promote programs exactly like *The Place*. Pretty soon the founding teacher of *The Place* went on the National Teacher of the Year talk circuit and never came back. So we were left looking for a new teacher and swallowing the reality that the media's darling was really a dog. Kids weren't learning at *The Place*. And the National Teacher of the Year wasn't even the best teacher in the Juvenile Court and Community Schools let alone the rest of the nation.

The new teacher at *The Place*, however, managed to secure a whole classroom full of computers and in time, created a strong curriculum for her students. She organized exciting learning opportunities with many different employers and prepared students for job interviews and college. But she still liked the school's location.

"I'll give you three reasons why I don't want to move, Dr. Riley. We are located right next to the trolley line so it is easy for the kids to get here. It is an understated building so the kids don't feel like they are back in school. And the Downtown Rotary has adopted us as a partner."

"What's the Downtown Rotary have to do with the location?"

"As long as it looks like we are living in squalor, they keep the donations coming! They love coming here because we are such a good project to sponsor."

"Oh, now I get it. Children who are homeless, or semi-homeless, or who just choose to come here for whatever reason they come here, are perfectly content in this location and since there are a lot of donations flowing…why mess with it?"

"That's right. Why mess with it?"

"For just one reason, I guess."

"And what is that?" asked the teacher who had replaced America's National Teacher of the Year at the school for San Diego's homeless children.

"Because our kids deserve better."

She could not disagree and neither could the altruistic and civically active members of the Downtown Rotary. Not long after that discussion, a large building was donated and a task force was formed to build a better school. It took a few years and a lot of effort from a lot of people...many of whom just wanted others to know how committed they were homeless kids in downtown San Diego. In time, a new school opened in a much cleaner and even more convenient place.

The students re-named it Monarch School. All the dignitaries were at the opening, sitting strategically located in the perfect light of the media cameras. Everyone had a comment. Everyone praised the visionaries and the pioneers and each other. I could not bring myself, even as the director of the Juvenile Court and Community Schools and the new Monarch School to inject myself into the spotlight. It seemed so disingenuous.

Just open the doors and get the kids in here.

GOLDEN BELL

The Golden Bell is awarded to outstanding education programs in the state of California. The Community Home Education Program, which was based at the San Diego County Office of Education, had won the award in 1998 and I couldn't for the life of me figure out why.

So, as always, I asked questions:

Why is there a *home schooling* program at the county office and why is it under my direction as the Director of the Juvenile Court and Community Schools? Why do eight *court school* teachers staff it if all of their students are learning at home? And if the program is for students who learn at home, why do they need two administrators and two sets of clerical staff to run two separate school facilities fully equipped with materials, books, desks, computers, and a lounge?

And why do the teachers work a 225-day calendar in a program that runs 180 days? And why do they take vacation when the kids are in session and work in the summer when the kids are off?

Do taxpayers in the state of California know they are paying so much money for the Community Home Education Program and for their high priced teachers not to teach? And since so many of these home school kids were being kept home from public schools and homeschooled for religious purposes, does that constitute a violation of our commitment to the separation of church and state?

As long as the Juvenile Court and Community Schools maintains facilities for homeless and expelled children in run-down strip malls and urine-stained tenement houses and grimy office buildings—there is this inexcusable dichotomy. White kids who stayed at home to go to school had immaculate classroom facilities that they never attended while children of color were taking public transportation for two hours to attend class in veritable shitholes.

I flipped on the light switch at the County Office of Education and even the highest officials seemed to squirm in explaining the inequities and near-immoral contrast between the Juvenile Court and Community Schools and the Community Home Education Program. The teachers union did its best to represent the interests of their eight association members with a straight face. I pushed back as hard as I could.

"Who the hell does this new director think he is?" the teachers and parents started to ask.

"What does he have to do with our students anyway? Isn't he in charge of the criminal kids and the Mexicans?"

"We need to organize and get this guy out of here."

And, of course, they did.

After all, they had won the Golden Bell.

ICARUS

I noticed that the programs with the greatest potential for success are the ones that always come under fire first. Everyone loves a new idea. But eventually ideas can become too avant-garde, too dangerous, or too numerous. Pretty soon, they push frightened organizations to the tipping point.

We were creating so many innovative ways of serving high-risk youth in the Juvenile Court and Community Schools that the system could not sustain it. The status quo was shaken to the foundation. Our ideas collapsed under the weight of their own immense potential.

We flew too close to the sun. When the wax melted, our wings disintegrated and scattered our feathers to the wind.

BUSTERS

Tattoo #10 says: When the sky is falling...be resilient!

Libi Gil, the superintendent of the Chula Vista Elementary School District, was in search of a new charter school principal to head one of her struggling charter schools. She was looking for someone who was both creative and passionate. She was looking for someone who would challenge the status quo and who was not afraid to take risks. One of her assistant superintendents was Lowell Billings, a friend of mine from the doctoral program at Northern Arizona University. He told Libi Gil that I was a crazy Tae Kwon Do black belt who kicked the ceiling lights out at Buster's brewery in Flagstaff, Arizona. He also told her I was getting burned out on the politics of the Juvenile Court and Community Schools and that perhaps I could make more of a difference for kids *before* they got sucked into the engine blades of the system. Evidently, that was good enough for Libi Gil.

Besides, she also remembered me from the day she visited Rancho del Campo High School when I was still their principal. I must have made a good impression when I gave her and several other school chiefs a tour of the facilities and introduced her to some of the amazing boys who were locked up there.

I interviewed at Mueller Charter School and emerged as their first choice. I knew only that Mueller Charter School was a complete disaster. It was in ruins. The adults were at war with one another, the parents were on the outside looking in, and as always, the children were completely forgotten in the struggle. The school was in horrible disrepair. There was no plan. No future. No likelihood of an ongoing charter renewal. It would take a miracle to resurrect Mueller Charter School.

I was moving to my sixth school district and eighth job in public education. I could have bought stock in Mayflower for as often as I had to pack up and move. But each time I had to box up my collection of lumps, bruises, and ass whuppings, I also got to box up the successes: the programs and services that benefited kids, the ideas and innovations that did not exist until I created them. I also had a deeper understanding of the skill set required to effectively lead organizational change.

Great leaders *lead* change. They build coalitions. They sell the mission. They convince people that they will sacrifice anything for the good of the cause. They create programs and strategies that last. And they learn from their past, however painful it might be.

And one more thing. When the glass and barroom lights fall out of the ceiling from a perfectly executed spinning crescent kick, know that this too shall pass. Good leaders are as resilient as children.

CHAPTER TWO

Our Children Will Change the World...
...or They Won't

It is absolutely essential that the oppressed participate in the revolutionary process with an increasingly critical awareness of their role as subjects of the transformation.

—Paulo Freire

FIRESTORM

I f in your deepest core values you believe you work in the service of children, and you are willing to exhaust your God-given skills and talents for them, willing to subvert your ego for them, willing to stand up to a freakin' firestorm for them...you can transform your school. And, oh, yes, somewhere along the way you may lose your job, may lose your place in line, and you may even lose your mind. But some things are worth fighting for.

I learned a lot from my mistakes and when I arrived at Mueller Charter School it was, in many ways, as broken as I was. But I am nothing if not resilient. I know whom I serve, and how urgent is the need. And while there may be countless unpredictable events and challenges inherent in leading an organization to greatness, there is one constant mantra that will never betray you:

Adhere to the mission...serve whom you serve.

Strong core values that individuals passionately share—drive successful organizations. That was my belief when I first began to teach the teachers of Mueller Charter School. When I met the staff for the very first time, they had no idea of the path that I took to stand naked before them. They stared and squinted and waved in the air, as if to clear the fog and smoke and get a better glimpse. The only thing they knew about me was my name. They heard I was an experienced administrator. They heard I had been recruited, drafted, brokered and ordained to be the next principal.

I wonder if they expected Teddy Roosevelt, all fat-waisted and bespectacled. Did they expect Bill Gates with money and Montblancs sticking out of my shirt pockets? Whom did you expect? *Pat* Riley in an NBA Armani suit, hair slicked back from the oil of the international media's unforgiving stare? Who is equipped to lead you? Would you have settled for Gandhi?

There was great anticipation. The room grew quiet. So I said something.

"Shhhhhhhhhhhhhhhhh. Hey....shhhhhhh. He's going to say something."

They measured the words. They came out like this:

"No matter what has happened in the past...no matter what happens in the future....you keep your eyes on the *children*...and you can never be wrong!"

And they began to murmur under their breath to one another:

"What? What was that?"

"Did you hear what he said? I couldn't hear him. Did he just say something?"

"I heard parts of it but he lost me on the 'no matter what happens in the future' part."

"Are we supposed to take notes? Does he want us to write this down?"

"I heard what he said. To tell you the truth, I wasn't all that impressed."

"I don't get it."

"Well I heard from Ms. Tucker that he said something about keeping your eye on the kids."

"Well that's because he was in the court schools. You have to really keep your eye on those kids. They'll steal your purse, your car keys. You can't trust those little bastards."

"No, that's not what he meant. He meant that we should stay focused on kids and not all of the other nonsense we have been distracted with."

"Really? He said that?" (Uncomfortable laughter.) "What did Mr. Drinkwater do? I'll bet he thought that comment was directed at him."

So I continued.

"Look. It's real simple," I said. "It's about children. If we are to go from here to El Milagro, it will only be by their lights."

"Ohhhhhhhhhhh," they said. "Ahhhhhhhhhhhhhh." As if they were watching fireworks explode out over the traffic and monotonous hum of Interstate 5.

"Our children will change the world as we know it. Treat them accordingly."

Some took notes like they did in their teacher preparation courses. Some elbowed one another to make fun of their colleagues. Some feigned interest or comprehension. But the ones who really listened sat quietly back in their seats and reflected. "He's right," said the contemplative teacher by the window. "It is about children. But what the hell is El Milagro?"

DISNEYLAND

You don't have to be at Disneyland long before you realize who the customer is. It is all about kids. They are the target audience. Everything about the park is aimed at engaging their imagination and keeping it: every ride, every shop, every employee, every toilet stall, every trash can, every souvenir, every show. But the kids don't bring the dough to Disneyland, their parents do. So if parents have to buy the $50 tickets and $20 hot dogs endorsed by Goofy, they must be engaged at the same time and in the same way.

Disney knew that when he first carved his 1950s-era theme park into the fragrant orange groves of Anaheim. So he created a world in which adults could be kids again too. And every generation that grew up on Grumpy and the Matterhorn would one day bring their own kids here, would relive their childhood, would weave family histories together, would pull their knees into their chest on wagon rides and remember what it means to be a child.

Disney wasn't content to just *serve* children, he required that we all become kids again—even if only for the duration of a day pass. As if powdered by fairy dust, he wanted child-like humility to be the great equalizer. Disney thought it would truly be a magic kingdom, if adults could see the world through a child's eyes again, could remember their fears and their dreams. Could put their needs first. Could remember how they learn, how they laugh, how they pray at night when they want only to sleep and wake up to unwrap another morning of infinite promise.

Disney's magic was not his ability to turn oranges into a billion-dollar corporate empire based on cartoon toys and illusion. Because the children his enterprise serves are no illusion. Their needs compel us.

They are real. None of his cast can afford to forget it: not Cinderella, Captain Hook, Mickey, or Geppetto. Disney's gift was knowing that if you forget who you serve, you vanish and die. You become obsolete.

Perhaps he would be pleased with the high-tech remix of his old feature cartoons now available on DVD. They capture generations. They never forget whom they serve either. They see who sits in the front row, eating popcorn in the dark and innocently farting when the theater is tittering with its own laughter and no one can hear. Disney believes in children and never surrenders to jaded cynicism that only adults are capable of when they lose their way.

"Clap your hands, Wendy. Clap your hands and Tinker Bell's light will shine... Tinker Bell will live again."

EQUALIZER

Educators — teachers, administrators, board members, custodians — would all do well to learn again from Disney: *schools are for kids*.

Obviously, the fundamental purpose for the existence of schools is to educate our children. How we educate them, for what purpose, and to what standards have been debated for centuries. But nowhere in the history of public education is there evidence that schools were established in communities to provide employment for the adults, opportunities for grandstanding politicians, or tax write-offs so that corporate leaders can assuage their guilt through altruism.

Schools exist to create thinking, skilled, caring, and literate citizens who can utilize the complex technological tools and systems necessary to be successful contributors to a twenty-first-century society. Schools exist to help all individuals reach their full potential and beyond. Schools exist as America's equalizer—where students can overcome the disadvantages associated with social class, family income, lack of English skills, or even significant disability. Schools exist so that the children who inhabit them may someday parlay their gifts and life lessons and make the world a better place.

In the great democratic experiment called America, the depth and breadth of a person's education can overcome generations of economic and social inequities. So why aren't schools producing more extraordinarily enlightened and productive citizens?

Why isn't your school?

SATELLITES

Every so often, some watershed event takes place that causes all the politicians and educators to come together in a shared, public panic and declare that our schools aren't good enough. It happened in the 1950s when the Russians launched Sputnik and scarred our national psyche.

"Holy Shit!!!...How are our kids ever going to compete with an unmanned Russian satellite?"

So we ramped up math and science for a few years. We had to compete in the rocket race and win. Our leaders and scientists all lined up and their things had to be bigger than the Russians' things.

Then it happened again in 1983 with the publication of *A Nation at Risk*. This one really scared the crap out of everybody. In perfect Reaganesque hyperbole, the report trashed the our schools and warned Americans that their children were falling woefully behind children from the rest of the industrialized world. The document even went so far as to say that if another country did to our kids what we are doing to our own kids in schools we would declare it an *act of war!*

I was working on my master's degree when *A Nation at Risk* was released and so naturally it became the subject of every class and every paper for the next several years. The "act of war" thing really got everybody's attention. Mine too. Most educators were really angry and felt betrayed by a report that seemed to so thoroughly discount all that they had done for America's children. But I knew it was true. We hadn't done enough, because schools were less and less about the children.

For example, America had led the world in its commitment to children's education after World War II. In the 1950s, American kids went to school for 180 days a year...more than any other industrialized nation. Then all the other industrialized and enlightened nations of Europe and Asia wised up and figured out that their schools should be for kids too. And if schools are for kids and you want them to learn... they have to spend some time at it. By the mid-1990s, those countries were requiring 220 to 230 instructional days a year—and in some places even more. But America has stuck stubbornly to 180 days! A decision that is not necessarily for the kids.

So *our* kids have fallen way behind *their* kids, according to the international comparisons. And they have been behind for decades. Maybe the Asian and European countries that produce more academically accomplished children are on to something: maybe having children attend school virtually year round might not be a bad idea. And the government of any nation that loves its children should know that too.

And now the sequel to the alarming charges of *A Nation At Risk* is the *No Child Left Behind Act*. NCLB is the President George W. Bush plan for engendering more competence and competition in America's schools. It is more prescriptive. In a framework of regulations and unfunded edicts, the federal government changed the rules of the game in the name of *accountability*.

So now, we have...

NCLB policies,
NCLB programs,
NCLB teachers,
NCLB commemorative sweatshirts,
NCLB schools,
NCLB conferences,
NCLB workshops,
NCLB threats and
NCLB sanctions,
NCLB data fields,
and the vaunted NCLB goals.

And what is the net effect of this effort around the President George W. Bush Administration's "commitment" to children?

Nothing.

The same children who always got left behind...are still getting left behind, mainly because they get left behind on purpose! Do you think Ozzie and Harriet's kids are getting left behind? Not only are they not getting left behind, they are catapulting forward like they were shot out of a hotel toaster. You know why? Because Ozzie and Harriet will not abide their kids being left behind with all of the other kids that are being left behind. They think its bad company. They would have to explain it at the country club.

"Hey, I heard your kid was left behind."

"Yeah. I don't know what happened. We got him a tutor, but he kept struggling in math. He just couldn't do the work. He failed all the tests and got an 'F' in the class."

"So what did you do? You aren't really gonna let him get left behind are you?"

"Oh, hell no. We had our attorney work with the principal and they changed his grades."

Long before President George W. Bush began his first term as president, states like California had already painstakingly identified its curriculum standards for each grade level and had developed an aggressive system for annually assessing the degree to which children were performing at or above those standards. Like many other states, California's assessment system featured rewards and sanctions designed to raise everyone's level of urgency. Mandates emerged that were intended to coax improvement out of the schools. The only thing missing was the critical soul-searching needed by elected officials in our state and federal levels of government.

They should have asked themselves:

"Exactly how committed are *we* to the idea of providing children with the highest level of education possible? Gee, if we started over from the beginning to design a school system structured around extraordinary academic achievement for all children...and money was no object...what would it look like? I wonder how we could design schools, for example, to overcome conditions like childhood poverty? And come to think of it...isn't money the antidote to poverty? And knowing that a highly educated citizenry is fundamental to the preservation of democracy... shouldn't we all turn up our sense of urgency on this? And if educators are going to be held accountable for academic results — shouldn't we, as legislators, be accountable for the community conditions that contribute to, or compromise, our children's learning? What about these charter schools? Don't they have a chance to do something special?"

The American public school system is not designed for engendering success for all children. Nor is it designed for the extraordinarily high levels of achievement that parents, business leaders, and the community at large so badly desire. Nor is it designed with children completely in mind at all.

We have been "restructuring" and "reforming" schools in traditional and predictable ways for a long time. But the more schools have changed, the more they remain the same.

Except, perhaps, schools like El Milagro.

HOUSTON

Back in 1985, I wrote my dissertation on the equal protection clause of the 14th Amendment. It was a 425-page essay on how a few simple words out of the United States Constitution have so significantly influenced modern public education. That experience shaped my beliefs about children and the obligation we have as educators to help every child reach his or her full potential.

I knew the history of the segregated South and that it eventually required the Supreme Court to declare that schools could no longer separate their students by race. I also knew that after decades of bussing, crying, cussing, firebombing, foot-dragging, fighting, resisting, and ducking, school officials were compelled to abide by the constitutional promise that all citizens enjoy the equal protection of the law.

I knew that if another nation had done to our children what Americans did to their own children in segregated schools it *should* be declared an act of war.

But as a lifelong beneficiary of the invisible powers of white privilege, I had no idea that there were two Constitutions: one that we salute as the greatest ideological framework in human history...and simultaneously, one that is more illusion than David Blaine's wild prime-time promise to make the Statue of Liberty disappear.

In either case, liberty is missing. Justice is the illusion.

In one post-graduate class or another, I had become fascinated with how the 14th Amendment was used like an immense social mirror—held up to compare what our collective consciousness told us equality should look like, versus what it actually was. The equal protection clause was the foundation argument in dozens of significant legal cases that defined equal educational opportunity during most of the 20th Century.

It was at the heart of a long line of school desegregation cases, for example, dating back to 1896, at both the K-12 and university levels. Thurgood Marshall placed all the judicial stock he had in the equal protection clause, piled his chips to the ceiling, then rolled the roulette wheel on the bet that the goodness of America would prevail. When the numbers aligned in *Brown v. Board of Education*, Thurgood Marshall and his team of NAACP lawyers exalted. America had hope.

The truth about *Brown* was that it wasn't the result of just a wild gamble. Thurgood Marshall had paid the price for this legal victory long before he argued in front of the Supreme Court that he would someday join. His mentor, Charles Houston, realized that education was the key to the full development of black youth in America, but that there were two school systems—one for white kids and one for everybody else—and they were not equal. Schools that served white children generally had better facilities, more money, better teachers, higher expectations...and a pitifully small patch of moral turf to stand on. It was 1954, the year I was born, and generations of white kids like me had no idea that we were coming into a world in which the most hallowed institutions were constructed on a lie. We were the post-WWII baby boomers. Our fathers fought for freedom and democracy in a segregated army. Over two million African American soldiers fought with bravery and distinction though they would not qualify for the same medals or commendations.

I wanted to ask the ghosts of our history: "Did you do that on my account? Did you think I could not compete in a system that was fair?"

Those who fought so stubbornly to perpetuate policies of apartheid have willed to their progeny generations of sorrow and division. Charles Houston was just one more in a long line of African-American giants intentionally obscured by history books. He paid for his hard work with his life but he must have known that Thurgood Marshall would carry the day. And he did. Before he died he gave to Thurgood Marshall all of his instincts and his sense of fairness. And he passed along the map to a secret treasure—one that you had to hold up to the light to see.

It is called the equal protection clause of the 14th Amendment. Read it yourself. It is written in ink. It is written in blood.

It goes right to the very heart of the constitutional provision that guaranteed equality for all citizens of the United States. It was the legal foundation for the arguments Thurgood Marshall successfully posed in *Brown v. Board of Education*. It was also used in the cases associated with bilingual education, special education, gender equity, and school finance schemes some thirty years ago.

Legal scholars argue that the equal protection clause is not intended to provide "equality" among individuals or classes but only "equal application" of the laws. It does not address results. It merely denies states the ability to discriminate. But I'm not a legal scholar. I'm an educator and a citizen of America, and in my view, the application of the equal protection clause in public education is our call to arms. In America, if we are going to be true to our own moral code, we have to create schools in which absolute equity is the only acceptable outcome. In America, there can be no achievement gap!

Ideally, if you take the time to develop a doctoral dissertation you should publish the thing and make some kind of contribution to the field. And so I did. But what it really gave me was a personal value system forged in iron. It clarified my beliefs in a system that should reflect the equality envisioned by the likes of Thurgood Marshall and Charles Houston.

In March of 1985, just one week after meeting Annie at the house Father Serra built, I successfully defended my doctoral dissertation at Northern Arizona University. It was dedicated, in part, to Charles Hamilton Houston.

FORGIVENESS

Every day people struggle with their higher purpose in this world: Why are we here? What is my role on this planet? How can I make my life meaningful?

Teaching children is missionary work. To excel requires a sense that you are *meant* to teach. That you bring something to the table that will inspire other human beings, at whatever age, to reach beyond their full potential...and in their greatness, you are fulfilled.

Are we called? Perhaps. But I never heard the telephone ring nor did I get an e-mail from God that I was to go to Chula Vista and lead a struggling people out of darkness. I just followed my own light as it lit the way past dead ends, insurmountable walls, and miles and miles of mind-numbing mediocrity and sameness—past Palomar Mountain School and Muirlands Junior High, and the Race and Human Relations Program, and Skyline School and the Juvenile Court and Community Schools. My light always seemed to find a thin crack in the maze and spill out into a giant room where I was headed next.

"Is this my next stop?" And, "Is this where I am needed now?"

Maybe I am more mercenary soldier than missionary soldier. I have been guided by the sense that I go where I am needed. At some point though, I realized that either I had a calling or I was called. If our values and beliefs come from our life experiences, then somewhere in my history I must have undergone an intense transformation. In either case, I had work to do. There was no moment of epiphany. I did not come by my enlightenment in the glow of a spiritual trance nor at the bottom of a peyote button milkshake.

As I reflect now, my career and life experiences seemed to weave along parallel paths. Others have come by their inspiration more honestly.

I've worked with thousands of teachers at schools and hundreds more as an adjunct professor at the University of San Diego. Teachers have consistently told me they knew they wanted to teach from the time they were little kids. Or they talk about having had that mysterious "calling" to serve others. Not me.

I went into teaching totally by accident. I truly must have been led. I was blessed as an athlete, but not as a student.

I was the youngest of three boys but the only one in my family to graduate from high school. My father and my brothers left high school early and finished their diplomas in the service. My mother went as far as eighth grade and never went back to school. She was of the "greatest generation." She reached adulthood at the height of WWII and married her sailor home from the sea. At the time, there was no urgency to complete her high school diploma. But it was a decision she regretted for her entire life.

I only went to college to play football and it somehow lead to an actual degree. Until then, the only career question I ever considered was which branch of the armed forces I would go into after high school.

My dad had served in the Navy for nearly thirty years and he would have liked me to jump in and carry the family flag up some embattled hill in Da Nang. Both of my older brothers had been prematurely discharged from the service and my dad had a hard time understanding how our generation perceived the Vietnam War. Michael, the oldest, was thrown out of Vietnam because he refused to play along and follow the rules of engagement, while Patrick's drug and alcohol demons made him unfit even for a wartime army. They were just kids that the '60s produced. So, like so many others, they were spit out of the service and they came home. My mom was relieved just to have her boys come home alive. My father was humiliated.

"Here, Boatswain Riley. Take your boys back. They keep fucking around and we are trying to fight a war over here."

Michael's darkest day—my family's darkest day—came in September of 1986, a few months after I had successfully defended my doctoral dissertation. Michael agreed to stay with my father, who was suffering from emphysema, while my mother took a break from caring for him and visited her family on the East Coast.

My father was tired of struggling against the inevitable, torturous lung disease that offered no relief or cure. On a smoky Monday night while the Denver Broncos were staging a comeback out in the living room, he asked Michael to help him get comfortable so he could breathe again. And so he did. Michael handed over the full bottle of valium and dutifully left my father alone at his request. Dad died within the hour in an apartment building less than a mile from Mueller Charter School.

FIRST TEACHER

My father was my first teacher and I watched what he did.

I can remember him crying only two times in my entire life: once when his mother died and once when Martin Luther King was assassinated. I was in eighth grade when the latter incident occurred. I wasn't aware of the civil rights movement or why it was necessary. I only knew that if my daddy cried for this man, as he cried over the death of his own mother, he must have been very special.

My father was a mysterious man with a deep intellect. He was always so pensive, cerebral, aloof. Sometimes I think I hardly knew him at all. I learned he had been a teacher briefly at the Naval Academy. I don't know who or what he taught but I always thought it must have inspired some subliminal longing in me to teach like him. He taught me one thing for sure. He cried only for people who mattered. I think my entire life was affected by that image...those fleeting seconds of him standing in the doorway, tears streaming down his face, his back to his boys so we couldn't see.

In that moment back in 1968, there was no such thing as Martin Luther King Day. There were no freeways or promenades or schools named for him yet. There were no MLK curriculum guides or Web sites with thousands of MLK quotes. He was still an enigma to most white Americans.

But our nation's history visited my home that day. Dr. King touched my father, and in that moment of deep sorrow, my father's conviction was revealed. I like to think it survives him. That these two who died as giants to me, live in a purely spiritual plane that still teaches and inspires me. The humbled warrior—part sailor, part preacher. Neither black nor white. Not of the 1960s or any decade of the distant past. But rather, a servant-leader—teaching children that might some day change the world.

LONG SHADOWS

Fifteen years later those same images stretched back toward me like long shadows. While I was researching and writing my dissertation, there were intense moments of personal discovery.

For example, I found the story of the desegregation of America's public schools to be painful, frustrating, and glorious all at once. And it hooked me. There were many heroes, most of whom never made it to the history books.

I also discovered that the legal principle of the equal protection clause was used to argue some of the most urgent and critical issues in modern public education. And that those issues seem to be every bit as unresolved as when they were first advanced.

But most importantly, I realized that we have a moral, legal, and constitutional obligation to engender high academic achievement for our children! And yet, white kids and Asian kids were outperforming African-American kids and Latino kids so convincingly, so consistently, and so universally, that it could be attributed to only one thing—public schools were simply not designed to accommodate our amazingly diverse student communities.

Or, we wanted them to fail.

Or both.

ACADEMIES

Serving as the director of the Juvenile Court and Community Schools provided me with an opportunity to take everything I knew, everything I was good at, and everything for which I had a sincere and passionate commitment...and go to work. It was an opportunity to test my conviction that all children were innately wired for greatness. Even the children everybody else had given up on.

When I started to talk with progressive leaders among San Diego County's juvenile judges and probation officers, I could hear a sense of longing for some kind of different approach for adjudicated youth. The traditional middle schools and high schools were not working for most of these kids. San Diego was always considered a leader in the state when it came to creating alternative "community" school programs — especially for kids who had been locked up or expelled. But over time, community schools had proliferated too rapidly and kids were housed wherever an inexpensive lease could be signed.

We had nearly 2,000 students in these community schools scattered around the city. They were self-contained classrooms that housed ten to twenty students, with a teacher and an aide. They provided children with a comprehensive high school program and the credits they needed to earn a diploma.

The classrooms were converted storefronts in strip malls, office buildings, churches, and warehouses. Some were nice. Most were horrible. Kids went to school next to liquor stores, X-rated theaters, chop shops and crack houses. I just thought they deserved better.

So we created a new kind of community school specifically for juvenile felons returning from incarceration. We called them "Academies".

We put one on site at the world-famous San Diego Zoo and designed it as an environmental studies magnet. Students were permitted to wear zoo uniforms and many got part-time jobs there. We then created a physical fitness academy at the Barnes Tennis Center in Ocean Beach. Then a science academy at the Ruben H. Fleet Space Museum in Balboa Park.

Then we tried to create a Marine Science Academy at Sea World. The CEO was reluctant because he was afraid to mix convicted juvenile offenders with his summer work force...all of whom were the same age. He wrung his hands and delayed for months until we could finally get a meeting with him and his staff. "What will I tell the parents of my summer employees?" he asked. "What will I tell our patrons when they want to know why Sea World is hiring juveniles who have been convicted of a crime?"

"What did you tell them last summer?" I asked.

"I didn't tell them anything."

"Did they ask?"

"No...why would they? We had a great season with our employees."

"Well you just proved that kids like ours will rise to the level of expectation we have for them."

"How is that?"

"Last summer, you hired thirty-eight convicted juvenile offenders as seasonal employees, all of whom had been placed here by probation."

The CEO looked at his staff incredulously as if to ask if I were bullshitting him.

"Is this guy bullshitting me?"

"No sir. We had thirty-eight employees from probation working in virtually every area of the park...without incident. This program will only be different because they will not only work here — they will also go to school to study marine science and get their high school diploma."

Our classroom opened a few weeks later at the Marina Village conference center across the street.

There were many more innovative academies in a planning stage. We negotiated with the United States Marines Corps to place a Leadership Academy at the Marine Corps recruiting depot. We were working on a Physical Therapy Academy for Qualcomm Stadium, a Tourism Academy at the Convention Center, an Economics Academy at Merrill Lynch, and a Technology Academy at Sony. Many business leaders we worked with said the same thing: "Wow...too bad you have to get arrested to go to these schools. My kid would love to be in an academy like this."

Around the state, other counties embraced the concept and were working to do the same kinds of things. And why not? What an exciting way to teach and learn. What a refreshing way to organize curricula for kids for whom the traditional curriculum never seemed to make sense. What a compelling way to think about educating the kids that the traditional schools never wanted in the first place. Engaging. Meaningful.

Who wouldn't support the academies and the tremendous potential they had to benefit high-risk kids?

Unfortunately, people's altruism goes only so far. I learned how hard it is to convince a community that all children are innately desirous of being good, and that they often just need another chance. A lot of people believe "it takes a village"...they just don't want it to be their village. But even that's not what killed the academies.

The real killer of the academy idea was the established old Juvenile Court and Community School *system*—the frightened teachers afraid of change, the administrators who merely wanted to quietly retire and not have to stretch, the militant court schools labor union, and the fundamentalist school board members who were preoccupied with their own trivial politics.

They all realized that if the academies continued to gather momentum, the old strip mall models could disappear. Out in the strip malls there were no expectations. There was no curriculum, no standards. There was also very little supervision and zero accountability. Teachers could come and go at will. Kids could come and go too. No one kept roll. No one accounted for anything to anybody. In fact, the community schools worked academically for kids only so long as they had a caring and conscientious teacher. Otherwise, they were not much more than a youth center.

The academies were true partnerships that got a lot of attention. They worked. And they raised the bar. Sooner or later, we would have moved out of every urine-stained strip mall classroom in San Diego County and into a state-of-the-art academy that you would want for your own child. But I have noticed that too much attention is never a good thing in public education. It was not a good thing for the Hispanic Reading Pilot or the Global Education Program. It wasn't a good thing for the academies either.

After a while, there were complaints that we were siphoning off all the JCCS resources for these creative programs. The teachers' union complained that the academies were a huge drain on the other community schools. They knew better. They knew that we had actually received a state grant that funded them and that the programs were precisely what legislators in Sacramento envisioned when millions of dollars became available to any imaginative educators who believed they could design a better school system for our most high-risk kids.

The academies were growing like a virus and if the opponents were going to control it they would have to kill the host. And so they did. And I was the host.

At the time, the County Superintendent of Schools had problems of his own with two whacky school board members that wanted desperately to fire his ass and send him to the desert. The union leaders liked the Superintendent but made it clear that they could only continue to support him if he could cure them of that academy virus guy. So he concocted a lethal inoculation against any more forward thinking that was going to advance the cause of court school kids.

I could have stayed and fought but there is a moment in every journey where you realize *you* are the very reason why an organization can't get out of its own way and move forward. I reached that point. I was fighting on too many fronts: Monarch High School, the Community Home Education Program, the academies. I chose to live to fight another day.

When I left the Juvenile Court and Community Schools, I had no hard feelings. I knew they would disassemble the academies as soon as I packed my last box and headed down the driveway. And they did.

In the end, I could not overcome the inertia and lethargy of a system so efficiently designed to resist change. And so I failed those children. I learned from that. When I came to Mueller Charter School, I was wiser for the experience. And more determined to develop not just creative programs, but my own capacity for leading change.

MICHELANGELO

For not following the well-worn path, I had been regarded as a maverick, a rebel, a warrior...and sometimes even a stubborn asshole. I guess it all depends on your point of view.

But I always counted on three personal attributes that just seem to lend themselves to creating change:

First, I was quite content in pirate gear. I was enough of a revolutionary to be comfortable with challenging the systems that I loathed as a kid.

Secondly, I knew I could write and that my words could fly. I knew that words could land feather-soft and make you weep, or they could explode, like nuclear warheads, raining fire from miles above the earth. And so I used them. And I wrote them down.

And finally, I had an active imagination fueled by the honest belief that we could create better schools. "I saw the angel in the marble," said Michelangelo, "and carved until I set him free."

I wanted to use these weapons and create a ruckus. I didn't want attention. I didn't want a spotlight. I just wanted to knock over the furniture and break things. I wanted to turn the party house upside down. I wanted to set free better schools for kids.

A CHILD NAMED OPRAH

A charter petition is the business plan for a charter school. It describes the goals, the strategies, and the metrics to prove that the promise of the petition has been kept.

Mueller's charter petition had already undergone multiple revisions and amendments before I had read it for the fist time. By conventions of the document, anyone could propose an amendment at any time. So, in my first year as principal, I set out to clarify the areas that I had struggled to understand when I initially read it. It took awhile but I was finally able to pinpoint my confusion: the charter petition was not solely about kids! It had elements of a labor agreement, elements of a strategic plan, elements of the education code requirements that were typical of a boilerplate petition. But it was missing the audacious vision that the children of Chula Vista so desperately needed.

Though creating clever slogans for schools in the form of vision statements was a little passé, we still felt strongly that we could develop a unifying idea that drove people. We adopted a statement that simply promised: *Our children will change the world.*

Then we thought about what that really meant.

Children from poor sections of Chula Vista rarely go on to change the world. To do so requires power and expertise and opportunities far beyond what would be offered to children with such modest means and ambitions. And, of course, the one and only path to power, expertise, and opportunity is education—at the highest level. From the most elite universities.

Business and political leaders can change the world. Eminent scholars and scientists and inventors can change the world. Design engineers and successful artists can change the world. But few former graduates of Mueller Charter School have filled these vocations.

We thought a lot about the portents of Mueller students positioned one day to create world change. We began to write this statement everywhere we could—on our letterhead, on our newsletters, in our performing arts center, on our Web site, in the front office. People got the meaning. It was challenging their expectations.

If you know you are teaching children who will one day have the power and opportunity and expertise to significantly change our world, it is bound to affect your expectations and your treatment of them? How do you want them to remember you? How might you inspire them to stretch and grow and discover the depths of their potential?

Imagine turning back the hands of time, and looking out into your fourth-grade classroom—down the neat little rows of fresh-faced children on the first day of school. Imagine there is a child named Oprah Winfrey or a scruffy-headed Irish kid who everybody calls Bono.

Imagine looking to the corner seat at the nerd with the big glasses and the nondescript name Bill Gates. "What a geek! Bet he can't catch a football."

Imagine you could see them in the future...among the most powerful and successful people in the world. For the fleeting moment that they are in your classroom, they are only children, inviting the adults around them to provide a positive influence to their development. They will become the products of our expectations.

Our new vision statement resonated with people who happened to believe, as I did, that our children mattered. We created a kind of creed around it. It became our anthem. In the difficult moments of struggle and challenge over the next few years, we would come face to face with our beliefs and core values and repeatedly have to choose to place our students' needs ahead of our own. Our actions would have to reflect these ideals or we would lose our way forever. This statement, published in our Charter Petition, was our lighthouse, even in chaotic moments and long periods of dense, dense fog:

- At Mueller Charter School, we believe that every child has the potential to change the world.

- We believe that a future president, a master engineer, a concert cellist, a groundbreaking oncologist, a space pioneer, a Nobel Prize winner—is currently sitting in a classroom somewhere in America, and therefore they could be any child here at Mueller Charter School.

- Our children will change the world.

- We believe that every child has unlimited potential for learning.

- We believe that we can create an elementary school that is a national model in its ability to meet the complex needs of our children and their families, to offer exciting and challenging learning experiences, and to engender extraordinary academic results by any measure.

- We believe that we can create opportunities for genuine parent governance and participation, and create options in which the community can become inextricably linked with the mission of our school.

- We believe that we have the ability, the will, the opportunity, and the obligation to reinvent the institution of schools, to challenge the status quo, to remove barriers to our student's success, and to make Mueller Charter School worthy of its children.

- We believe that our children will change the world.

Eventually we laced the charter with references to our students, their goals, and our belief in their capacity for amazing accomplishments. Though I did not know how the Charter Petition had been used in the past, I was determined to make it our roadmap now. So, it needed to reflect the collective child-centered values of our organization.

It didn't speak for everyone, but it spoke for a critical mass. And it sent a strong message that Mueller Charter School would no longer operate its business as usual. We now had a focused, specific, inspired mission. It was non-negotiable. It was urgent. And it had been captured in writing.

Amending our Charter Petition requires two-thirds of the staff to vote in favor of the proposed change. So we had an election. The vote was unanimous.

BULL'S-EYE

Once the amendments to the Charter Petition had been approved, we referred to it constantly. We had our child-centered business plan... now we needed the actions to back it up. I sensed that not everybody held the Charter Petition in the same esteem that I did. I got the feeling that it was a document that people used only from time to time, either when they wanted some leverage on a plan they were proposing (or opposing) or when they wanted to argue for personal advantage. I felt that every teacher and every staff member needed to read, understand, internalize, and believe in the charter as a document that elevated our children as the center of all school business.

We quickly got better at framing questions and discussions around "what is best for our students." As our perspectives changed, our language changed...and eventually our ideas and expectations changed too. Then our results.

The majority of our teachers embraced the notion that a charter school was a kind of ever-evolving action research project...a petri dish in which to try to grow cool things. They accepted their role as entrepreneurs with a willingness to challenge the status quo in all aspects of our school.

We started to ask:

"If money were no object and you had full control over all decisions—and the implementation of decisions—how would you design a school *for your own children?*"

This was our guiding question that called for the development of child-centered systems and programs. As we created innovative alternatives for even the most routine of organizational tasks, we began to slowly transform Mueller Charter School into a place that seemed to realize for the first time that it existed for its students.

We created changes that affected everything about our work— from our expectations for our students to the expectations we had of ourselves. We agreed that our students were worthy of a better effort. We agreed that we were collectively capable of a better effort. We agreed there was something very liberating about working in a charter school. We agreed that we had really just scratched the surface of our infinite potential.

There was a lot we didn't agree on too. And it's too often upon what people don't agree that they are so willing to wage their wars. Before I could unpack my boxes and my baggage hauled in by Mayflower from the Juvenile Court and Community Schools, I saw the scope of Mueller's raging turmoil. I can tell you this, I needed to learn a whole lot more about charter schools if we were going to salvage El Milagro.

CHAPTER THREE

The Covenant

It is impossible to create a healthy culture if we refuse to meet, and if we refuse to listen. But if we meet, and when we listen, we reweave the world into wholeness. And holiness.

—Margaret J. Wheatley

THE LAUNCH

Charter schools are created in an atmosphere of tremendous emotion and expectation. They are a rocket launch at Cape Kennedy.

Like any new business, it is not uncommon for the concept to exceed the capability of the designers. Whether educators, community citizens, NASA engineers, parents, or some combination are behind a charter initiative, there is, if nothing else, hope and optimism. There is sometimes the euphoria of having launched the rocket, of getting it off the ground before it explodes and falls back to earth in a self-consuming fire. In that glorious moment when we look skyward, seeing a vaporous trail of spent white fuel pushing our grand design straight into the heavens, there is even the hope that a mission will somehow be defined as it hurtles through space.

And there is a change. By design. And where there is change there are the inevitable forces that oppose change.

Mueller has been a charter school since 1994. It is one of California's original charters...a pioneer of the movement. Through three renewal cycles, the school has been distracted and torn by internal conflict, lawsuits, union pressures, attempted coup d'etats, hostile takeovers, and community indifference. Staff has come and gone. One principal was removed. And because it is a place rife with revolt, it has been ground zero in testing legal precedents on multiple fronts.

Through it all, the children came too...and even in troubling times...some have excelled beyond any legislator's keenest imagination. But back in July of 2000, Mueller was at a crossroads. We had one more chance to be extraordinary—to be El Milagro—or to revert back to an ordinary neighborhood school that promised only to trap children in eternal mediocrity. It was the moment of truth—the rocket launch when all systems are go but the weather is threatening. If there was ever a time to ignite the engines it was now...and the spark was provided by our Charter Petition.

THE FRANCHISE

A *charter* is simply a contract, a covenant—an agreement between two parties.

You can charter a limo. You can charter a plane or a fishing boat. You can charter a corner 7-11. Run it yourself. Pay the headquarters a fee for using the name 7-11 and then make your own decisions about where you want to put the Red Bull and what magazines you want to display on the corner racks.

And you can charter a school.

Charter schools are independent, public schools, created and operated by the educators and parents whose dreams live or die on the strength of their resourcefulness.

They set forth their goals and operating procedures in the Charter Petition, and present it to their local school board. There is a simple quid pro quo: in exchange for your freedom, you must produce a miracle.

The school board says:

"Here's the deal: We promise...no more micromanagement, no more red tape....and no more meddling from the district office. How's that sound?"

"Uhhh, no offense but it sounds a little too good to be true. How are you gonna control yourself?"

"Easy. We are going to wait for you to self-destruct...or produce a miracle."

Charters are free from many of the constraining obligations of local, state, and federal forces. They operate like a private business. Like a franchise. All of the policies, programs, decisions, resources, and energy can be focused on the needs of the population of the school. The traditional monoliths of the status quo—the idea killers—are neutralized through charter law. This includes governing boards, the teachers' union, the district office, and in our case, the educrats of

Sacramento—none of whom know a single child who attends Mueller Charter School.

There is an alluring appeal inherent in the promise of academic freedom. There is also the obligation to deliver results that could not be achieved had the yoke of diligent oversight never been lifted. In California, as in many of the states with charter laws, there are all kinds of charter schools. There are start-ups and conversions. There are fiscally independent charters. There are charters that have declared themselves the employer for purposes of collective bargaining. There are innovative charters and charters that are charters in name only. There are successful charters. And there are failed charters whose bones litter the landscape, piling higher by the year. They feed their critics with ammunition and hope that the whole charter movement is just a temporary nightmare that will soon go away.

Just when you think there is really no good news about how charter schools and their children are performing...just when you are so sure you have them all figured out...just when you think there is nothing unique about them at all...along comes Mueller Charter School.

VOUCHERS

Most schools have a business plan in one form or another. There are the ones that are required by law in order to secure specific funding, and there are internal ones that are agreements on how business will be conducted. There are even the unwritten business plans that define the culture of how people interact and what goals they seek to achieve.

In the 1990s, public school leaders embraced a growing trend toward creating community-generated strategic plans. We were told it was a model "borrowed from the business world." This has always been a surefire way to get educators to implement something. The promise that we might be adopting some secret weapon of corporate America is irresistible. Never mind that many of the businesses that touted their 1990s-era strategic plans boarded up their windows and sold back their leased office furniture a long time ago.

Nevertheless, days were spent in retreats with the broad representation of a school community: parents, teachers, administrators, board members, community citizens, and students. We called them stakeholders. During the strategic planning, an outside consultant guided the group through a process—the fruits of which typically included a written vision statement, a mission, organizational goals and objectives, and strategies for achieving their miracle. And a consultant's bill that featured breakfast rolls and decaffeinated coffee.

Whenever organizations bring their stakeholders together to articulate a mission, it inevitably improves communication and morale, even if only for the moment. It builds that all-important buy-in and unity of purpose. It establishes a kind of marketing plan. Ultimately, it even sets the tone for nurturing and growing a kind of group character that helps a team to more efficiently weather adversity as time goes on. But not all organizational models transfer so efficiently to schools.

After their facilitated strategic planning sessions, school stakeholders were faced with the realities of actually implementing their infant plan. Stained by continental breakfast and catered Caesar salads, the *plan* showed up in spiral-bound notebooks disseminated for all staff members who weren't fortunate enough to have participated in the *process*. There were dedication ceremonies during which superintendents and board members publicly congratulated themselves for their progressive business sense and for successfully formulating a strategic plan.

But board members come and go. Superintendents, like students, come and go too. Pretty soon you could hear people in the faculty lounge asking "whatever happened to that strategic plan and that big mission statement we were all supposed to memorize?" Then that sarcastic laughter—that kind of "I-told-you-so" laughter. Like, "I told you this too shall pass." And a heavy-throated *whoosh* blows through the room, sucks all the air out for an instant, and kills the potted plants.

"That, my dear friends," says the most seasoned and cynical teacher camped out by the microwave, "is the pendulum swing."

Charter plans, however, are not just strategic plans on hotel stationary. They are not just doorstops to prop open the door of the faculty lounge during the next pendulum swing. They are flight plans. They drive the bus.

As greater external pressures are brought to bear on schools for producing results, these organizational road maps are more critical than ever. Besides, a business plan must be carefully conceived and published as a prerequisite for local board approval. Any group of people who wish to establish a new charter (*start-up* charter) or convert an existing school into a charter (*conversion* charter), has to create their explicit business plan, which is described in the law as a *Charter Petition*. In California, this petition must detail specific features of the school design, as listed in the Education Code. The law requires that a charter petition describe—for example—its vision, mission, goals, metric for determining success, governance model, role of parents, and relationship with the school district.

It was from this law that charters were born in California.

By 1992, public education was essentially adrift in mediocrity, as it had been for decades. There were many ideas about school "restructuring" and school "reform" that everyone knew were necessary to blast the American school system out of the doldrums.

But the stranglehold of the teachers' union, coupled with a general lack of vision and audacity, had routinely thwarted any threat of dramatic institutional change. Anyone could see an ever-widening performance chasm that was developing along racial, ethnic, and economic lines, and if that did not get the attention of the greater community, the gaps that existed between American students as a whole and their international counterparts did. In comparison test after comparison test, it seemed, and in every academic area, our kids were outperformed by kids in countries with far fewer resources and far less commitment to lofty ideas like *equality*. The more we tested, the more the gap persisted.

Legislators who were not beholden to special interests wanted a better model, and so did voters. All across America, those same voters were electing representatives who had the courage and ideas to fix their schools. All across America, state legislators were simultaneously arriving at the same conclusion: if our public schools were going to significantly improve, we were going to have to let the air out of the tires on that old pile of crap that wasn't running very well and leave it where it died on the side of the road. We would have to abandon her like a beloved old '63 Impala—with the familiar seats and the old floorboards ground to grease from gum and oil and French fries. We would have to trade her in for that new edition we have been hearing about...the one called charter schools.

SHANKER

The initial vision of a charter school was articulated by Albert Shanker, the president of the American Federation of Teachers, on March 31, 1988, when he spoke to the National Press Club in Washington, DC, on the subject of restructuring American public schools. He said:

"Districts could create joint school board-union panels that would review preliminary proposals and help find seed money for the teachers to develop final proposals. The panels would then issue charters to these groups and commit themselves to trying to waive for the charter schools certain regulations that legitimately stand in the way of implementing their proposal, if the faculty so argue. The faculty also would be allocated their share of the per pupil budget spent in other schools, as well as the space and resources they might ordinarily

have. All of this would be voluntary. No teacher would have to participate, and parents would choose whether or not to send their children to a charter school."

Not exactly "I Have a Dream" on Lincoln's steps but extraordinarily visionary for the times and the industry.

History is filled with strange ironies and this was one of them. Here was the president of one of America's two largest teachers unions dreaming out loud about a school concept that could one day be the undoing of his labor union.

From the beginning, the whole vision of charter schools was to free groups of educators and parents from the perceived micromanagement of state boards and school boards and let them create their own destiny, through signed agreements with their districts. Charters wouldn't just free up the teachers. Administrators, too, would be free of central office restrictions, union-negotiated straightjackets, and even state-level polices and laws.

These ideas were inspired by the early work of educators like Shanker, and Ray Budde, a New England educator who experimented with a charter model in the late 1970s. But they also had deep roots in other innovative structures that in one way or another pushed back against the status quo. As more and more children failed to fully benefit from their public schools, we saw the emergence of alternative schools, voucher initiatives, site-based management, magnet schools, public school choice, privatization, community-parental empowerment, and the school-within-a-school option. Charter schools could cherry-pick whatever structure and model they wanted, depending on the strengths of their teachers and the learning needs of their students.

The idea of independent *charter* schools, run like private businesses, appealed to conservatives because they believed that charters could trigger the debate on vouchers and perhaps even begin to loosen the union monopoly. If this could happen, they believed they could hasten the emergence of free market competition, greater teacher empowerment, and ultimately, authentic parent choice in schools.

Liberals liked the charter concept too but, of course, for different reasons. They believed that charter schools could potentially satiate the general public's hunger for vouchers, which they feared would siphon public dollars off to private schools. Charters would inevitably lead to democratic renewal—a kind of grass roots movement toward less-centralized, local leadership. Thus the liberals saw teacher empowerment as a by-product of charters too.

The city of Philadelphia pioneered elements of the charter idea in their school-within-a-school model of the late 1980s. But it wasn't until 1991 that Minnesota became the first state to actually adopt a law enabling groups to establish charter schools. California was right behind them, writing and adopting their charter law in 1992.

Within five years, there were twenty more states with strong charter laws on the books. There were some common themes in those laws—a common vision of public school models that would be nothing short of revolutionary:

- Each school would run like an independent business, free of district and confining state laws;
- While freed from the laws that constrain, charters would willingly adhere to the common set of laws that preserve the welfare of our students—laws that address their health, safety, and civil rights;
- To promote innovation, there would be very few barriers or restrictions in the start-up phase;
- Each state developed their own guidelines for the number of charters in the state, as well as a number, type, process for approval and appeal;
- Charter schools would be designed to engender student academic success. Period. Rather than focus on methods and regulations, charters would be judged solely on student outcomes;
- Significantly, charter schools would also feature a model of financial independence.

And, just as there were common design features as charter schools began to emerge, there were also some common challenges in actually getting them opened. In California, for instance, charter organizers had to inspire approval from more than 50% of the school staff who would work at the charter, and ultimately, win approval from their local governing boards. Both processes hinged on a clear and succinct business plan that described the charter vision—thus, the Charter Petition.

The petition became a public covenant, a promise that the school staff and community would work together to achieve the vision described within. New agreements and working relationships evolved between the charters and their sponsoring districts.

The autonomy—combined with the inherent ambiguity that had been built into charter law—created an immediate demand for a new style of leadership. In charter schools, the traditional elements of instructional expertise would not be sufficient. Charter leadership now demanded visionaries with a rare combination of business acumen, a knack for creating innovative solutions, a rebellious streak, and just enough knowledge of law to be dangerous.

NUMBER 64

Meanwhile, Robert L. Mueller's elementary school was sitting inconspicuously in its cozy corner by the borders—barely in California but not quite in Mexico. Thanks to a law approved in Sacramento called the Charter School Act of 1992, it became Mueller *Charter* School.

The author of California's charter law was a former high school teacher named Gary Hart. At the time, Hart was a state senator, a Democrat from Santa Barbara who possessed degrees from Harvard and Stanford, and who paid attention to what leaders from around the country were saying about charter schools. Perhaps he was inspired by some East Coast guy with the same name who once wanted to be our president. But more likely, he was inspired by Albert Shanker, whose work he regularly read in the *New York Times*.

As the chair of California's Senate Education Committee, Hart sought a charter design with three nonnegotiables: 1) Charters would get the same funding as the non-charter public schools, 2) there could be no religious affiliation or motive, and 3) there could be no discrimination in the selection of students for admission to the school.

Hart had lots of believers. Many California legislators liked the idea of removing the regulatory burdens from schools. They wanted to see what could happen when you set communities free to create new school designs...ones that actually worked for *their* kids...and for *all* kids. They were prepared for the fight that inevitably comes when hallowed institutions like the state Legislature turn the status quo on its head. And a fight had to come.

California had longed for a "school reform movement," but there was little real reform. By 1992, it was still business as usual in the Golden State. But then along came charter schools and the prospect of an exciting alternative to otherwise moribund bureaucracies. They promised the perfect blend of local entrepreneurialism and self-imposed accountability. In exchange for complete autonomy and an opportunity to design schools according to the needs of a specific community, charter schools were encouraged to inspire risk taking. They are to operate like a "laboratory" for school innovation. Charter schools are expected...

- To improve student learning;
- To increase learning opportunities for all students;
- To expand learning opportunities, especially for pupils identified as academically low achieving;
- To encourage the use of diverse and innovative teaching methods;
- To create exciting new professional opportunities for teachers and engage them in designing the specific learning programs at a school site;
- To provide students and parents with expanded choices in the types of educational opportunities traditionally available within a public school system; and
- To provide the flexibility to promote organizational innovation and expand students' educational options.

You don't necessarily have to be a charter school to promise these benefits to families. We did them all at Skyline School in Solana Beach. We did them because we chose to. It was our collective nature to experiment and create innovative methods. We were the rebel school.

In the Charter School Act of 1992, these expectations are understood. They are preconditions for any community that chooses to open its own charter school.

The California Teachers Association (CTA) didn't much like the new charter law. Albert Shanker notwithstanding, they sensed a monster on the front lawn that would stomp on their authority as the preeminent guardian of an ethos defined by "the way we have always done things around here". They fought hard to contain the potential damage of the new law. In smoky union offices across the state, local officials got the bad news in the form of digestible executive summaries from their legislative analysts...sort of *School Law For Dummies* that regularly come to union officials and administrators alike.

There was the ominous specter of charter schools spreading like weeds all across the state. There was panic in the halls of the CTA: Teachers and administrators being set free to actually work together? Fiscal independence? Freedom from education code provisions? Which provisions? Freedom, potentially, even from the provisions of collective bargaining and contracts that had been signed in the blood of our union forefathers? What about our contracts?

Clearly, this charter upstart had to be stopped. Or at least contained.

So, following the successful passage of Hart's Charter School legislation, the CTA managed to restrict the number of charters that could be started in the state. But the damage was done. The movement was officially born. And though it would take fifteen years to come to full fruition, the seed of El Milagro was planted.

By 1999 there were 250 charter schools in California.

By 2007, there were more than 600 charters serving 221,000 students. There were six charter schools in the Chula Vista Elementary School District alone. Fully 3% of the children in the state were now enrolled in charter schools. Of those, 70% were start-up schools, while 30% were conversions of existing schools, like Mueller.

Nationwide, charter schools were experiencing explosive growth as well. Increasing by a rate of 13% a year, charter schools now comprised 4% of all public schools nationally. And by the start of the 2007-08 school year, there were more than 3,000 charter schools serving 700,000 children in over forty states.

The original law permitted the development of only one hundred charter schools in all of California. Mueller was number sixty-four.

NUCLEAR FIRE

Charters emerged about the same time that state testing programs and federal grandstanding in the form of No Child Left Behind began to devour the spirit and innovative energy of educators. Perhaps the convergence was inevitable. But in reality, the sky-high achievement goals now in demand can likely not be achieved *except* in charter schools.

Like the magnet schools that were developed in the decades before, charters started to create unique programmatic features. Some had a creative and performing arts focus, or literature, or marine biology. Others were designed specifically to provide opportunities in technology or leadership.

Many charters were established for specific populations of children trapped in inner-city malaise. On the theory that the public schools aren't doing a damn thing for their kids, parents and entrepreneurs demanded to take their children back and educate them themselves. Many of these schools featured curricula that presented the humanities in an ethnic context that could for once make sense to their children.

Some charters thrived and some didn't.

But one thing seemed consistent in all of them. The more they pushed the envelope, the more unique and effective they were at getting those measurable academic results—the more of a target they were for any agency with a vested interest in slowing their progress. So there has always been tremendous pressure on many charters, including El Milagro, to restore the status quo. The pressure takes on many forms:

- The demand for teachers and administrators, to train like, work like, and behave like all other teachers in the state;
- The demand to conform to restrictive and tedious regulations;
- The effort from labor unions and their representative legislators to restrict charter freedoms;
- The media's insistence on defining charters as if they were all one in the same;
- The fallout from charter school operators who have failed to be innovative, unique, or effective;
- And, of course, the charters' own well-earned reputation for lacking the acumen to manage either a school like a business or a business like a school.

Like nuclear power plants, charter schools often incubate as a brilliant source of light. Powered by their own creative energy, the kinetic and sometimes violent forces push so hard, simultaneously and in all directions, that they create a delicate equilibrium that hovers precariously between infinite brilliance and utter catastrophe. The by-product of this fusion is more energy—as innovative charter schools seem to either flourish or implode.

For nearly a decade El Milagro lived on that razor-sharp balance... seeking purpose. Who are we going to be? Why are we a charter? What's in it for kids? What's in it for me?

The stakes have always been high because children on the western, impoverished fringes of Chula Vista—like poor children all across America—can no longer afford second-rate schools collapsing like plastic straws in the heat of their own fire.

ROAD MAP

The difference between Mueller and many other schools, and even between the school it used to be, is that, by conventions of charter law, it now has an operable business plan called a Charter Petition. We *live* by that plan.

The Charter Petition reflects the vision of El Milagro. It is our rudder, whenever we remember to use it as such. Unlike all of those "strategic plan" notebooks now safely tucked away in dusty filing cabinets from previous decades...this rudder is still in the water, steering us to wherever it is that we are going, so long as we can keep one hand on the wheel and one eye on the horizon.

It has managed to keep us on course, even through tremendous chaos and turmoil. The Charter Petition is the Constitution of El Milagro:

- It articulates our **core values**—especially our service to children. Sometimes eloquently and sometimes more clumsily, the words are a constant reminder that schools exist for children and not as employment agencies for adults.
- The Charter Petition consists of fourteen chapters, each of which is required by charter law. One of those chapters defines the **goals** of our charter. Nothing ventured nothing gained: they unambiguously set the organizational bar so high, that the one might regard Mueller as either extraordinarily ambitious or delusional.
- The Charter Petition establishes the climate in which **change, ambiguity, innovation, trial and error, and risk taking** are a cultural norm and expectation.
- The Charter Petition describes our efforts to build **teacher efficacy** and to create a unique organizational design that lends itself to **efficient governance.**
- The Charter Petition is framed by **programmatic solutions**... ideas...the creative capital that makes it possible to overcome immense challenges within our community.

And the Charter Petition provides the ultimate measuring stick for accountability—in effect, the ground rules for *keeping* the charter. It reminds us that the district could revoke our agreement and turn us back into a traditional district school if it is determined that we have somehow lost our collective marbles and

- Committed a material violation of any conditions, standards, or procedures set forth in the Charter Petition; or
- Failed to meet or pursue any of the pupil outcomes identified in the Charter Petition; or
- Failed to meet generally accepted accounting standards of

fiscal management;

- Or violated any provision of law.

Ultimately, the free market is driven by outcomes—not just strategic plans, corporate off-sites, or shiny new buildings with 3,000-square-foot exercise rooms. Results matter. Outcomes are influenced by strategies; strategies are influenced by ideas; and ideas by the passion to achieve greatness on behalf of others. These are all contained in the Charter Petition of Mueller Charter School. This is our road map.

SPEED OF LIGHT

At first glance, Mueller's Charter Petition looks like many others. It was written to the state's formula, but two very distinctive ideologies influenced its development and its potential as a map for deep revolutionary change. Like some ancient European city that had been fought for and divided and colonized for centuries, the influences can be peeled back in generational layers; the differences clearly pronounced:

"See the architecture of those buildings? That is the influence of the invading Celts. Remember those guys, with their kilts and their bagpipes? And the next block over is the Moorish roof structures. And then the heavy mortar-laden walls that were used to discourage bilge rats when the pirate ships pulled up. On that horizon is the post-WWI neighborhood and to the East, post-WWII..."

The architectural themes of Mueller's Charter Petition, reflected the best and worst of our intentions. Time passes and some of the earlier efforts seem a little disingenuous—like reading the Constitution knowing that the framers held slaves. The problem wasn't in the drafting, but rather, the execution of ideas.

There have actually been *two* charter movements at Mueller.

The first influence was that of former employees who sought to utilize the document as a uniquely flexible contract for teachers. The staff had sought to build on all of the protections and benefits of the teachers union agreement, coupled with the flexibility and freedoms of charter law. It was a vision of how the charter would benefit employees, how adults would behave toward each other and who would steer the ship. It was a marriage of convenience. There was language that defined procedures for filing grievances layered together with teachers' scope of authority as defined by charter law. Over several years, new language and new agreements were added into the document. With each new edition, with every amendment, the purpose of the charter became more obscure.

Then came the Migden election, the state-mandated process through which Mueller teachers declared that they would be their own employer for purposes of collective bargaining. In that decision, they tossed out the teachers union and touched off a civil war that created turmoil, divided and distracted the staff, and prematurely ended a number of careers.

By the time I pulled up to the front curb at Mueller Charter School there was still blood flowing in the streets. I rescued a copy of the Charter Petition from the bulldozers and even after I read it a dozen times, I still had no idea at all what this charter school stood for.

And perhaps that was by design. Perhaps to the early Mueller charter designers the Petition itself was not the point. Perhaps the Petition was a merely a formality—like just another *strategic plan* presented to the board and then tucked deep into the shelf space of the faculty workroom.

I didn't see it that way. I saw a lost opportunity for clarity and direction. I saw a living document that should be treated with the same level of reverence and awe that we treat our federal Constitution.

The obvious components missing from the Charter Petition were the obligation to parents and advocacy for children. So we converted the Petition from a labor contract to a prescription for transformational change that was so desperately needed. We laced it with an unmistakable bias toward serving children. We created our own rules of engagement. We empowered our staff to be brilliant. We designed a governance model built for moving ideas at the speed of light. We scripted our revolt before we staged it. We established sky-high goals that have rarely been achieved in demographics like ours. And we staked the future of our charter on achieving them.

PHILADELPHIA

As El Milagro began to rise from the ashes, so too did the quiet leadership of Maureen DeLuca. As a young teacher Maureen DeLuca was caught up in the churning politics of Mueller Charter School and swept to wherever the waters would carry her.

Our teachers come from all over America and Maureen DeLuca came to Mueller from Philadelphia. She graduated from West Chester University and then headed west with her fiancé. They didn't know anybody in California. They only landed in Chula Vista because that is where she was meant to be. The original charter advocates captured

Maureen DeLuca for her energy and idealism; and maybe because she was from Philadelphia. There was some sweet symmetry in including a child of the patriots in the process.

She read the charter law and listened to the ideas of the veteran teachers and then voted for change. Then she started to attend the committee meetings and helped them write the first charter drafts. And then she stood in the doorway when the walls were caving in. And while the original Mueller settlers packed their farm implements and exited in droves...Maureen DeLuca stayed. She maintained her deep faith in the idea that teachers and parents and administrators could operate schools independently and achieve prodigious outcomes for their students. She quietly resisted self-serving ploys from various factions to capture the charter for adult interests. She maintained her belief in the academic potential and fundamental goodness that was everywhere in our children and in our community. She bided her time. And the whole while, she honed her skills as a teacher.

We went through four literacy coaches before we realized that our most skilled reading teacher was already here. We didn't have to import any more experts from the outside...veterans who failed to grasp the uniqueness of living in a charter school. So Maureen DeLuca became our literacy coach and our teachers benefited mightily from her expertise.

Then we searched for an Associate Principal to replace the line of others who left for one reason or another. So Maureen DeLuca became our Associate Principal and again our teachers benefited mightily from her expertise.

And as El Milagro continues to evolve, it will do so on the energy and spirit of teacher-leaders born for revolutions. Like Maureen DeLuca, a founding author of the charter vision—not so far removed from the forge of the liberty bell and a city called Philadelphia.

LIBI GIL

The life cycle of a charter in California is five years. After the fifth year, the charter proponents can request that their charter be renewed, or they can pack up all of their hopes and dreams and return the building to whatever it was before the charter was granted...be that a converted 7-11 in a strip mall, or a fifty-year-old elementary school tucked into the corner of a rapidly changing community like Chula Vista.

Mueller Charter School was first approved in 1994. Five years later, in 1999, they were granted their first renewal. The second renewal came in 2003.

A lot happened at that school during those formative years.

It may not have been evident what they were trying to accomplish, but El Milagro owes its existence to the foundation created by the educators who preceded us here. One thing is certain, like many schools across America, they desperately wanted to insulate themselves from the fierce determination and expectations and supervision of a strong superintendent. In our case, that was Libi Gil.

Throughout the 1990s and on into the new millennium, Libi Gil was regarded as one of California's rising stars. She was aggressive, laser focused, bright, and creative. She was a lethal adversary for those who were none of these things. For the principals and staff who could not stay true to the district mission of serving *children*, Libi Gil was their worst nightmare. Moreover, she surrounded herself with an inner circle of strong assistant superintendents who faithfully carried the company flag. When principals veered too far off course, it was one of the assistant superintendents who lopped off their heads or other body parts. "Off course" was never officially defined, and that made the job of principals a little trickier. All anybody ever knew with certainty, was that Libi Gil was committed to children, academic achievement, and progressive leadership. Principals had to fill in the blanks on the rest of it. It was kind of a guessing game...but you either had the stuff to lead in the climate she created or you didn't. If you didn't have her same core values, you could never consistently guess right and do the things that she thought you should do as a principal. Those who didn't were thrown overboard into a rapidly growing pool of *former* administrators splashing frantically around looking for a floatation device to save their careers.

Libi Gil and her cabinet were beholden to no one...especially the teachers union...whom they saw as a political force committed to preserving archaic systems and agreements that prevented positive change. She remained an excellent leader because she was convinced that as long as she did the right thing, stayed true to core values built on the capacity and potential of students, she would survive anything. And she did.

Libi Gil liked innovative ideas and the people who created them. She realized that sometimes innovative ideas collide like a train wreck and when there is a train wreck, the best ideas are the ones that are resilient enough to withstand the test of time and sabotage. During the 1999-2000 school year, in the dawning hours and days of the new millennium when charter schools like Mueller were searching for a new way, and when principals were desirous of keeping all of their body parts intact, there was a defining moment of truth.

Mueller had two interesting innovations that were coming together on a collision course: the Charter Petition, and the "Orchard Plan." The future and the past. The village peeling like an onion, exposing architectural mysteries that had been buried along with the hands that built them.

ORCHARD

The Orchard Plan was adopted from a strategy successfully used in Orchard, Utah, to stretch school resources. Basically, it was a five-track year-round calendar, funded by the state as an experiment that legislators had hoped might save California millions of dollars in new school construction costs.

In the Orchard Plan, the school operates all year round, but one-fifth of its students are always off on vacation. When they come back, the next group rotates out. In the meantime, the teachers stay to teach the students who are in session—4/5 of the overall school population. Every nine weeks, six or seven students from each classroom go out on vacation and six or seven return.

Teaching a class with constant turnover just doesn't make much sense as a strategy for improving academic achievement. But that wasn't the objective of the Orchard Plan. The benefit was that it enabled the school to enroll 20% more students than it might otherwise be able to accommodate. It generated revenue without the accompanying construction costs. In addition, it provided an additional twenty-five working days on the teachers' contract so the employees made a lot more money than anyone else in the entire school district.

Teachers quickly realized that their retirement pensions would be dramatically improved if they finished their teaching careers at Mueller and retired with the high salary that was part and parcel of the Orchard Plan. California's teacher retirement system bases its pension payment on the highest earned salary. It is figured in terms of the total salary, not a per diem, so you could work at Mueller for a year or two and retire with a great pension. Simultaneously, by conventions of the union-negotiated contract, teachers in the Chula Vista Elementary School District could select which school they wanted to teach at based on their seniority. The more senior the teacher, the more likely that their request to retire at Mueller School would be granted. You'd think it would be a tremendous benefit to have a steady stream of veteran teachers coming in to teach children desperately in need of their expertise. But most of them weren't coming for the children.

Even though the Orchard Plan was a huge headache, and it was never proven to be good for kids, the senior teachers liked the year-round calendar, and they fought to preserve it for nearly ten years. Midway through the first five-year cycle of the charter it was abandoned. But the benefits of working 225 days were not. The salary scale was adjusted, and Mueller teachers continued to earn more than anyone else in the district, so teachers looking to retire continued the migration toward Mueller.

Creating a charter school to escape district accountability, to make more money, or to expedite one's retirement is truly a creative use of talent and intellectual energy. But it was never the intent of charter law. As the state's testing and accountability system gathered momentum in the late 1990s and into the new century, schools driven primarily to serve the needs of the adults would be harder and harder to sustain.

CALL THE QUESTION

At least once a year, or upon reasonable request from their authorizing board, charter schools are required to report in. The school board members call the meeting to order and out come the marching bands and PowerPoints and children dressed up like it's picture day. Propped up by raw theater, the charter school is invited to lay open the bones. The drum rolls.

In the meantime, school board members try to come to terms with their charter schools any way they can. Who calls the shots? How do we reel them in?

Not in Chula Vista, though, where the school board can be as revolutionary as the revolutionaries out running the schools. They want change badly enough to allow their schools the space to make it happen. They want it badly enough for children, that they are willing to suspend their own doubts and let innovative ideas have a fair chance to blossom.

The governing board members of Chula Vista Elementary School District are as exemplary in their authorization of charter schools as they are in their patient monitoring of them. They follow the law, they do their homework, they read every word of the charter petition, and they ask the tough questions when it is time to do so. But for them, once they approve a charter, it is "hands off". Like all board members, like all educators, they want results yesterday, but they know how slowly real organizational change takes place...and who will ultimately make it happen. They too are seeking El Milagro but they know they can't legislate brilliance from a school board dais.

Still, I imagine that many communities reconcile the madding ambiguities of charter law any way they can. I imagine board members, elected to do the right thing, stretch to interpret the full meaning of the law and to inspire their schools to be everything they can possibly be. I imagine that somewhere, in some community torn by the tantalizing promise of charter schools, they may have had a board meeting that goes like this:

"And...I am pleased to report...that we saw gains of 13% across the board in all areas, including mathematics!" says the remarkably dispassionate charter school principal.

The crowd "ooooohs" and "ahhhhs". There is applause. The board members smile approvingly. All are suitably impressed with the children's account of their experience on the field trip to Legoland or the district's speech contest.

"And our teachers are the best in the whole world," reports the student body president—as if anyone would doubt the children.

And parents are equally as effusive in praise of the principal's coffee klatches. "He's such a good listener," they say.

And just when they are about to wrap it up and move en masse to the parking lot—just when they are about to exhale in deep relief, shake hands, and pat each other on the back for another successful board presentation—one recently elected board member clears her throat and leans forward into the microphone. At first she speaks softly as if she isn't sure of herself.

"I just want to compliment you and your entire charter community for your presentation tonight. I think you are a lovely group and you seem to really enjoy your school. But I have one question."

Oh-oh. Here it comes. That one leading question. The monster from the deep with its thousand possible tentacles and snares. There is silence and the principal swallows. Hard.

"Maybe it's because I'm new on the board. Or maybe I missed something, but your school seems so...well...ugh...*normal*. I guess I am a little confused. But, again, I am new. Could you tell me again, Mr. Charter School Principal...what's the whole point of a charter school? I mean...what's the difference between what you are doing and what is going on in all of our other schools? I guess I just don't get it. What can you do as a charter school that a regular traditional school can't do?"

Sometimes it takes a fresh set of eyes to ask the searing question:

What is your charter school doing that it could not have done had it not been for Gary Hart's charter law that was chaptered back in 1992?

Good board members are like lawyers—they never ask a question that they don't already have an answer for. And you have to know, new board member or not, that this lady knows the answer.

If it is possible for an entire room filled with civically literate people to suddenly and simultaneously fall into stunned and incredulous silence...they just did. And all eyes fall, not on little Joey Hopper who did the bit on the school's new computer lab or Ms. Austin's explanation of how all the grade levels collaborate on the state standards. Indeed, the eyes fall on Mr. Charter Principal. It is the moment of truth.

"Tell 'em, Mr. Principal...tell 'em. She's anti-charter—we can see that right now, or she wouldn't have asked that question. So let her have it. What is different about our school?"

"Ugggggggggggggggggggggggggggggggggggggggh. Well, we have our own logo and letterhead and...ugh...there are some laws that we ignore. That's different."

"Oh, yes, that is definitely different," says the new upstart board member. But that was clearly the wrong answer. So she fills in the blanks.

"However, there seems to be a lot more to it than that. You know, as a new board member, I get all kinds of cool stuff in the mail to read. And believe it or not...I read it. Like this report from March 16, 2007, that described problems in how schools in California are organized and financed. Have you seen this, Mr. Charter School Principal?"

"No, ma'am. I...ugh...I read a lot but.... I haven't had a chance... well...I had a chance but I don't know which study that is..."

It doesn't matter. The new board member is on a roll and the charter principal is merely a prop.

"Oh, no...don't apologize. It's okay. I know how busy you charter principals must be. But I *did* read it. And I noticed in the report's executive summary that—oh, I'm sorry—is this okay, Mr. Board President? I don't want to waste everyone's time here. I know it's getting late for these students."

"No...go right ahead, fellow madam board member," says the board president. And so she does.

"Thank you, Mr. President. Well, here in the executive summary, it says that:

- *Increasing student achievement in California will require a fundamental overhaul of how schools are operated and financed...*
- *That the current finance system is "deeply flawed" and contributes to the problem...and that...*

- *Funding gaps across districts are substantial and haphazard, with no regard to costs, student needs, or meeting state achievement goals."*

"You haven't had a chance to read this yet, Mr. Charter Principal, but I just wanted to bring it up because it is relevant to your work. Are you familiar with the...let's see...I had the name right.... here...oh, yes... the Institute for Research on Education Policy & Practice at Stanford University. Have you heard of them?"

"No, ma'am...I mean...I'm familiar with Stanford University, of course...but not..."

"Oh, yes, Stanford's my alma mater," she announces proudly to an audience who does not seem to be surprised.

"Well anyway, in 2007 they published their research on California's current K-12 public school governance and finance systems. Twenty-three independent studies, and some 1,700 pages of information later, they produce these findings on the inadequacy and inefficiency of our state's schools. Basically, what the heck ails them. And the report says, among other things, that:

- *California's education system is not making the most effective use of its current resources...that*
- *Resources are distributed in an irrational and ineffective method across districts and schools...that*
- *Staff time is allocated haphazardly and there is a lack of transparency and evaluation...and that*
- *The state's schools may need more resources to meet student achievement goals, but to have an impact, increased funding must go hand in hand with reforms."*

"Let's see...it's a long study but these are the points that jumped out at me. It also says that:

- *Any new system that would produce a dramatic improvement in student learning would require that the state create a new infrastructure that would support an educational system committed to continuous improvement."*

"It says that:

·

- *Tinkering around the edges of reform will not work. The system should be redesigned from the ground up. "*

"Do you see my confusion here? Anybody?"

Actually the audience is spellbound. And they know where she is headed with this. But of course, now she is delivering the goods so she has tuned them all out.

"Now this part gets me," she says...

- *The public school system in the state has excessive regulation, which makes it difficult to be creative or innovative. People working in the schools are seeking more flexibility at the local level."*

"Hmmmm. More flexibility. You know what that immediately makes me think of? Charter schools! Your school, Mr. Charter Principal. And all of the schools like yours."

She holds the report up to the audience as if it were the morning paper. The *New York Times* perhaps. Stained at Starbucks and folded clumsily over crumbs from hastily eaten coffee cake. Reduced fat.

"This whole report describes schools in straightjackets! It says:

- *Highly prescriptive finance and governance policies thwart local schools and districts in their efforts to meet the needs of students and promote higher achievement."*

"It describes schools without adequate funding:

- *California's K-12 spending is below the national average...*
- *California spends far less on disadvantaged kids than other states...*
- *We are underinvested in funding for the poorest students...*
- *EL (English Learner) is the fastest growing student demographic group in the state...and*
- *Two-thirds of EL students live in poverty. These kids are poorly assessed, they don't get enough instructional time or the proper materials, and they are housed in the poorest facilities."*

"And it describes frustrated school administrators:

- *A survey of principals found that they needed less paperwork and more flexibility in allocating resources...*

- *Current teacher policies do not allow state and local administrators to make the best use of the pool of potential teachers, or to adequately support current teachers...*
- *Dismissing ineffective teachers is difficult...*
- *California principals spend more time on non-instructional tasks than their colleagues in other states...*
- *They serve more students with fewer district specialists...*
- *Very little time is spent evaluating student data or in students meeting with their teachers..."*

"I imagine you have heard some of these complaints from your colleagues Mr. Charter Principal," who by now recognizes a rhetorical statement when he hears one. "And finally, this report offers one very interesting antidote:

- *There is no one "best practice" for an educational system. What is needed is more data, more flexibility, better use of technology and time to be innovative."*

Perhaps for effect, or perhaps from sheer exhaustion, the new board member slams the paper down. At the beginning of the meeting, she seemed so demure. She smiled at students and looked like she wanted to pat them on the head and say the sweet and sometimes patronizing things that board members say to kids who are up past their bedtime. Now she is slamming her paper down. But she has everyone's attention.

"It occurred to me when I read this—and especially when I read your advanced materials in the board packet and when I heard you speak tonight, that you don't experience *any* of these problems. And that is the whole point of having charter schools!"

"Well, you're right. We actually are in much better shape than..."

"Excuse me, sir. I don't mean to cut you off. I just want to see if I understand all this. 'Cause you already know this stuff. Like I said...I'm new to the school business. So let me see if I have this right. As a charter school:

"You have your own budget?"

"Yes, ma'am."

"It comes in its entirety...$7 million directly to you?"

"Yes, ma'am."

"You and your own governing board—and nobody else—decides how it is to be spent?"

"Yes, ma'am."

"There are no negotiations, no collective bargaining, no quid pro quo, no backdoor deals, no reading between the lines, hidden costs, finder's fees, or attorney fees?"

"No, ma'am."

"And with regard to governance...you create your own policies, systems, programs, guidelines, and rules?"

"Yes, ma'am."

"There is virtually NO outside interference of any kind? No regulations or grievances or bureaucracy? Even this board has no authority at your school?"

"No, ma'am."

"Neither does the teachers union, the county board of education, the state or federal government—or the president of the United States?"

"That's correct, ma'am, except when it comes to assessment and accountability."

"Right...you participate in the statewide assessments, which is a hugely significant factor. Because, as I understand it, your mission is to get academic results that can be measured by those state assessments. So no one can question your metrics. You just get the growth...by any means necessary! Am I correct?"

"Yes, ma'am."

"And, sir, you don't see the significance of being a charter school?"

"Well, I see the advantages...of course...but what I thought you asked me is..."

She interrupts again not because she is rude but because the dam has broken and her enthusiasm is pouring over the sides like torrents of pure water and river fish.

"Sometimes lay people like me have to put it in our own terms to comprehend this. The truth is, I've been reading reports about how screwed up schools are in California since I moved here twenty-five years ago. I've been reading about the need for reform. The need to redesign schools. The search for a better model that is still fair and democratic. A model where the authority to make substantive decisions and innovations is pushed right out on the edge where our students are standing. The search for a school that will close the achievement gap. A school that is ultimately accountable for the measurable gains their students are making. Am I really the only one seeing this?"

"No, ma'am...that's exactly why we want to be a charter school."

"Yes, but with all due respect, you may want to *be* a charter school—but you don't want to *perform* like a charter school! You have an opportunity to be amazing but all I see is colorful graphs and logos to show for your efforts. This is a lost opportunity. And it's tragic to me as a community citizen. Read this report, Mr. Charter School Principal. The antidote to the stifling bureaucracy of California's public school system is the charter school model that allows individual schools to fully exercise their opportunity to be brilliant!"

"Well...now that you mention it perhaps we could try to be a little more daring."

"Daring? You should aspire to produce a freakin' miracle!!! Our kids depend on it!"

In that final moment, pregnant with silence and the quiet pencil tapping of a board president who lost control a long time ago, the charter school principal saw clearly, even if for the first time, that he was in the wrong line of work.

The newly elected board member finally flipped off her microphone, sat back, and took a sip of water. Once again, she looked so tiny in the large executive chair that swiveled and swallowed its host in black leather. There was a moment of catching one's breath. There was an awkward silence. The superintendent and the rest of the school board suddenly realized that their cozy monthly board meetings will never be the same and that what they should have been doing all along is asking people tough questions and challenging their assumptions. But she got the answer to her question: *What can you do as a charter school that a regular traditional school can't do?* She defined the revolt.

"Thank you, fellow madam board member," said the board president at the end of a long pause. Then he turned to the principal, stunned but still standing at the modest lectern. "Is there anything you'd like to add, Mr. Charter School Principal, before we move to the next item on the agenda?"

"Just a recommendation. I think I know what you are looking for. You should visit El Milagro."

And with that, an otherwise underachieving charter school principal left to catch his train.

IMAGINE THEY BLOSSOM

Imagine Mueller Charter School.

Imagine a public school that has complete control over its entire $7.5 million budget.

Imagine having complete authority to invest your resources any way you choose.

Imagine absolute freedom from outside influence of any kind—no state bureaucracy, no meddling school district, no teachers union, no boilerplate contracts, no negotiated agreements, no political agendas, no labor force distractions, no competing agencies.

Imagine no second-guessing.

Imagine being held to account solely by the quality of your results.

Imagine that with every positive step, however small, toward the vision of excellence—more autonomy is earned.

Imagine an opportunity to create a high-performance school-business fueled by the very latest technology in organizational development.

Imagine a mission so righteous it promises to define the career of every employee.

Imagine cultivating the talent you need to achieve what others can only imagine.

Imagine a school where families stand in line for two city blocks just to get a seat.

Imagine children striving against peer group norms and cultural morays just to excel.

Imagine teachers so intrinsically driven that they will walk through fire to help children blossom.

Imagine a culture, balanced by some internal gyroscope, that keeps kids and their teachers whole.

Imagine a spiritual center that hums. Invisible. Hypnotic. Transformational.

Imagine El Milagro.

CHAPTER FOUR

A Blinding Fog

One evening, an elder Native American was talking with his children by the fire. He said to them, "A terrible fight is going on in my heart between two wolves. One wolf represents fear, anger, regret, greed, guilt, and pride. The other wolf stands for joy, peace, love, hope, empathy, and truth. This same fight is going on inside of you too."

One child asked, "Well, which wolf will win?"

The wise man simply replied, "The one we feed!"

—Native American Story

THE ROAD WITHOUT YOU

From the very beginning of the journey at Mueller Charter School, I knew that there were long and difficult battles ahead of us. We had too many nonbelievers. Too many who sought a different "prize." Too many on a different mission. Too many, for whom the years had tainted their sense of joy and excitement and optimism when it came to teaching anybody other than the kids who looked like their own kids. They couldn't take the journey and they knew it. They didn't have the strength or stamina or stomach for the challenges that lie ahead on such a long and arduous trail. They would die on the side of the road. They had to either step aside and let others go in their place, or they had to try to distract us long enough to get us lost down an altogether different trail. They figured that if they could just keep us circling on the same road, another few years would pass and we would be inevitably at the place that they began thirty some years ago. Then they could retire and save face. Call it a career.

We could not get 90% of our students to grade level if we did not believe in them, or if we didn't believe in ourselves, or if we didn't think the mission was worthy of our commitment. We could not evolve as an organization until every single teacher and employee was ready to set aside his or her own ambitions and agenda in an effort to achieve a greater common good.

In charters, everything must be transformed. Even relationships. It is hard doctrine for those who cling to traditional views of power and influence. But charters succeed when they protect their autonomy and tame those external forces that refuse to behave. In our case...one of those external forces was the teachers union. To say that that they did not go quietly would be an understatement.

Looking back, it is amazing that the charter survived at all.

UNION WORLD VIEW

When the charter movement was unfolding in the 1990s, there was initial support from some of the more progressive elements of the teachers union. Albert Shanker was the president of the American Federation of Teachers when he started to envision a world in which teachers could have more autonomy, more freedom from the bureaucracies that constrain their energy and their passions, and an opportunity to have a more authentic role in determining how public schools spend their money in the service of children.

In 1996, when individual states across the nation were exploring the concept of developing charter schools, an AFT report identified what was considered to be essential criteria for good charter law. The union's view of charter schools was that they:

- Must be based on high academic standards;
- Must take the same assessments as other students in state and district;
- Should hire only certificated teachers;
- Should have the approval of local districts;
- Should have to make financial and academic information available to the public;
- Should be covered by rigorous, enforceable evaluation and accountability measures;
- Should submit the same reports that school districts are required to submit
- Must meet same performance standards other schools must meet; and finally,

- *Charter employees should be covered by collective bargaining.*

It would make sense that the labor unions would envision a role for themselves within the charter movement. They would argue that the mission of the charter movement and the mission of the teachers unions were not in conflict with one another and were not mutually exclusive. Perhaps it was the inevitability of the oncoming charter wave crashing on the beach that sent them scurrying under the cabana. Or perhaps they knew all along that much of the momentum behind the charter movement came from a desire to release creative teachers from the many onerous and suffocating bureaucracies of which *they* were one of the biggest. In fact, until that moment in school history, the unions may have had the monopoly on suffocating bureaucratic constraints.

No one at Mueller Charter School had ever imagined that we would become a kind of ground zero in the battle for control of public schools in California. But we did. California moved to create charter schools as independent, experimental laboratories where innovation could perhaps one day lead to a whole new model for public education. And, of course, California had nothing to lose by encouraging start-up charters to be the lightning rods for a revolution. Overall, too many of our schools were failing miserably by any measure.

The Chula Vista Elementary School District had nothing to lose either by encouraging their most creative people to explore charter models. Over the past several decades their demographics shifted dramatically as housing developments exploded in all directions. This was now the largest elementary school district in California, and by all accounts, one of the fastest-growing communities in America. It was also, by virtue of its proximity to the US-Mexican border, the beneficiary of one of the most massive international migrations in our nation's history. But through it all, the schools had not responded to the needs of their student population as evidenced by the persistent underperformance of their elementary school district and the even more unimpressive results of the high school district they fed into.

"What do we have to lose?" Libi Gil asked. " If some of our schools want to apply to be charters, let's help them."

And she did. Her district had five charters by the year 2000 with more on the drawing board. In the meantime, she faced daily, nonstop criticism and resistance from the local affiliate of the teachers union, the Chula Vista Educators Association, also known as CVE.

After the Rodda Act went into effect in 1976, California's teachers unions faced a steadily rising level of power and influence and control.

They accomplished many good things in terms of raising the status and standards of teachers as professionals. They were fierce advocates for the rights of teachers. They won excellent benefit packages, significantly raised salaries, advocated for safer school environments, exposed incompetent administrators, and contributed to the gains—such as they were—in the knowledge base that defined teaching excellence.

And as the unions grew and evolved in California, they learned how to fight. They learned how to protect their turf. They learned how to sniff out a potential enemy and they learned how to crush any opposition... whether that opposition came in the form of legislation, legislators, superintendents, community groups, or upstart entrepreneurs.

Their tactics were so effective that they became predictable. Even now, as contract negotiations become acrimonious from district to district, you can predict with amazing accuracy the next move they will make. In fact, most administrators have the *Here Is What Your Teachers Union Is Likely to Do Next* monograph so that as rough times visit themselves upon the school district, the governing board and the superintendent need not take anything personally and they can continue to steer the ship with some clarity of vision.

One thing that became clear to the union leadership in the state of California was that this rising charter movement was, to say the last, an ominous development. That message was definitely communicated to the Chula Vista Educators Association. In fact, with five charters in their house and others on the drawing board, a clear memo from CTA headquarters was in order—something along these lines:

What the hell are you guys doing down there in Chula Vista? You better kill those freakin' charter things before they grow and eat us all! (Or at the very least...could you slow them down a little?)

MIGDEN

The good soldiers at the helm of the CVE dutifully followed the advice and direction of the CTA. Between the fall of 1999 and the spring of 2004, Mueller Charter School faced attack after coordinated attack from a panicked labor union...and survived.

Mueller wasn't alone. There were many legal challenges, differences of opinion, public attacks at board meetings, and backdoor tactics to devalue the efforts of all of the charters in California. But the final decisive battle—the winner-takes-all world championship—emerged when teachers themselves were asked to decide the fate of unions in charter schools.

For Mueller, it began with a mandatory election that was held on Friday, February 28, 1999, in what was to become known as "The Migden Vote." The results of the election would determine the future of Mueller as a charter school and ultimately, its future as an innovative school for children.

A California state senator named Carole Migden had authored a bill that required all charter schools to—once and for all—declare their intentions with regard to the teachers union. This law posed a simple question to the certificated teaching staff: *who is your employer?*

They had two choices. The **school district** with which the charter was affiliated could be declared the employer, and the charter would continue to come under that district's jurisdiction for all matters related to collective bargaining. As such, the existing contract between the district and the local teachers union affiliate would prevail.

On the other hand, by conventions of our own Charter Petition, if two-thirds (67%) of the certificated employees elected to declare **the charter** as their employer, they would have to terminate their relationship with the local teachers union. Existing contracts and agreements with the labor union would no longer apply. It would be like creating a brand new school district that had not yet established a contract with any labor representative. Employees would be free to seek representation from any union of their choice: the CTA, the AFT, the Teamsters...or none at all.

The California Teachers Association and National Educators Association recognized that this was a crucial vote. If the charter schools voted to be their own employers and nullify all existing union contracts, the CTA could be faced, at the very least, with the logistical hassle of simultaneously managing countless organizing elections all over the state.

At worst, charter schools could opt out of unions altogether. They could lose thousands of union members and hundreds of thousands of dollars in their war chest that they would otherwise use to oppose such fledgling movements as the charter schools. But perhaps the greatest danger was the risk that charter schools might actually work! There was a fear that in California, there might one day be public schools that serve kids better, serve parents better, and treat teachers better...without the presence of a labor union to keep everyone in line. They feared the likes of El Milagro and its potential as a new model for employee relationships. Pretty soon there could be a wave of pressure coming from communities that were tired of second-rate schools. The teachers union and charter schools would be sent spiraling down opposite paths, as perpetual philosophical opponents. And that is exactly what happened.

By the margin of a single vote the Mueller staff elected to be their own employer. They had opted for more independence from the school district, and ultimately, from the labor union too. Around the state, many other charters did the same. The result of that Migden election in 1999, was a crushing defeat for California's once powerful teachers union.

But labor unions don't roll over. Whatever their motivation, they are led by resilient and pugnacious fighters who love a good brawl. They are the antithesis of teachers, who by and large are the peacemakers of our society. Teachers encourage children to walk away from trouble, to live and let live, to advocate for others, to celebrate the legacy of non-violent resistance. It works for nine year-olds in the schoolyard, but not labor unions.

If you are placing bets on fights in Las Vegas, put your money on the union leaders. They almost always win. They win because they have the history, the resources, and the will to prevail. They win because they represent teachers...the peacemakers.

But they could not prevail at El Milagro, where for once, *children's rights* to a quality education won out over the *employees' rights* to be protected by unions; a decision made possible by the employees themselves.

A PREMONITION

The staff at Mueller Charter School had made a bold statement by voting to be their own employer. It was a leap of faith. It was a stunning victory...but any celebration would be short lived.

Many of the newer teachers had just wanted to vote and get on with the business of teaching.

"I am so sick of the politics," they said. "I am tired of people coming up to me everyday on the playground and asking me how I am going to vote. I just want to teach." Their frustration was understandable...even if it was a little naïve. They may have cast a vote for labor peace and a return to calm, but peace was never promised in this election.

In fact, after the election, the staff at Mueller was even more bitterly divided. There were three groups of teachers: those who were pro-union, those against the union, and the new teachers who were oblivious and just wanted to pursue their dream of teaching without the distracting politics.

Mueller Charter School was convulsing toward a revolution that, at the time, the younger teachers were incapable of seeing and the veteran teachers were loath to prevent. It was a philosophical showdown for the soul of the school.

On the one side, there was the growing group of idealistic young teachers who came to the charter because they believed it to be a progressive school that cared for its students. They had read the Charter Petition before they came. It said that the charter was designed to better serve children, not for the convenience of adults. But when they were hired and reported for work, they were faced with union recruiters and the inexplicable climate of infighting over adult issues. And there were plenty of adult issues.

Because on the other side, there were the veteran teachers who had cleverly utilized the provisions of the charter for their own personal and professional gain. They were good people, loyal to the school district and loyal to the union. They cared about children and had a career of successes to look back on. But they were intensely motivated to protect their financial and employment security interests, and the teachers union could always be counted on to be their advocate. In a way it seemed duplicitous. While their hearts and minds were really motivated by the material benefits of employment, they could disguise that motivation behind their service to kids while the union did the dirty work.

By the end of the Charter Petition's first cycle, teachers had managed to maintain an extended school year of 206 days and a pay scale that remained 3.85% above the district's negotiated scale to compensate for what they said was a longer school day.

These arrangements were made unilaterally by Mueller's own governing board made up of...naturally...senior-level teachers. But the decision was made without the blessing of their friends in the union, because "Mueller was a charter school" and they were free to do whatever they wanted to do with their budget. So to keep the union close by, they made sure that the Charter Petition defined and secured the union's role. They trusted the union to protect the sweet salary deal...even though they created it without the union's help. Perhaps it was by accident, but they were creating an interesting organizational model in which they truly had the best of all worlds: the freedom and control over a budget that could be used for their own personal gain, and the protection of a labor union that would fight for their evolving rights.

In fairness, the senior teachers didn't want to perpetuate the union model just to protect their own salaries and benefits. Deep down, they believed in the role of the union on a personal, professional, and patriotic level. They felt a teachers association was as much a part of America's public school system as those little American flags that stick out from the wall in every classroom across the nation. Unions were a slice of Americana. Like singing the *Star Spangled Banner* before a baseball game.

You teach...you pay your union dues.

And besides, they felt all teachers needed a strong union to protect them from the arbitrary and capricious decisions of unscrupulous administrators who could never be trusted. Of course the union wanted to stay in the charter picture too, even though their leadership was indignant that the teachers had voted on their own pay raise. It was a bad precedent but they figured they could tame that tiger later. There were more immediate concerns lurking like storm clouds on the horizon. The union leadership had a bad premonition:

"What if charter school teachers didn't need us anymore?"

"What if they created their own salary arrangements?"

"What if they even veered from the district calendar?"

"What if they started running the schools and there was no longer an administrator-boogeyman to protect them from?"

What would stop teachers in non-charter schools from wanting the same kind of arrangements as charter schools? Schools would fall like dominoes. You could hear their collective panic: "Oh my God!!! It is the cold war all over again."

NO FEAR

Across the state, charter teachers were abandoning their unions in droves. The Chula Vista Elementary School District alone had five charter schools with a combined total well in excess of 200 teachers. At $750 per year per person in dues, the loss to the Chula Vista Educators association was over $150,000. Not enough to break the organization perhaps, but certainly enough to pay for an executive salary or two.

Aside from the immediate loss in revenues for the war chest, teachers in charter schools were beginning to have real authority for decision making in their schools. They were standing on their own feet, with no fear, and no apparent need for the protection that is bought from a traditional labor union.

For years, good teachers opposed the union mentality. They let their professionalism and their competence speak for themselves and bristled at the notion that they needed to pay union dues for protection from the boogeyman sitting in the principal's office. But even good teachers were obligated by "agency fee." They had to pay into the union, and belong to the union, whether they agreed with their strategies and politics or not.

So the charter movement offered freedom and teachers accepted it in the form of the Migden vote. But with so much at stake, and with their substantial war chests and long successful history of political advocacy, the California Teachers Association and local CVE, were determined to prevail against the charter threat.

WILD WEST

In their panic, the CVE filed a grievance, complaining that *the school district* had violated the provisions of the union contract by allowing Mueller Charter School teachers to establish their own calendar, salaries, benefits, and transfer policy without utilizing the collective bargaining process. It was an interesting argument. All the teachers at Mueller benefited from those decisions...especially the veteran teachers who enjoyed the biggest salary increases. They participated in all of the salary discussions knowing that their union was preparing to file a grievance against the district.

After the Migden election, however, the union changed its strategy. They started to get wind of some juicy rumors about the behavior of the principal and how the election was conducted. They heard that the principal interfered with the election process by intimidating teachers.

They heard that the principal had threatened teachers to "vote for the charter" or they could lose their jobs. They heard that he told one very pro-union teacher that she *owed* him her vote, and that if things didn't go his way he would expose the affair that she'd had with a parent. Then, according to the complaint, he told her that he had some Hell's Angel friends who were going to come in and break some arms if they didn't vote his way!

It's hard to believe that anybody would have actually said these things. He denied it. But the truth of what may have been said hardly matters. The union office was abuzz with excitement. The union soldiers felt the election results should be invalidated. They had a winnable battle on their hands and the prospect of taking down a charter along with a salty old principal whom they never liked. What's more, they had a chance to demonstrate just exactly how the union could protect teachers from a bully.

Then they filed a second complaint against the district—the original grievance coupled with the complaint that the former principal interfered with a legal election and the district did nothing to reel him in.

The proposed union remedy was to conduct the Migden vote again. This time, they expected to prevail and put this horrible scare behind them. But the district leadership refused to permit another vote. "A card laid is a card played," said Libi Gil. And the members of her cabinet nodded. They weren't giving in to any union demands because, as a result of the vote, Mueller was now its own employer and the union no longer had jurisdiction over the charter.

"You just wait, Libi Gil," said the union leaders. "We are going to go to court and find a judge to overturn these election results…"

"So let's go to court," said Libi Gil.

And again, the members of her cabinet nodded.

The chaos wrought from the election convinced Libi Gil of one thing though; it was time for a change in leadership at Mueller Charter School. So one of Libi Gil's cabinet messengers sharpened the ax and paid the former principal a visit. After hearing his options, the former principal agreed to step aside, and finish out the school year at the district office. It was only May and Mueller Charter School had to survive another month choking in the sulfuric gun smoke of a Wild West shoot-out.

FOG

The union set its sights on Mueller Charter School and was not going to concede the loss of forty-one potential dues-paying members. More importantly, they could not abide a group of teachers with the self-confidence to make their own decisions on issues that had always come within the scope of collective bargaining. They had the money, the patience, and the legal clout to gum up the works and embarrass the district leadership. And, of course, they thought they had a great test case for the entire state, one that could potentially cripple the rapidly rising charter movement.

So they initiated a series of legal challenges in an effort to throw out the results and vote again…and again…and again, if necessary.

None of this, of course, had anything to do with children. The school was now officially adrift in a blinding fog.

"STAY ABOVE IT"

Carole Teall hired me twice: first as the principal of Rancho Del Campo High School and then again as director of the Juvenile Court and Community Schools, She was the strongest, most focused, most organized, most intimidating woman I had ever met in education. As the assistant superintendent at the County Office of Education, she had tremendous organizational power and she would use it to cut off your knee caps if you didn't perform to her standard. She expected school leaders to be resourceful and efficient. She expected them to follow through on the tasks that they had been directed to complete. And as if school leaders didn't have enough to do, Carole Teall had "to do" lists for everybody.

When you went to a meeting in Carole Teall's office, you could count on emerging with another freakin' list. You could count on her barking orders through her morning yogurt, scribbling lists upon lists, checking off completed items with her long arms waving through the air for added emphasis. Everything was urgent. Everything was a priority. She was exhausting. But she was also tremendously loyal to those few who could keep up.

After a while it wasn't so intimidating to meet with Carole Teall because I started coming to the meetings with my own lists. I learned where to sit so that I wouldn't get hit with flying chunks of granola or get my eye poked out from the pencils and note pads at the ends of her flailing arms. I learned to manage up.

Eventually Carole Teall became a friend and a colleague. At the age of 55, she ran her very first marathon with my wife. Cross that off the list. Then she remarried and started to travel all over the world to lots of new places that she crossed off other lists. Then when so many new "to do" items began piling up on her yellow legal pad she decided that the only way to get to them was to retire. And since retiring was on her list, she crossed that off too.

Carole Teall left a huge void in the leadership at the San Diego County Office of Education. She walked out the door and it was like everyone exhaled for the first time. "Phew. Finally. No more goddamn lists!!!" There was celebration. Relief. But it was short lived. Carole Teall would be deeply missed—but no one knew it until she was gone.

So the search was on for a new assistant superintendent at the San Diego County Office of Education. And soon they found one. And if they thought Carole Teall kicked everybody's ass...they hadn't yet met Claudette Inge.

But I had. I knew that she was the director of the court schools in Alameda County for many years. I knew that she and had been one of the real state pioneers in alternative education. She was a tiny, soft spoken, woman who, upon first impression, seemed kind of timid—a

definite contrast to Carole Teall. In reality, Claudette Inge was a
force....extremely bright, very experienced, and guided by an internal
fire that burned hot as the core of a nuclear reactor. "Make no mistake",
I promised everybody, "Claudette Inge will kick your ass too." And she
did.

Claudette Inge didn't collect lists. She kept those in her head.
There was only one item for her anyway: what are we doing for our kids?
She was politically savvy and knew the court school law because she had
helped write so much of it during her years in Alameda. Claudette Inge
knew about me too. She knew about the academies and the innovations
and how much fire I was taking from the entrenched "good old boys"
of the juvenile court and community schools. We worked together
for nearly a year until it became evident that the good old boys and
the county superintendent had reached an accord: "Either you go Mr.
County Superintendent, or that freakin' Kevin Riley and all his academy
ideas go."

At politically-charged County Offices of Education in California,
you protect the General—the Superintendent. Personally, I didn't
much care about the General, but I did want to protect Claudette
Inge because at this point, she could be far more effective than me in
transforming the Juvenile Court and Community Schools. So one day,
being ever the good soldier, I told her I had been recruited to run a
dysfunctional charter school that had imploded in Chula Vista...and
that I had accepted.

On my last day as director of the court schools I sat with Claudette
Inge in her office and asked her how she would approach this crazy
place I was going to—this Mueller Charter School. I asked her how to
balance all of the feuding groups, the misplaced priorities, the politics,
the twisted legal issues, and all the adult drama. She didn't hesitate with
her advice:

"Isn't that what you have been dealing with for the past five years?
Hell, it's the same everywhere! You're just going to a scaled-down version
of this place, is all. Just stay above it, Kevin. Don't get caught up in the
emotion. You stay about kids. Stay above the bullshit."

And that became my mantra. *Stay above the bullshit.* Stay about kids.
And I pursued it with the same myopic tenacity as the one-item "to do
lists" urgently scribbled by Carole Teall.

TEAMSTER GOONS

In the beginning, I didn't know anybody at Mueller Charter School.
I knew a little bit about the turmoil but I didn't have a dog in their fight.

And I certainly had no knowledge of any of the goofiness that resulted in the job opening that I eventually filled.

But I have to admit that I was a little sensitive on the union issue after the unraveling of the court school academies.

As a classroom teacher, I had organized the Pauma Teachers Association in San Diego's North County region, and was their chief negotiator. I wasn't exactly the next Jimmy Hoffa though. In fact, I had only just learned about teachers unions and collective bargaining and the Rodda Act that came to define management and employee relations in schools since 1976.

Upon arrival at Mueller, I had no real preconceived idea about their union...nor had I given it much thought. I was fully prepared to argue and fight for any settlement that would bring peace and unity to this staff. It was actually a school ripe for unique and innovative relationships — even between charters and their unions. But that did not seem to be in the cards. Once I read the first grievance that challenged the authority of charter employees as a legitimate and autonomous governance body, I realized that the goals of a labor union and the goals of an ambitious charter school were probably incompatible.

When it comes to general discourse about improving the quality of our schools in America, there is an enormous "elephant in the living room" in the form of the teachers union. And when it comes to school policies and programs...unions must advocate for what is best for adults...not what is best for children. After all, that is their purpose.

THE JUDGE FROM SACRAMENTO

The Chula Vista Educators' grievance took several years to resolve and meandered down some fascinating (albeit distracting) legal paths.

In January 2000, just after my first Christmas as principal of Mueller Charter School, an administrative law judge flew down from Sacramento to meet with the various parties to the mess that I had inherited. I was invited to the meeting since, as the new principal, I would be charged with the responsibility of acting on the court's ruling. A number of Mueller's teachers were invited too, teachers from both sides of the issue. And if it wasn't already hard enough to find a seat around the conference table, there were also representatives of the governing board of the Chula Vista Elementary School District and CVE advocates. And there was Jackson Parham.

JACKSON PARHAM

Jackson Parham was the attorney for the Chula Vista Elementary

School District and one of the most knowledgeable attorneys in
California on charter school law. Such as it is. It was from Jackson
Parham that I started to realize how ambiguous the law really was when
it came to charters.

"You may very possibly find yourself in the middle of the test case
on charter law, Kevin."

"Wow," I said. "What the hell does that mean? And what does that
mean for trying to actually achieve the mission of the charter...you
know...getting 90% of our kids to grade level?"

"It means until some of this gets resolved, you may likely find
yourself swimming in some very rough legal waters. I suggest you set
your sights first on *not drowning*...then you can consider the possibility
of swimming fast enough to break the course record."

It was the first piece of great advice I got from Jackson Parham. He
had decades of experience in working with the teachers union through
the collective bargaining process. He worked with school districts
throughout the state, and could predict their next move before they
could even get a fix on the fix they were in. But his political savvy and
knowledge of law weren't the reasons why Jackson Parham was so
successful in dealing with the teachers union. His greatest asset was the
fact that he was just so damn likeable.

Jackson Parham is the classic, modern-day Renaissance man—
former college football player, English teacher, writer, voracious reader,
superdad, and private airplane pilot. He is witty, engaging, and extremely
articulate. He knows the law and—perhaps even more important—he
knows the holes in the law. He knows what the law doesn't say. And
when it comes to the subject of charter school law in California, you can
look it up yourself. The law doesn't say plenty.

So while the administrative law judge flew American Airlines
from Sacramento to San Diego to resolve what he assumed would be
a minor irritant on his otherwise long list of labor disputes occurring
in California, Jackson Parham threw on a pair of cowboy boots and a
tailored suit and flew his own plane right into the CVE meeting room
crowded with an agitated rabble of charter school pioneers.

The purpose of the meeting was to begin negotiating the terms for
a new election. The judge had already decided—perhaps on the flight,
somewhere over Oxnard or Santa Barbara—that this case would go
away in a hurry with a new election. It was a simple fix. The former
meddling principal was gone and the district, under the supervision of
the state's Public Employee Review Board (PERB) could manage the
election more responsibly. The pro-union folks would feel like they had

a fair shake. And the teachers who had prevailed, and had voted for the charter to be the employer, had every reason to assume that they would prevail again. There. It's decided.

"Excuse me, sir, we're landing in San Diego in about twenty minutes, would you like one last cup of coffee?"

"No thanks...but you may want to keep the airplane engines running after we land. I am just running down to Chula Vista to settle a little labor dispute and I'll be back to the plane before the crew even finishes refueling."

"You sound pretty sure about yourself. Where is the dispute?"

"Some little backwoods school district called Chula Vista. They are squabbling about a charter school election or some damn thing"

"Is that the school they call El Milagro?"

"El Milagro.....no, I don't think so. It is....let me see....where is the name...oh...here it is...Mueller Charter School."

"Mueller Charter School? Twenty minutes to resolve their labor dispute? With all due respect, your honor...that is El Milagro. And you aren't solving anything in twenty minutes. In fact, you're gonna need more than just this cup of watered down coffee by the time you're done. We'll see you back in Sacramento."

TOXIC MESS

What I initially lacked in my grasp of Mueller's political turmoil I made up for in my awareness of organizational momentum...and organizational toxicity. I believed deeply that if there was one thing these good people did NOT need, it was another election. Like all elections, this vote would be preceded by a campaign. During that campaign, there would be a tremendous amount of aggressive lobbying, persuasion, and tumult. And while teachers are whispering and cajoling each other to vote one way or another, the mission would be forgotten.

So I argued that Mueller Charter School could not survive another distracting vote. Jack Parham argued that though there may have been inappropriate comments by the former principal, a secret ballot was taken, and in the end, every teacher was free to vote according to his or her conscience. And they did.

I appealed to the judge to allow this school to heal and to get on with the business of serving children. Meanwhile, he spent the entire day meeting separately with all of the different teams. He brought us together at the end of the day and tried to make sense out of everything he had heard.

"The union wants a revote because they are convinced that they have been cheated. The teachers that prevailed want to be left alone. Jackson Parham claims I don't have any jurisdiction over a charter school. And this wacky principal keeps talking about getting 90% of the kids to grade level..."

The only thing that made sense in the end was that he had a flight to catch. Translation? The flight attendant had been right. This was a freakin' mess and the administrative law judge from Sacramento couldn't get back to the airport fast enough.

SIMPLE MATH

A few weeks after his meeting with all of us in San Diego, I decided to be proactive and not wait for a disappointing outcome from the administrative law judge. So I boarded an airplane to meet with him in his office in Sacramento. I was now engaged in the legal fight...and, thanks to the inspiration of Jackson Parham, I started to ask lots of questions that didn't seem to have easy answers:

- What is the purpose of Charter Schools as defined by the state Legislature in California?
- What is the consequence when a state agency like the Public Employee Review Board (PERB), develops a process that compromises the spirit of our legally adopted Charter Petition and the Charter School Act of 1992?
- What, if any, is the role and jurisdiction of PERB as it relates to charter schools?
- Who is accountable for damage suffered by children and their parents as a result of the ongoing legal haggling?
- Can the charter file a countersuit against the labor union for creating a hostile work environment and/or causing us to violate the conditions of our charter?
- Who exactly is "the Charter" anyway?
- What recourse is available to a charter school that is committed to (and legally obligated to) an established goal of getting their students to grade level in a climate of intentional outside distraction?
- Given that we currently have an Academic Performance Index (API) of 603, and the state expects an API of 800, what role will the courts play in protecting our school environment from union meddling?

On another front, Jackson Parham aggressively argued that the results of the Migden vote should be allowed to stand. Specifically, he posited that:

- There had been aggressive "campaigning" from both sides on the issue;
- The DA investigated threats but never found sufficient evidence to file charges;
- The vote was conducted by secret ballot;
- Those who claim they were threatened by the former principal later indicated that they still voted for the union;
- The charter required two/thirds of the staff to vote to be their own employer, which they did.

He also argued that the union's proposed remedy of holding the election over again was not appropriate because:

- The Migden law required an election by March 31, 2000, and that date had passed;
- The principal whose conduct was in question, had already been relieved of his duties;
- There are more than thirty-three other schools in the Chula Vista Elementary School District that have a union, and teachers at charter schools have transfer rights and could freely opt to go to any of those schools (since, after all, the district cannot assign someone to a charter against his or her will);
- Some of the teachers who participated in the original vote had already left the school;
- PERB law permits staff to organize anytime they want so they can still vote to have a union if they choose to; and, just for kicks...
- No new election was declared as a remedy for proven voting irregularities in the Florida presidential election of 2000!

The union's insistence on rewinding the tape and starting over on the whole vote was understandable. It was simple mathematics. The threshold for victory for the union was so much lower under the Migden rules, where it would take two-thirds of the teachers, a minimum of twenty-eight votes, to establish the *charter* as the employer. If there were fewer than twenty-eight votes , the *district* would remain the employer and the union would stay at Mueller. So ultimately, the union needed only fourteen votes to prevail.

A vote to "organize," on the other hand, would be much more difficult to win. Though public employees in California are permitted under PERB law to organize and be represented by a union, 51% or more of the staff would have to agree. The process to unionize would require some twenty-one votes. The union went down the list of names on Mueller's staff roster and they could see that their base of senior, pro-union teachers had dwindled. They would be lucky to get the fourteen votes, even in a new Migden election.

I woke up one morning and as I prepared for the school day it occurred to me that I was a long way away from the quiet solitude and simplicity of Palomar Mountain School. I also realized the wisdom of Claudette Inge when she told me to stay above the bullshit. It was so hard to do now. I thought the whole future of the school depended on us getting this thing resolved once and for all. And I was right.

SEVENTEEN MONTHS

As a staff, we had made a promise to each other that we were going to pursue one mission: we were going to get our students to grade level.

We might as well have promised to "send astronauts to the moon by the end of the decade!" The pro-union teachers went along with adopting the new mission because they knew they had some scud missiles coming in from over the horizon. They figured a few scud missiles would back off the new principal in a hurry. They were ready to go for broke. Many were close to retirement anyway. They didn't really care about getting kids to grade level at all. They wanted retribution.

Claudette Inge would tell you that we could never in a thousand years get our children to grade level if it wasn't important to everyone to do it. And Claudette Inge would be right.

To overcome poverty let alone all the other variables that cripple our kids, was going to require a singular focus. There could be no other mission. But clearly, for some of our teachers, *the mission* was to save the union at all costs. This was disappointing, but it was another one of those battles worth fighting. While everyone else was going to their schools and investing every second of their time in training teachers, analyzing data, strategizing for improved student learning, we faced a seventeen-month tug of war for control of our school. The uncertainty hung over us like a stifling black cloud.

It became an intense chess match that required multiple moves to conclude.

On January 17, 2002, PERB ruled in favor of the union when they adjudged that the Migden election had been improperly tampered with. The ruling specifically found that the Chula Vista Elementary School District was at fault for not thoroughly investigating teachers' complaints that they were being harassed and threatened by the former principal. That was the bad news. The good news was that the remedy which was requested by the union—the opportunity to revote on the issue of "who should be the employer"—could not be applied. Why? Because the union failed to name Mueller Charter School in their complaint! They sued only the Chula Vista Elementary School District. And the legislation did not require Chula Vista Elementary School District to conduct the Migden vote—it was only for charter schools. Whoops.

The judge said: "As separate employers, a charge against CVESD is not the same as a charge against Mueller Charter School. Only named parties are entitled to the benefit of a remedy."

In other words, if you win a lawsuit, you only win against the person you are suing.

Further, CVESD would not compel Mueller Charter School to have another election as a remedy for the complaint filed against the district, because Libi Gil was the superintendent and it was her call and she didn't want to. The union had made a major tactical mistake in not amending their original complaint to include Mueller Charter School. So even if they could prove there were some inappropriate shenanigans when the former principal threatened to bring in the Hell's Angels, there was no consequence to the school.

Then in February, pretending not to have read the judge's rationale in the previous ruling, the Chula Vista Educators filed yet another appeal. This time they argued that since "the district" (by way of the former principal) interfered with the election, the district should be compelled to set aside the results and hold a new one. They weren't going to take no for an answer. Even if the very teachers they wanted to represent were telling them no!

HUEVOS

For good measure, in a parallel strategy to bring the union back by any means necessary, CVE filed a *"Request for recognition as an association to be named Mueller Charter School Teachers Association."* It was a petition to organize the employees of Mueller Charter School into their own union. When I read the initial letter I immediately thought three things:

First, that this was a great tactic by the union because Migden vote or no Migden vote, public school employees can vote to form a union whenever they choose to—they aren't at the mercy of any judge's ruling or any litigation.

Second, that this promised to be just one more crippling distraction to our school…especially with testing just one month away.

Third, I thought that they might really have us by the *huevos* this time.

The request, which came from the office of the Public Employee Relations Board, included a timeline for the voting process. It also required that Mueller Charter School send them a list of all staff who were eligible to vote for a certificated union.

And it had one more additional strange feature.

The PERB directions offered the "employer" an option:

Since the employees had submitted their *intent to organize*, the Charter School, as employer, could either 1) request that an election be held, during which employees would vote to be represented by a union of their choice or continue with no union at all; or 2) forgo the election altogether and just automatically ordain the Mueller Charter School Teachers Association as the employees' representative.

We all kind of wondered at this point, "What is it with these freakin' people and their preoccupation with Mueller Charter School? And what is it with their elections?!"

Initially, the local organizers couldn't even muster the "proof of support" they needed to conduct a vote. We were dumbfounded. You gotta be kidding! Though the union organizers had tried to rally the Mueller teachers, they failed to get even the minimum number of signatures required to authorize the vote.

So, PERB stepped in and permitted the local organizers ten more days of arm-twisting and cajoling until they could acquire enough signatures to warrant the election. Within the next few days, they had their signatures. Another vote was on.

THE CONFERENCE CALL

As they had done before, PERB moved quickly to organize the election. Their representative, Jeri Hopper, clearly didn't get the anomaly presented by the collision of charter law, the education code, and the government code. On May 14 she called me to invite my participation in a three-way conference call that would include her office, me, and the union officials.

"And you are inviting me to participate in this call?" I asked.

"Yes, well, you are the principal and that is who I normally work through on these elections," replied Jeri Hopper.

"But this isn't a normal election."

"So I noticed. Nevertheless, I'll call on May 17 at 3:00. How does that work for you?"

"It doesn't." No matter. She had already hung up.

Ms. Hopper had also sent a memo to all parties called the "Consent Election Agreement" which outlined a few of the election details. Provision #16 stated:

The Voting Unit shall exclude the principal, psychologist, student advocate, and all management, supervisory, and confidential employees.

Something really didn't match here. I understood why they didn't want the principal to vote. I could even understand why they excluded the school psychologist. But our student advocate, Greg Valero, was a certificated teacher serving in a leadership role for students. One of his responsibilities was student discipline, so he had similar responsibilities as an assistant principal. But he didn't have an administrative credential. He was officially a teacher with over thirty years of experience in the district, all the while, paying his union dues. Why wasn't he considered in the voting unit?

It was clear that Greg Valero was being excluded for reasons other than his job description. First, like all elections, this was a numbers game. The union officials counted their potential votes and knew it was going to be close. And secondly, they knew Greg Valero was not going to vote for the union.

"You want to be in the union, Greg Valero? Get back in a classroom! Otherwise, you have no say in this process."

A FEW CLARIFYING QUESTIONS

I didn't want to complicate what was already a convoluted process, I just wanted to know why the student advocate couldn't vote. And I wanted to know just exactly who was included in the category of *"management, supervisory, and confidential employees"* that Ms. Hopper referred to in her memo. It seemed like this was a boilerplate memo that PERB sends out to every organization that requests an election to unionize and I wanted them to know this is not a boilerplate organization. It's a charter—and our working relationships are different.

So on May 17, 2002, when Jeri Hopper called to connect all the parties on her conference call, I told her that I had a few preliminary questions.

"Dr. Riley, this is Jeri Hopper in Sacramento, how are you today?"

"I'm okay."

"We have the union representatives and several teachers on another line…are you ready to conference with them?"

"Well actually, I have a few questions before we bring them on the line."

"Oh…okay. What is your question?"

"I was reading your May 14 memo, and it says 'the voting unit is to exclude all *management* employees.'"

"Right, that is standard for a union election."

"I understand. Why is that?"

"Well, the government code does not allow *management* employees to be represented by the union."

"I see. And why can't the student advocate vote?"

"My understanding is that he is a member of *management*."

"Really? How is he a member of *management*?"

"Isn't he in on a team or a cabinet that makes your *management* decisions?"

"Well, yeah, technically he is. *Management* decisions are made by our Leadership Council. He is on the Leadership Council, but he, like me, is one of the few members that doesn't even have a vote there. He is considered "staff." He is in an advisory role to the members of the Leadership Council who actually make management decisions.

"So who is on your Leadership Council?"

"It is teachers and parents."

"But are they really making *management* decisions?"

"Well, let's see. I have a list here of some of the decisions that the Leadership Council has made recently and they include decisions about the school budget, salaries, working conditions, approval of contracts, program development, approval of textbook series…shall I go on?"

Jeri Hopper stammered on the other end of the phone about how decisions like these are typically reserved for *management* employees and how difficult it was to believe that teachers were actually making such critical decisions at a public school.

In the meantime, the union representatives were still patiently waiting in another room for her to come on the line and nail down the procedures for the upcoming union election. For now, they small-talked quietly while waiting for her to come on and break their long and sometimes awkward silence.

I continued.

"Ms. Hopper...are you still there? I don't want to be an obstructionist or a smart-ass or anything, but I still have a few more questions."

"Okay...ugh...well, I am still processing your point about Greg Valero. But go ahead, what other questions do you have?" I could hear that she was not happy with me.

"Well, actually there are several. Can I just read them to you? I think you'll get the idea..."

"Okay...go ahead. What are your other questions?"

So I read my list of questions:

"Ms. Hopper, I just wanted to know—What is the legal definition of *management*, according to PERB?

"And secondly, based on the scope of decision making that our Leadership Council is responsible for—To what extent do teachers who serve on the Leadership Council act in a *management* capacity?

"And in light of Provision #16 in your boilerplate 'Consent Election Agreement'—What conflict of interest is presented for this particular charter school by having teachers in the bargaining unit who are simultaneously serving on the Leadership Council?

"Are you still there?"

"Yes, I am here. Do you have more questions?" asked Jeri Hopper.

"Yes, I do. I was wondering...

"...Who should be (or who should not be) in the bargaining unit...and...Who should be (or who should not be) on the Leadership Council...according to these PERB provisions?

"And for that matter—What is the legal scope of authority of the teachers association as it relates to charter law?...which, as you know... is quite different from the regular education code.

"In other words, Ms. Hopper, neither the teachers union, Libi Gil, our school board, the governor, the president, or the pope is authorized to influence decisions made by our Leadership Council. Our charter gives them full autonomy. And, as I am sure you well know, the Court is admonished to consider the scope and intent of charter law when settling disputes that rise with charter schools."

"Was that last part a question or a statement, Dr. Riley?"

"I guess that was more of a clarifying statement. But here's another question:

"Given the authority of individual teachers on the Leadership Council to establish and implement school policy, especially as it relates to access to the budget and salaries—Does the presence of the union present a potential violation of the Mueller Charter School petition?

"And finally—for now—If there is a violation of our Charter Petition, could that violation result in the revocation of the charter? And does PERB or any other entity have the jurisdiction to compel us to take an action that will knowingly violate our own charter? And if so, what legal recourse might there be to protect the children of El Milagro?"

HOPPER'S LETTER

I was genuinely surprised that Ms. Hopper could not respond to any of these questions. In fact...for a moment there, I thought she might have hung up because of the vacuous silence on the other end of the line. Eventually, though, I heard her say, as if to herself, that perhaps a conference call was ill advised at this time.

"Excuse me?"

"I think perhaps a conference call is ill advised at this time. I need to do a little more research into charter law. Can you send me that list of questions along with a memo stating why you do not want to go forward with the conference call?"

"Oh, I'm sorry, I may have failed to communicate clearly. I'm okay with the conference call, Ms. Hopper. I just need you to reconcile those questions first. Can you do that?"

"No, I have to admit, I am not real well versed in charter law."

"Then would you agree that it might be a little premature to hold conference call to establish the procedures for an election that could potentially compromise our school's charter?"

"Yes, I think we need to research these questions."

"Then, since you don't have answers to these questions as a representative of the State of California, perhaps you could write the memo explaining why the union discussion is on hold."

"Okay...you are right. I will do that. And I will let the union folks— who are still patiently waiting for our call—know that we are postponing the conference call for now."

Fair enough. It turns out Jeri Hopper was angry that all of these questions were coming up that she couldn't answer. And, as a government bureaucrat, she was unhappy that this Mueller Charter School thing was on her "To Do" list and she couldn't make it go away. And she was agitated that we were a charter school and we didn't fit in the box that every other organization of state employees fit into. And she was livid that our Leadership Council had sent a letter back in April requesting that an election for union representation take place.

"If you had all of these questions, why did you request an election?" she asked me.

"I don't think I did."

"Well, you sent that freakin' letter!"

"Yes, ma'am. That was because you gave us only two choices: send the letter requesting an election...or the union is automatically authorized."

"Well, I need another letter. From...ugh...let's see...how about from your attorney. Yeah, send a letter from Jack Parham indicating that you are having second thoughts about the union or something. I don't know, Kevin. Just make it up."

That was actually the last we ever heard from Jeri Hopper. Even as she got one last bureaucratic request in. But Jackson Parham dutifully sent an amended letter in which he detailed the potential conflict looming between the government code and charter law. By PERB's own definitions, there were significant conflicts presented when management employees are represented by a labor union, especially when the members have the entire school budget in their hands.

The CVE tried to rebut by arguing that Jackson Parham's letter didn't really describe a potential conflict with teachers at Mueller Charter School serving on the Leadership Council. To the union, we were just obfuscating and delaying the inevitable. Initially PERB agreed (as always) with the union and ordered the election. However, their solution was to exclude the teachers who were currently serving on the Leadership Council. Jackson Parham pointed out that this was nearly half the teaching staff and that membership on the Leadership Council rotated from year to year.

So the PERB decision went all the way to the docket of the State Board of Appeals.

HEY IDIOTS!

Nearly eight months later, on March 5 of 2003, a new administrative law judge from the Public Employee Relations Board issued an order to proceed with the election. Though there were a number of interesting and confounding contradictions between bodies of law, there was no clear reason to believe that the Leadership Council would make decisions that necessarily represented a conflict of interest. There were ways to avoid such conflicts.

We didn't see it that way, of course. But by then, we didn't care. The staff had undergone additional changes. Fully half the teachers who were here for *Migden-gate* were now gone. The teachers who were most recently hired were 100% behind the charter mission. Most were brand new teachers who knew very little about what the union does or doesn't do for them. It wasn't an issue.

More importantly, I had eight months to prepare for life at Mueller Charter School in the event that the union was voted back in. We began to develop different strategies in anticipation of the court finding for the union:

We could accept the election results.

We could contest the election process.

We could ignore the election—and thus ignore the union.

We could restructure the Leadership Council so that *only* those who do not wish to be in the union could serve as "management employees" on the Council.

We could somehow overturn the election and initiate the process to decertify the union.

There were, no doubt, many other potential options. If you play chess, you probably thought of a few that we didn't think about. And, whether you play chess or not, you are probably exhausted by this exercise. You are probably reading this screaming at your bookmarker: "Hey, idiots! What about the kids? What about the mission? Remember what Claudette Inge said? Stay above the bullshit!"

And you'd be right. We caught ourselves often doing the same thing. Checking ourselves. A lot of intellect and energy clearly went into this chess match. But I also made sure we put the same amount of energy and attention into the service of our children and the development of our school. In a way it kept us far more focused than you might ever realize.

Throughout the entire process, the academic achievement of our students was steadily improving.

CAPOEIRA

I started to formulate lots of ideas about how to create a unique and powerful alliance with the Mueller Charter School Teachers Association that would serve everybody's interests: the CTA, the charter, the teachers, and especially the kids. If we were compelled by charter law to be innovative and we had so successfully transformed every other aspect of our organization—from structures and processes, to systems and relationships—why couldn't we develop a new paradigm in how the union and the school partner?

One of the cornerstones in the relationship between labor unions and management is that they are, by design, adversarial. With varying levels of militancy, gamesmanship, and obstruction, the union exists to represent the interests of the employee vis-à-vis management. In our case, regardless of what PERB said, *our teachers on the leadership council were management.* They would, as *management* employees, inevitably have to sit across the table from the association that they pay to represent their interests as teachers.

As the principal of Mueller Charter School, I wanted the union drama to go away. I longed for the day that every discussion, every meeting, every interaction, and every ounce of creative energy was spent on forging a new path toward achieving the charter mission. Period. On the other hand, I was also quite fascinated by the possibilities of creating a new reality around this historically adversarial and conflicting relationship.

No matter. We will never know what new frontiers we could have discovered together at Mueller Charter School—with management and labor...charter and PERB legislators...union leaders and children... Libi Gil and all the judges in Sacramento combined...our Leadership Council and Jeri Hopper...teachers and themselves...all walking into the sunlight...hand in hand.

On April 4, the union election was held and the California Teachers Association along with their local affiliate, the Chula Vista Educators Association, failed to muster the votes required to sanction the upstart Mueller Charter School Teachers Association. It wasn't even close. The CVE followed with a few weak letters and memos trying to rally behind potential grievances and appeals, but the election killed whatever appetite anybody had to push against the rapidly changing culture of Mueller Charter School. With dwindling membership and finite resources, the CVE decided to take the fight elsewhere.

PERB sent one final memo at the end of May. I noticed that it was not signed by Jeri Hopper. I now had volumes and volumes of letters, memos, grievances, depositions, complaints, arguments and counterarguments, judges' orders, and other union hand grenades. I had them neatly organized in tall file cabinets. But in the end, the final verdict came to five unceremonious words that mattered. I thought there would be a more dramatic conclusion.

I expected that we would wind up on Court TV, shuffling down Broadway and Front Street on our way to the courthouse in downtown San Diego. I'd have one of those little silver carts on wheels, piled to the knuckles with official-looking briefcases and boxes from Home Depot. We'd be arriving for the final disposition of the court—trying to beat the CVE guys for a better seat in the house.

For all the piles of paper and paper and endless paper...the final word from the court would fit on a single yellow Post-it. Dated May 27, 2003, the Public Employees Relations Board (PERB) certified that, as a result of the election, there will be no exclusive representative at Mueller Charter School. So quit asking! And the gavel hammers down.

I expected the microphones shoved into our faces by Court TV reporters as we left the judges chamber. "Ask Maureen DeLuca," I would say. "I don't do interviews."

But of course there was no Court TV, no reporters, no judge's chambers and no need to take still another day away from our students for all of this nonsense. There was just a final decision and the words written on the single yellow post-it that I shared with others:

"This case is now closed."

And it's just as well. There was something anachronistic-sounding about the Mueller Charter School Teachers Association. Even worse, from there we could only ever be Mueller Charter School—never El Milagro. Our dance, the capoeira, would be lost on those who cannot hear the music...or imagine the violence of a single stunning blow delivered by a flying heel kick.

CHAPTER FIVE

The Whispers of Heretics

Change ain't lookin' for friends. Change calls the tune we dance to.

—From the character of Al Swearengen, *"Deadwood"*

REVOLUTION

The *I Ching* is an ancient Chinese manuscript that contains teachings that are over three millennia old, stretching back to the Shang and Zhou dynasties. It speaks through the ages about people and systems and the chaotic nature of change. The *I Ching* says, "Before there can be great brilliance...there must be chaos."

I realized that my work—the work of transforming schools—was mostly about our life tattoos and the inevitability of chaos as a means to an end. So I had the Chinese symbol for "chaos" tattooed on my arm... strategically centered between the symbols for "revolution" and "peace." Thus I have the cycle of deep organizational change permanently calligraphied in the morning mirror so that every day, as I get ready for work, I can be reminded of the essential stages of change:

Revolution—Chaos—Peace...Revolution—Chaos—Peace...

Maybe there are a few other steps for deep change too. But you can count on these to play the tune we dance to.

There seem to be at least these two kinds of change in public schools:

The slow and cautious kind that is all *cosmetic*. The kind of change that is safe. Where patio furniture is rearranged or a new course on contemporary music is added or we rewrite the school fight song. Where everyone can feel good about the process and the outcome and the prospects for long-term viability. Where there is buy-in. The kind of change that is meaningful to the committee that conceived it...but in the bigger picture...becomes all but insignificant. Where change is an illusion.

Then there is the kind of change that results in deep, deep organizational *transformation*...right down to the bones. Right to the very soul. It is most rare. It is painful and exciting; unsettling and uncertain. And it pisses people off.

That's how we changed Mueller Charter School. Transformed her into El Milagro. The only thing left untouched was the ghost of old man Mueller and the freeway symphony that grew in pitch and volume and tempo with the technology of each new year. The rest we disassembled brick by brick. We consistently challenged every structure: Do we still need this pillar? Do we need it here? Does it have to look like this? What if we painted it? What if we pushed it over and broke it into tiny pieces on the ground?

In times of transformation, nothing is sacred. In fact, the more permanent and secure a structure might seem, the more urgent is the need to destroy it.

The safe, secure, and comfortable parts are replaced by uncertainty and by ambiguity. No wonder such complete transformation is rare. But before there can be brilliance, before there can be El Milagro, the debt we owe is paid in utter chaos.

CHANGE 101

The first law of school change is that *schools are designed to never change*. They have a built-in aversion to creative transformation, a natural barrier structured to ward off even the suggestion that there might be a different path...even a better path. You have to *want* to change. There has to be a compelling need and a nearly unnatural sense of urgency. The buildings have to all but be ablaze.

America's present-day public schools were influenced mightily by the industrial revolution. We still have a factory-like model of mass education: neat rows of plastic chairs all sliding like pucks along linoleum floors. There are the cookie-cutter texts and tools and store-bought inspirational posters displayed on otherwise mundane corkboard walls. All interchangeable parts—from the obsolete spinning globe to the students and the teachers.

Schools are the same everywhere (or at least remarkably similar). Though there is tremendous variation in physical appearance—campus landscape and building design—what goes on inside the classroom and faculty lounge is nearly indistinguishable from one community to the next. From one school to another, one district and one state to another, all across America, they rise as if they are extruded from preformed molds and spit out somewhere in the Midwest. Classrooms look the same, smell the same, and sound the same—from the physical space to the routines, patterns, practices, and behaviors that we call *teaching*. As times have changed, our schools have not. They are like ancient temples from a bygone era—frozen in space and time and born not long after Lincoln was shot.

And it is not as if we have a winning formula here. This is not the hundred year old recipe for Coca-Cola or magic motor oil. If the medical profession progressed at the same pace as teaching, we would still be in search of the cure for smallpox. We know our schools are failing to serve too many kids in too many places, but the ingenuity and energy required to change them is wasted on just keeping the boat afloat. Instead of ideas, we confront clichés spun to justify the status quo. I've heard them all:

"We don't want to change things just for the sake of change." Or—

"We have a little something here we call 'tradition'...and kids these days need some consistency in their lives." And, of course, that colorful equine banner for self-fulfilling prophecy—

"After all, you can lead a horse to water..." And my personal favorite—

"Let's stick with the tried and true...let's not reinvent the wheel!"

Bullshit. Let's reinvent it. This wheel wobbles if it spins at all. It's time to create a new one. Create a better wheel. One that doesn't look like it lost its hubcaps and rolled off of Henry Ford's production line.

So we started looking outside of schools for a better metaphor for change.

John Kotter studies organizations and the process of change. He is an expert on the common dynamics that occur when some of our nation's most well-run companies adapt to their market realities and make wise and sometimes painful adjustments. He has discovered a lot of similar patterns in the organizations that changed effectively. You know the changes worked because the companies still exist. And, of course, the companies that failed to change, or just didn't do it right, don't live in the same building anymore. That's the free market for you. You grow or you die.

Not public schools though. They can nearly be as bad as they choose to be. They can afford to ignore John Kotter and all the research on change. They just can't achieve greatness. They can't be effective with the richly diverse populations of children they serve. At El Milagro, we figure we can't afford to ignore the art of organizational transformation because that's what miracles are: transformations. So we pay attention. We study "The Dynamics of Organizational Change-101." Here is the syllabus:

Professor Kotter says you have to establish a sense of urgency.

We did. We saw our former students, our children, drowning in the middle schools and dropping out of high schools because they weren't going to those places fully prepared to swim. We resolved that they could do better. We could do better. We resolved that they would be at grade level by the end of the year and that we were the right people to make that happen. You grow or you die.

Professor Kotter says you have to create powerful guiding coalitions.

We did. We found a critical mass of teachers and parents who believed our children were worthy of our energy and effort—and from that point, the revolution was on! We soon discovered the kinetic power of the coalition: when the *unity of purpose* grows and feeds off the urgency. Eventually, a critical mass emerges, teams develop, communication improves, the coalition become stronger, the spirit overtakes you...and eventually the nonbelievers begin to disappear.

Professor Kotter says you have to create a compelling vision.

We did. What could be more compelling than working to overcome the adverse effects of life circumstances that prevent poor kids from learning? We recognized that many of our children come from impoverished homes and that some 60% speak English as their second language. Many have huge holes in their school history or have bounced from school to school. Many come from dysfunctional home environments. Many have witnessed violence or abuse. Many have been exposed to drugs or alcohol or so much garbage television that their imaginations are as discolored and brittle as their teeth. We gave a name to all these variables—we called them symptoms. Then we promised each other we would treat the symptoms, and mitigate their effects on teaching and learning. While others might use them as stock excuses for their students' stunted levels of academic achievement, we structured a system to overcome them.

We created the vision of resilient children. With 90% at grade level. We proclaimed: *Our children will change the world.* But every day we have to give them the foundation that enables them to go on and compete in middle school and high school. Then they have to have the goods to go to the colleges that kids who grow up and change the world go to—like Berkeley and Brown and Stanford and Dartmouth. And after they get out of Berkeley they have to go to law school or get an MBA or run for public office or become a school revolutionary. That's how our children will grow up and change the world.

Professor Kotter says you have to communicate that vision.

We did. In every parent letter, every meeting, every publication, every board presentation, every goal session, every discussion with newspaper reporters. It's on our Web site, on our letterhead, and on our marquis. It's on the tip of our tongue. It's imprinted in our psyches. It's written in stone and tattooed to our bodies. We write articles about it.

This whole book is about it.

Professor Kotter says you have to empower others to act on that vision.

We did. We realized that having a compelling school vision isn't terribly progressive...but that *acting* on that vision is. And acting on that vision means every action, decision, policy, program, interaction, service, assembly, expenditure...every lesson and every day is devoted to the transformation of El Milagro. By conventions of our charter, and by virtue of our mission, every person is not only empowered to act...they are *compelled* to act. They are required to. We must each lead change, eliminate the barriers to learning, create new paths. We must each experiment, pioneer, take risks, break something, fall on our collective faces, rise up, and overcome. We must model the resilience we seek to cultivate in children.

Professor Kotter says you have to plan for and create short-term wins.

We did. We knew we could not go from having 18% of our students at grade level in the year 2000 to having 90% at grade level in 2001. Not that our students couldn't do it, but we didn't know how to get them there. We hadn't fallen backward on our butts enough times to learn the way. So we developed a five-year plan. Then we started to find every sign and omen that signaled improvement. We sung our successes from the rooftops. We celebrated. We celebrated our students and we celebrated each other. We told stories, we exaggerated, we rode the tide. We replaced our fears with informed optimism.

Professor Kotter says you have to consolidate improvements, seize the momentum, and produce still more change.

We did. The more we learned, the more the rivers rose. We created new systems for everything: from how we provide materials and copies to teachers to how we hire new staff. Process excellence. We created new programs and services and new ways to tell our story. New optimism. New reason for hope. Carpe diem! Then we rode El Milagro like a runaway cable car headed down Stockton Street with a mind of its own.

Professor Kotter says you have to institutionalize new approaches.

We did. We took everything that worked, every process or system or method that contributed to our forward momentum and we wrote it down. We memorialized it. We created charts, notebooks, slide shows, handouts, presentations...anything that would help anchor it into the culture of the "way we do things here." The culture of El Milagro.

JENNIFER'S PROJECT

Kotter isn't the only academician to pin back and label the various anatomical elements of the change process. There are other models too. They come from many sources. You can even make up your own. I did.

I received an e-mail one day from a student named Jennifer at the University of San Diego who found us by accident as she researched the Web sites of charter schools. She was studying the school reform movement and needed some input on a research project. They were learning about how change happens in schools where real change actually happens.

She came to the right place.

I agreed to participate in her research project so she sent me my assignment:

Dear Dr. Riley:

Thank you for your willingness to help on my research paper for my leadership class at the University of San Diego. I realize that you are very busy and appreciate you taking the time to respond. It should be self-explanatory. Here it is:

Today's schools are faced with the need to implement continual reforms to improve student achievement and ensure school safety. Research has indicated that sustaining a change once it is implemented is a critical need in schools because most innovations fail over time.

Please study the list of the "Nine Factors for Institutionalizing Change" that are listed below. Rank them by degree of importance as they apply to sustaining a successful charter school initiative. (1 = Most important to 9 = Least important)

The Nine Factors are :
- *Planning and preparation*
- *Timing*
- *Congruence with mission*
- *Environmental sensitivity*
- *Clarity and simplicity*
- *Unpretentious realism*
- *Sufficient, not indulgent, resources*
- *Strong, central leadership*
- *Reduced individual proprietary interest*

Thanks in advance, Dr. Riley. BTW, I loved your school's Web site.

I considered Jennifer's academic list of nine factors necessary for institutionalizing change, and dutifully prioritized them according to my experience at El Milagro. But I sensed that something significant was missing. At first I considered adding a few different factors that weren't on her list. Then I realized it was bigger than that. Academicians may need to keep things simple, but organizational change, at least in my school, was far more complex. I realized that the list wasn't just missing a few factors...it was missing dimension. So in a moment of inspiration, I seized upon a teachable moment:

Dear Jennifer:
I read through your Nine Factors and have ranked them according to their influence on the change phenomenon—at least here at Mueller Charter School. (I can't speak for other charter schools!) I have also attached a brief rationale for my rankings:

1...Strong, Central Leadership: First and foremost you have to have somebody who's imaginative enough to envision a brighter future, who has the tenacity to pursue it like a cranky pit bull, who is wacky enough to think success is inevitable...but who isn't afraid to fail. The leader can't waste energy on self-preservation. Leaders can't worry about getting fired. In fact...they have to push back so hard on the system that they are always teetering on the edge of not being invited back for the next year! The leader has to be consumed by a ferocious fire called moral purpose...the flames of which become: the mission. The essential question is this: *Where, in the development of organizations that have achieved greatness, did the first vision of greatness come from?* There are managers, and then there are leaders. There are leaders, and then there are visionary leaders. Throughout human history, visionary leaders have been blessed with the imagination to conceive a better way. They are haunted by a nagging belief that they can always do better. And if their motives are pure, they have a very good chance to affect an element of change that is so dramatic and rare that the culture itself is transformed. Their depth of vision inspires the depth of change.

2...*Congruence with the Mission:* The mission is the driving force. All ideas, resources, energy, processes, systems and routines are invested in achieving it. Anything else is a distraction and a drain that keeps an organization from reaching its full potential. If you have no mission, you have no direction. Think "True North!"

3...*Clarity and Simplicity:* We cut right through all obfuscation and whining: 90% of our students must be at grade level. No excuses.

4...*Reduced Individual Proprietary Interest:* One mission. 90%. Every employee at this school is pointed toward the same mission. There are many other potential missions and agendas, but you just can't pursue them here. The mission is too big. It is bigger than any of us.

5...*Timing:* There is no right sequence for the change process. The sequence happens. There is no road map or itinerary. You just know when it is time to launch the next initiative or lob the next grenade. But then again, sometimes you can't wait. Kids can't wait. Sometimes the mission carries you.

6...*Planning and Preparation:* We do our homework and are in a constant state of serious research. We study every data set, every trend, every model, every metaphor. But we have also mastered the art of implementation. We could research and plan until the cows come home, plan and prepare to a point of utter paralysis! We don't wait. We do our research, then roll the dice.

7...*Environmental Sensitivity:* We are not so good on the sensitivity side because we are compelled by our circumstances and the urgency with which we pursue the mission. We are the toro in the china shop. We break stuff and sometimes wish we hadn't. We work to communicate better, establish timelines, monitor and report progress to whomever will listen. But we don't stand still or apologize for the deafening volume of our forward momentum that rattles the dishes and knocks pictures off the walls.

8...*Sufficient, Not Indulgent Resources*: Perhaps this should be listed number 10 on your list of "Nine Factors for Institutionalizing Change." Why shouldn't we have "indulgent resources"? Especially in a community where indulgence is a rare commodity. We have an indulgent mission. By design and by necessity our reach exceeds our grasp. Resources should keep pace with the development of rich ideas.

  9...*Unpretentious Realism*: I hate this component even more than the last one. I don't agree with it even being on the list. Why be realistic? Be audacious! Be fearless! "The tragedy is not that we set our goals too high and fail...it is that we set them too low and succeed!"

As I was prioritizing your list, Jennifer, some thoughts came to me about organizational change that I would like to share. So I am attaching some additional notes that you may use or discard at your discretion:

  ...The nine items on your list are very similar to what you find in other change models (like John Kotter's, for example). They are all generic components of a change process. But your list is entitled "Nine Factors for Institutionalizing Change." If you institutionalize a practice, it becomes, by definition, an established and long-term organizational norm. It becomes permanent and sustainable. It becomes...*institution*-alized. Any list of change ingredients will be deceiving because change is neither sequential nor linear. It is not predictable. It is not even always replicable.

  The truth is, you don't necessarily need any of these Nine Factors to create change at a school. You can change where the soda machines are located, for example, and you can make that move whenever you want. You can change the logo for the newsletter or the night you hold the talent show. We make plenty of adjustments in the management of this school but most won't contribute to an outcome of getting 90% of our students to grade level. They won't neutralize the effects of poverty or accelerate a child's command of English as a second language. So, for us, they just don't go wide enough or deep enough. We seek change so deep it will ignite a revolution. We cannot achieve greatness for children without transforming our school and the community that contains it.

  El Milagro, has never been about school reform, school restructuring, or school change for the sake of change. It has never been about test scores or avoiding the scarlet scourge associated with failing to meet some externally imposed standard of competency. It is about complete transformational change, where the academic outcomes, the people, the community and the entire profession is better because of it. Change so deep that our spiritual core is altered. For us, such transformational change has occurred in integrated waves...and in multiple dimensions.   .

So think about a change model with three distinct dimensions:

- Change at the **Foundation** level
- Change at the **Systemic** level, and
- Change at the **Spiritual Core**.

This first dimension, *Foundation Change*, represents every modification we made to the *operational* structure of our school. We had to change the foundation before we could go any further.

These components have to evolve first, especially in a charter school where the locus of control rests within our own immediate governance structure. They include changes to the infrastructure, and the daily business of schools. Foundation changes include those that address organizational philosophies and direction, programs and services, policies, guidelines, materials, and resources. They require less creativity and are, as a whole, less controversial. With a clear vision, they are adjusted quickly and efficiently. They contribute to our sense of organizational agility. Suddenly the gears turn better.

But at Mueller Charter School we expanded our scope of innovation and widened the *breadth* of change we were seeking. We examined the whole cosmos of systems that we had in place—the ones that impact routines and academic outcomes.

So the second dimension of this change model addresses the *Systems*.

From the very beginning, we began to craft the systemic alignment and integration of change initiatives. El Milagro is very much a composite of multiple innovations that have been implemented to get different results than we had ever achieved before. Some innovations are more significant than others. Some are more complex. Some work and some fail miserably. But they all contribute to a constant cycle of organizational self-reflection and continuous improvement. And in some way, they are all connected, even if only by the promise they hold for moving us closer to our mission.

To change organizational systems requires long-term, creative, and coordinated initiatives. Systems are hard to change because they are complex and often affect the adults—and adults are the ones who call the shots in schools. The systems that I am referring to include everything from salary and compensation packages to calendars and the daily schedule. I am also referring to systems for improving communication, employee attitudes of competence and efficacy, even morale, professional practice, pedagogy, and training. And systems that lead to more efficient processes for recruiting, hiring, and evaluation of staff.

Systemic change is on-going. It reaches into every corner of the organizational practice. It is a function of *breadth*. It feeds forward progress. There is a palpable new energy. If you can sustain and build on it something remarkable happens. The deeper the change, the closer you come to permanently influencing the culture and even that **Spiritual Core** I talked about.

Organizational culture is the sum total of how people, think, behave, communicate, collaborate, support, disagree, innovate and play. If you transform the culture of an organization, you change the genetic code of who they are collectively and who they are destined to be. Few schools have experienced this deep cultural transformation and perhaps that's why change has not been lasting or significant as it relates to children and their academic results! In fact, few organizations of any kind have done it. Just when some Fortune 500 company is held out as the paradigm, it disappears...

So Jennifer, when you and your classmates there at USD are discussing organizational change, remember that it has to include not only the "process" of change but also the "products" of change. This will help you to understand those dimensions of depth and breadth. Perhaps this is more information than you bargained for. But I thought an authentic organizational change model might be interesting for you to consider. This is how we have experienced change at El Milagro. I hope it helps!

ADVANCED CHANGE 301

At Mueller Charter School we changed the location of the salad bar, sure enough. We moved one of our softball backstops too. We even re-striped the parking spaces in the faculty parking lot. And in a temporary moment of focused brilliance, we bought our own electronic ball pump and issued equipment passes to each classroom.

Not exactly the stuff of revolutionaries. But these actions are all visible alterations. They are child and service centered. They are totally consistent with our mission. They required collaboration and discussion and the investment of resources at one level or another. And they represent the extent to which many schools re-invent themselves only to later wonder why their change initiatives did little to influence the achievement of children.

But we created *deep* change too:

- We invested $7 million in modernizing our fifty-year-old buildings
- We voted for autonomy;
- We empowered teachers with the authority to make management decisions;
- We invested hundreds of thousands of dollars in a long term and on-going training effort for our staff;
- We replaced 75% of our original staff with teachers committed to our mission;
- We created sky-high performance goals for children and adults;
- We trained our parents to be more effective at home and at school;
- We built a wireless, infrastructure for state-of-the-art technology;
- We created a literacy center that provided 20,000 book titles in English and Spanish;
- We rewrote our charter;
- We created a middle school Leadership Academy that serves students to the eighth grade;
- We created a comprehensive assessment system to monitor the progress of *every* child *every* day;
- We developed an instructional approach so compelling, it immediately began to change the very essence of teaching— from the industrial-era, one-size-fits-all model, to the personalized, custom-designed differentiated learning plan in place for every child; and
- We somehow rescued a school that smelled bad...where the adults would pull the chair out from under each other just to watch people land with a groan—right on their asses;
- and in part, that's how we transformed Mueller Charter School.

And we are just warming up. All change is not the same. There are the layers:

- The *Foundation* Changes, explained below;
- The *System* Changes, explained in chapters Seven through Thirteen; and
- Changes in the Organizational Culture, the *Spiritual Core*, explained in Chapter Fourteen.

LAYERS

It wasn't as if we started to change Mueller Charter School in a logical or preplanned sequence. We did not paint by numbers. We had no navigation system. We could not deconstruct fifty years of entrenched history like Lego bricks. In fact, that there is any sequence at all to what we did, is evident only now in hindsight.

Looking back, there were elements at the Foundation Level that we changed immediately. We didn't use a checklist. Some things were just easier to change than others. For example, it was easier to change the mission statement than it was to get the teachers and students to accept the notion that the mission was about them! The major elements that we changed at the Foundation Level include:

- Mission and core philosophy
- Programs and services
- Policies and operational guidelines
- Resources
- People
- Clients

Here's how it happened:

The first and easiest component to change at Mueller was our **Mission and Core Philosophy**. It only took some imagination. It cost nothing. Whatever the philosophy was before, it wasn't about kids. So we thought about it: "our children will change the world" if *we* give them the academic foundation they need to compete. We said: "Everyone stop right where you are, take a deep breath, and point to the mountaintop. Look around the room leaders! Is everyone pointing to the same mountaintop? Can you see yourself standing on that mountaintop some day? If so, we are on our way."

And we were on our way.

So next we created new **Programs and Services**.

Our kids, products of public education, had been languishing in the swamps of low expectations for decades. They had been underachieving, dropping out of school, becoming juvenile offenders, becoming teen moms, spray painting graffiti on freeway signs, joining gangs, joining unemployment lines. But to achieve a radically different outcome for our students first required a change in ourselves: toward focus, unity of purpose, resilient energy, and innovative alternatives to the status quo. All of the creative energy of the organization had to be channeled toward achieving the mission. The new currency of exchange became *fresh ideas*.

When we started to channel every ounce of our creative energy toward our mission, three things happened:

First, we began developing better programs and services that our students benefited from. It was exciting for teachers to contribute ideas to new initiatives that were quickly implemented. There were immediate and palpable changes occurring in our school, so things were happening and everyone could see and experience it. There was newness.

Within two years, we had created a multiage program and a dual-language program. We established a program to promote the arts. We started looping so teachers committed to staying with their classes for multiple years. We developed programs to recognize and award academic excellence in our students. We held school-wide ceremonies every Monday morning where we could sing and celebrate our students, where we could publicly promote learning. We developed a Student Services and Counseling Program, reached out to community resources, and hooked up our families.

In time, every program and service that we created started nudging us that much closer to the mountaintop. We called it alignment.

Second, for most people, the creative energy that once went into more subversive and counterproductive activities (like bitching about the principal, or plotting a coup, or backstabbing the grade-level chair, or undermining the "enemy") was now redirected toward creating exciting ideas that benefited our students. We eliminated our natural impulse to explain our failures with stock excuses. We slowly replaced our doubts and fears about what we were capable of as a staff with a willingness and urgency to innovate, to reinvent, to recreate, to redesign virtually every service and program we provide.

Thirdly, we saw immediate results, albeit by degrees, in the attitudes and outcomes of our students. Creating new programs and services to ensure that they were absolutely aligned with the mission, resulted in an immediate improvement in our teaching, and in our students' learning. But it was not enough to result in the kind of complete transformation required to produce El Milagro.

So we began to rewrite Charter **Policies and Operational Guidelines**.

Creating new programs is still fairly surface-level stuff. We would have to drill deeper. And then deeper.

As change began to manifest itself in all aspects of our organization, and as it became expected, many of our daily processes and procedures and guidelines began to change too. They take longer to develop because they are generally addressed on an as-needed basis.

They are our "rules of engagement" and they are significant because they contribute to a sense of common purpose.

In our charter model, we had created a streamlined governing board—minus the bureaucracy that goes with most political bodies. We tossed our encyclopedia of board policies and administrative regulations. We tossed Robert and his famous Rules of Order. Though sometimes these tools may come in handy, we decided to codify only three kinds of policies. We kept only the operating guidelines that would:

- Significantly contribute to the safety and welfare of our students;
- Contribute to access and distribution of resources for all staff and programs; and
- Clarify procedures that are not already described in the Charter Petition.

Eliminating hundreds and hundreds of board policies is, in itself, liberating. We defined our own conditions and debated the extent to which they impact the organizational mission.

Then we **Aligned our Resources**.

Once we started to create programs and functions that could better serve our kids and energize our staff, we had to align all of our resources to make sure those new ideas could survive. As a fiscally independent charter school, our budget comes directly to us. We don't get a discretionary subsidy from the school district. We are not like some teenager standing with our hat in our hand and asking for a pittance to buy some new skateboard gear:

"Ugh, Dad, do you think I could borrow ten dollars from my own personal fortune to go to the mall with my friends?"

Not Mueller Charter School. We get $7-something million a year from the State of California and we decide what to do with every penny! We control our own destiny with regard to the budget, and so we make sure everything is spent to better serve our students. We scrutinize every penny. We study the ledger. No stone goes unturned.

But money isn't the only resource. Time is a pretty important one too, and teachers never feel they have enough of it. So we started with a premise that we have more control over time than we think. We decide what time to start the day and what time to end the day. We determine when to have recess and how much time to commit to it. We control our calendar, our vacations, our staff development days. *We* decide what kids do for homework and how to use instructional time during the day. Since we really can control time, we harness it as a resource and make sure every minute counts. Every second is used to serve the mission.

There are lots of other resources we control too. The physical plant, for instance—our school facilities. We started to look strategically at every building, all of our playground space, and even the landscaping. Always the question was: "How can we better utilize this resource to meet the charter mission?"

All the texts, library books, manipulatives, playground equipment, and learning materials are resources too. So is every component of our extensive technology inventory from computers to sound systems, document cameras, big-screen televisions, and other tools.

We aligned all of our resources.

Then we saw **Changes in the People**...

It's one thing to create new ideas and policies, but it's another thing altogether when organizational change becomes dependent on the degree to which you can influence the people in an organization! In the end, the "school" is really the people.

There are two ways that the *people* change. Either they go away and we replace them with new people who very badly want to participate in El Milagro. Or, there is a change in the hearts and minds and attitudes of those who choose to stay. In either case, the people, like the organization itself, cannot remain static, if they are to remain at all.

As if it is not difficult enough to change the hearts and minds of those professionals who pursue the mission like a holy grail, in the next level of complex organizational change, you have to get to the hopes and dreams and values of the **clients** too. This means the kids and their families and their friends and their pets.

They have to believe. In the face of what may very well have been generation after generation of school failure and underperformance, *these* children are all that matters now. It is their time. And though parents may get first dibs on shaping their children's value system, we cannot be successful if children themselves do not have a positive vision of themselves gloriously achieving all that they are capable of achieving.

After all, this is the unambiguous contrast that exists between children of El Milagro and my former students from Skyline School. In Solana Beach, school success is not optional. It is expected. From the day children are born in these more affluent and mainstream homes, parents study them for the first sign of giftedness.

"What school are we going to send Junior to? How about Princeton? They have an excellent pre-law program and I am very good friends with a lady who has an aunt who works with a man whose cousin once designed the Web site for their West Coast alumni association."

"Honey. Junior is four days old. He can't even poop without help yet. Hand me that towel, will ya?"

In Solana Beach, Junior is expected to go to Princeton. At El Milagro, too many parents are willing to settle for Junior corralling the shopping carts at Wal-Mart and too many children have never even heard of Princeton.

And though there are many who argue that college is not for everyone and we still need electricians and plumbers and soldiers for the 82nd Airborne, I notice that given the choice, they want their own kids at Princeton. Dying in foreign wars is a little too arbitrary. My kid is going to Princeton.

So college is, among other things, an American metaphor. The discussion represents hope and achievement and resiliency. In even the poorest of America's communities and villages there are paths to Princeton. El Milagro carves the path. And children must *believe*, even when their parents' lives may be living proof of a nation that is patently racist or unequal or unfair, or selfish.

It is their time to find the path.

Of course, in the pursuit of El Milagro we went even wider and deeper again. We had influenced change in the mission, programs, policies, resources and even people's hearts; change even in children's sense of efficacy. Depth and breadth.

But the next level, if we wanted long-term, sustained, replicable, and radical change, was to reengineer the very systems that drive our school and begin to peer out on to the future.

Too many schools slog along— slow, inert, or at best, reactive. So we adapted a business model for long range planning. We started imagining our needs and our gains as if spread out across multiple horizons. "What are your strategic priorities for autumn, three years from now?" my wife asked me one day. As one of Intuit's corporate vice presidents, she thrives in a business that survives on their ability to anticipate and plan and allocate resources across a multi-dimensional time continuum. "Three years from now? Hell, I'm just trying to meet our AYP goals for this year!"

"That's why it's a scramble every year," she said as she simultaneously read the back of the cereal box and swallowed another spoonful of

Lucky Charms. "You don't have an instinct for long-range innovation. Seat of the pants, my friend. Seat of the pants."

And she was right. Now we think ahead. Two year, three years...even more. What are our priorities for training, curriculum development, technology infrastructure, long term data analysis, leadership, children's health initiatives, community relationships, political activism, etc. etc.?

We are managing and driving the change that happens at Mueller Charter School. We are engineering our own destiny...and not waiting for politics or economics to determine the fate of our students. We are proactively planning our path to greatness right down to the victory celebration. We can't leave it to the Lucky Charms. Trust me, in the staid milieu of public education, that is in itself revolutionary thinking.

Si Se Puede!

LA JARDIN DE PAZ

A few weeks after corresponding with Jennifer I heard from her again.

Dear Dr. Riley:

I wanted to express my gratitude for all the time you took to help with my research paper. My professor was very interested in the two additional factors that you proposed and he said he was going to add them to his model for next semester. He said the 3 Dimensions of Organizational Change reminded him of Neapolitan ice cream, but he understood the model. He shared it with the class too. So your efforts not only helped me get an A, they may have altered a course on school leadership at USD. I guess that's what change is about.

As a token of my appreciation, I wanted to share with you some seeds that came from my school's community garden. I don't know if you have a place to plant them at your school, but perhaps they will be a nice reminder that we are all connected in some spiritual way.

Thanks again. Best wishes on your journey for kids!
Jennifer

We have the perfect place for Jennifer's flower seeds. Our "peace garden" is not only a tribute to 9/11, it is symbolic of how children processed that whole horrific series of days. "Let's plant a garden," our student leaders said. "Let's plant two trees for the two buildings that fell down." And so we did.

They didn't know how two trees could ever really memorialize all of the lost lives. But seven years later, our two cypress trees have grown so tall you can now see them from the other side of the freeway, rising like skyscrapers over our sound wall.

This is our garden. There are the two trees, a plaque, and 400 square feet of boundless potential. The flowers we planted never bloomed but they were a nice idea. Change works a lot like that too. Some ideas grow and rise taller than the freeway overpass. Others never quite take hold in rock-hard soil that gets plowed over by children's tennis shoes.

CHAPTER SIX

We Are Our Wheels

The flapping of a single butterfly's wings today produce a tiny change in the state of the atmosphere. Over a period of time, what the atmosphere actually does diverges from what it would have done. So, in a month's time, a tornado that would have devastated the Indonesian coast doesn't happen. Or maybe one that wasn't going to happen, does.

— Ian Stewart, *"Does God Play Dice? The Mathematics of Chaos"*

WHEELS

There are common threads that run through every epoch of human history and the development of our wheels is one of them. Civilization may ultimately rise or fall on the strength of perhaps our greatest technological development: the evolving efficiency of the wheel.

We are our wheels. They drive our toys and cars, they move us bike and rail. They land space rockets and jets that fly at the speed of imagination. They climb. They float. They carve like fresh rink ice manicured by Zamboni. They bounce like Super Balls in Chicano Park—where low-rider wheels have been hip-hopping since before their drivers were even born.

We have wheels within our wheels. Like rollerblades—small as replicas and banana yellow. They float in their oily capsule of liquid ball bearings then roll across street surfaces like late-night whispers.

There are even wheels that separate the freeway overpass in Mission Valley in the heart of sprawling San Diego. Built over the Rose Canyon fault with enough steel and concrete to cast a small city, the wheels are buffers, designed to roll when the earth rolls. And when tectonic plates finally release the fury of the earth—trapped for millennia in the force of an 8.1 earth tremor—the wheels are our last hope that the Interstate 805 overpass will rock and roll but not come tumbling down.

Personally, I don't thinks it's going to work. But then again I'm not a bridge engineer. I build change, and my expertise is in designing new and faster wheels that carry our organizations like a NASCAR trophy.

So we invent and reinvent our wheels. We polish them with magic snake oil purchased on an impulse from the booths at the Del Mar Fair. They are chrome and rubber, plastic and wood and hard as rocks. They really roll better when they're greasy and smeared with traffic sludge, but we like our wheels clean. Perhaps when we can see our reflection in them, we are somehow transported to our own roots. Even our ancient ancestors were driven toward a faster roll, a rounder rock, a tougher tread.

I wonder: who was the first to coin the expression "let's not reinvent the wheel!"? For those who would defy the inevitable reach of change, it has become the Loser's Creed.

Change happens and it rolls on wheels.

Disposable, washable, inflatable, inflammable wheels.

Plow wheels, rocket wheels, four-wheels, wooden wheels, wagon wheels, flywheels, Ferris wheels, Wheel of Fortune, roulette wheels, steering wheels...

We are our wheels.

SYSTEMS

The organic state of El Milagro produces energy that is committed at a molecular level that absolutely matters.

And it is not random. We are, by design, a multiplicity of ever-evolving *systems*. The systems interact. They are like the gears of an engine. They are our wheels. They fit together. They channel the efforts of people so that there can be order out of chaos. They drive our efficiency.

And so on we roll.

We roll on systems that improve components of the greater whole: internal and external communication, quality of teaching, staff training, governance and decision making, student celebrations, assessment and program evaluation, and personal goal setting. And we roll on systems that engage our students and our parents. We roll or die on systems that will protect our freedom and our independence with a vengeance.

The more skilled we are in analyzing and aligning existing systems, and the more creative we are in developing new ones, will determine our ability to drive deeper and deeper levels of transformational change.

As the strength of our foundation evolves over time, there are ideas that begin to link in complex structures and delivery models. They inform our routines and our services. Mostly they come together by accident.

Systems become *systems* for Mueller Charter School when they demonstrate some defining features:

- They can stand alone
- They directly lead to sustained student academic growth
- They integrate with every other program, service, or person in the organization
- They consist of multiple structural components
- They link to other systems
- They influence our communications, routines, and operations
- They were born of necessity
- They are robust, resilient, responsive to external changes
- They facilitate transformational change

El Milagro has advanced on seven powerful systems that align like planets circling on somewhat elliptical orbits around a very, very bright light. They include:

- *The First System:* The Charter Mission
- *The Second System:* The People
- *The Third System:* Governance and Decision Making
- *The Fourth System:* Instructional Strategies
- *The Fifth System:* Assessment
- *The Sixth System:* Resiliency Quadrants
- *The Seventh System:* The Role of Parents

Each system is placed on this model in a hierarchal way. The center, the light in this solar system, is generated by the perfectly contained energy of the charter mission: to get our children to grade level. Each of the systems that follow lean to that light.

PART II

THE SEVEN SYSTEMS

CHAPTER SEVEN

The Mission Light

For the way we have to go words are no preparation. There's no getting ready, other than grace.

—Rumi

THE FIRST SYSTEM

We articulated our mission, shaped it, and internalized it. Then we pursued as if it were the only light.

MONSOON

By now you know that our mission is to get 90% of our students to grade level. We would rather get 100% to grade level but we have never seen more than 50% there so we'll settle for 90%.

Schools that get 90% of their kids to grade level are typically not in places like the western end of Chula Vista. They are in affluent communities where the students are mostly white and they have inherited the privileges of the generations that preceded them.

After the Orchard Plan, and the retirement schemes, and the Migden debacle, and the union issues, and the Hell's Angels, and the incessant conflicts between teachers...we *needed* a mission.

We needed a mission that would allow us to lead and innovate. We needed a mission that would guide us through the rough spots and turmoil and failed attempts to be brilliant. We needed a mission to raise our game. And we needed a mission that reminded all of us of why we entered this profession in the first place—to help children reach their full potential in their lives; to help our nation fulfill its promise of greatness; to change the world.

But having a mission isn't nearly as important as living it. It is a journey. We will always seek to harmonize our behaviors with a mission that compels us to be better collectively than we can be alone. Besides, the mission didn't just materialize from dust. It came from our community and our teachers and our students themselves. It was inspired.

My only role was to deliver it...and then create a *system* to make it happen. It was the first transformational change under my leadership at Mueller Charter School and it began before we even moved into the newly modernized facilities.

The mission had to be unpacked, like boxes thrown off the moving van and stacked on the driveway. Then it had to be infused in everything we did—our thoughts, our actions, our plans, and our innovations. It had to become part of us all. It had to soak through the ceiling and into the walls and drench the place—as if we had just been deluged by monsoon rains.

KNOWING YOUR STUFF

Getting kids *to grade level* is a big deal. Being at grade level means you have learned whatever it is you are supposed to have learned for that particular academic year...and you can prove it. It means you know your stuff. Especially in basic areas of literacy.

The state's curriculum standards define specifically what kids should know and be able to do by the end of the year. Then, at least in California, the annual California Standards Test determines to what extent each individual can demonstrate what he or she knows. There are about seventy questions on the math portion of the California Standards Test, for example. Students who answer approximately seventy percent or more questions correctly, are scored at the **proficient** level, which is the minimum threshold to be considered *at grade level*. They have to know their stuff.

If you know your stuff in grade four, it is a lot easier to acquire the stuff you need in grade five. And when you know your stuff at each level of elementary school, it is much easier to maintain your momentum on through middle school. If you know your stuff in middle school, it is much easier to get the advanced placement classes you need to pump up your GPA. If you can keep your GPA up, it becomes a lot easier to get into the college that you really want to get into and a lot easier to study a field of discipline for which you have a particularly keen interest or talent. If you know your stuff at the college level it becomes easier to complete a degree, and then maybe even an advanced degree. It becomes easier to go to work in a profession that rewards college students who know their stuff. Then it becomes easier to live in the community that you want to live in, in a house that is reflective of your dreams, and ultimately provide for a family you so richly deserve.

To be at grade level is to know your stuff; and to know your stuff is a necessary component in the circle of life.

OZZIE & HARRIET

Like many standardized assessments, the California Standards Test is a multiple-choice format. There is a question followed by four possible answers to choose from. There are all kinds of questions on the California Standards Test and you just hope they are field-tested, and research-based, and that they are actually reflective of the curriculum standards that we teach.

There are a lot of questions that aren't on the California Standards Test too. But the scores that students produce often answer, through indirection, a lot of those questions anyway—questions that public schools are afraid to ask.

For example:

"How many babies would have to be dropped on their heads at the local children's hospital before a public outcry would demand that someone be held accountable for their inability to care for children entrusted to them?"

And here are your answer choices:

A. 40%
B. 90%
C. 100%
D. Any of Ozzie and Harriet's kids

Give up?

Of course the answer is D. Any of Ozzie and Harriet's kids.

Schools were designed for Ozzie and Harriet's kids. They were the baby boomers born right after WWII. Ozzie and Harriet raised their kids in the glare of their cheesy sit com and they came to symbolize middle class America. They became a protected class. And though their fictional tv children may have grown up and long since moved out of syndication, the benefits of white privilege remain.

So to answer the question: children from middle-class and upper-class white America would simply not be permitted to fall down at all—let alone fall on their heads. They are treated with a standard of care that ensures their safety. Like they were born with special handles or something. But this doesn't seem to be the case for all children. And it doesn't seem like the case for many children in places like...let's say... our public schools.

In fact, according to the Children's Defense Fund, nearly 2,300 children will be dropped out of school and onto their heads every single day. And children of color get dropped on their heads in disproportionately higher numbers than children who look like they could be Ozzie and Harriet's kids. The "drop-'em-on-their-heads" rate is 7% across the United States for Ozzie and Harriet's kids, 12% for African-American students, and nearly 24% for Latino students. Those are just the cases that could be calculated. Children of color are dropped on their heads at such a ridiculous rate you'd almost have to think it was intentional. Like there was some silent conspiracy. And that's just not possible...is it?

That "drop 'em" rate actually reflects the volume of children abandoned and pushed out by our public schools. And it reflects a national indifference for the children least well served by our schools. Like we don't know what happens to kids who fall out of our classrooms? We do. They fall on their freakin' heads!!! They show up in all kinds of statistical columns and most of those are not good. For example:

- Young people who drop out of high school are unlikely to have the minimum skills and credentials necessary to function in today's increasingly complex society and technological workplace.
- The completion of high school is required for accessing post-secondary education and is a minimum requirement for most jobs.
- High school dropouts are more likely than high school completers to be unemployed.
- A high school diploma leads to higher income and occupational status.
- Studies have found that young adults with low education and skill levels are more likely to live in poverty and to receive government assistance.
- High school dropouts are likely to stay on public assistance longer than those with at least a high school degree.
- High school dropouts are more likely to become involved in crime.

So says the *Child Trends'* calculations from U.S. Census Bureau.

Many of the kids who drop out of high school and onto their heads actually survive. One study found that 63 percent of them had earned a diploma or GED within eight years of the year they should have originally graduated. They did it themselves, thank you.

Even these alarming trends have failed to inspire significant reforms in how schools operate. They have barely even gotten anyone's attention. And that's my main point. These are institutional failure rates that would not be tolerated in hospitals where these babies were first born. Nor would they be tolerated if white children were affected in such high numbers.

It seems to me, as soon as one child gets dropped on his or her head, there should be an investigation. There should be outrage. I'd like to think that *No Child Left Behind* was a federal initiative designed to send a loud and righteous message to every community across America that dropping even one child, anybody's child, out of our schools and onto his head is no longer acceptable. I'd like to think that the message reads: "Drop Kids on Their Heads and We Shut You Down! (Then we prosecute you for criminal negligence!)"

The problem is that No Child Left Behind isn't really about improving schools or improving the future for children at all. If it were, it would represent a singular national voice of outrage that says:

"We will not abide the loss of even one more child from our schools!

"We will not tolerate these persistent gaps between white children and children of color...

"We will not tolerate these profound gaps between poor children and affluent children...

"We will not tolerate the horrendous conditions for children born to adults who lack the resources to raise them...

"We will not tolerate you setting children on the table, only to have them roll off while you're not looking and landing on their heads!"

No Child Left Behind is little more than a shrill and annoying yelp to do better. Like the Saturday morning AYSO soccer coach chiding his ten-year-olds during halftime of another lackluster and dispassionate performance.

Some of us have been working in public schools for decades and have seen the damage done to generations of jaded kids. But now we have established standards. Some kids meet the standards and are said to be *at grade level* while others struggle as they have for decades. In the meantime, we know exactly what we have to do for children if we want them to excel. We know—with 100% certainty—that if we continue to do the same kinds of things and operate our schools in the same way as we always have—we will continue to get the same results. And our babies will continue to fall on their heads.

And, oh, by the way, kids that are *at grade level* can roll off the table and fall onto their heads too.

VERTIGO

Long before I had ever heard about Mueller Charter School, I read about "90-90-90 Schools." These schools were so named because 90% of their students were poor, 90% were children of color, and 90% were at grade level. They are significant because they prove what we all know: that kids (and their schools) can excel in spite of any circumstances! That if our expectations are sky high and our intentions are honorable, we just might prove that the debilitating correlation between poverty and learning is merely a myth.

The 90-90-90 Schools disproved the correlation between poverty and academic achievement. They seemingly defied the odds.

The more I read about these schools, the more amazed I was by the lack of any one program or strategy. They did some cool things, but nothing revolutionary. To this day, I don't know how they got their results. But it doesn't matter.

When I first proposed that we build our charter around getting 90% of our students to grade level, it was inspired by a belief that Mueller Charter School could be in the 90-90-90 club, too. Nearly 90% of our students were children of color, over 75% were poor, and for good measure, another 60% were learning English as a second language. All we needed was the academic proficiency. At 90%.

So our newly adopted mission was not so random. It wasn't arbitrary.

Our performance bar was so high it promised to consume everyone at that school. It would be a daily reminder of why we ever came into this profession. It would keep our teachers so preoccupied with their students' needs that they would have no energy left for adult issues. It would drive away the malcontents and leave us with only a committed core of idealists willing to work their butts off for kids every day. And it would raise our children's expectations of themselves, because we were going to tell them what the mission was too.

Our students deserved that.

This school had been torn apart by politics and acrimony for too long. Students and their parents were all but invisible. Teachers were adrift in organizational vertigo. They were good people, but they had lost their way. Our mission would lead us back to the trail.

QUINCEAÑERA

When Latina girls reach the age of fifteen, their parents often take out a second mortgage on their homes and throw a giant birthday party called a "Quinceañera". It's just like a wedding except the girl doesn't have a partner and there is no lifetime commitment. Everyone dresses up in tuxedos and wedding gowns and goes to mass. Then there is the reception where the old folks drink a lot and make fun of the kids dancing. They say:

"Back in the day, we used to listen to Smokey Robinson singing at the low-rider shows at the Community Concourse. Now that was dancing. These vatos don't know how to dance. They sure dress nice though."

On June 16, 2000, Mueller Charter School held another kind of celebration on a warm and sunny Friday morning. It was Graduation Day. There were 125 beautiful sixth-graders sitting in neat rows squinting in the morning sun. The boys were all dressed for church in dark pants and ties. The girls looked beautiful. Some dressed for church too. Others, however, looked like they were going to their senior prom. Or their Quinceañera. They were stunning. They were elegant. Their parents held balloons and flowers and stuffed teddy bears with caps and gowns and signs that read "Congratulations Class of 2000!"

They shouted support when their child's name was called to receive the certificate. The cameras rolled. There were hundreds of pictures. It was in some respects a typical elementary school promotion ceremony.

And it isn't at all what I expected to find at Mueller Charter School. It just didn't square with what so many people had told me. I had heard that the parents didn't really care what happened at this school and that they weren't involved with their children's education anyway. I had heard that they were all poor and that they didn't value our school and that they never showed up for school events. And that the kids were indifferent too. I should have known better. That wasn't even true in the Juvenile Court and Community Schools where parents and friends and families attended graduation ceremonies right in the middle of jail cells if that's what it took.

I figured I was hearing from the wrong people. And sure enough, I was.

On graduation day I saw 700 proud parents and grandparents and older siblings and family friends. I saw children who had tears in their eyes. I saw lots of smiles and students who looked like they knew that they had accomplished something.

I was invited to attend and to say a few words even though I had just been hired a few days before. No one knew me. I was introduced to polite applause as the new principal. I was at this point the only principal they had because the guy I was replacing had been replaced two months earlier. I have no idea what I said. I probably congratulated the children for not becoming collateral damage in the war that had been raging among their teachers—all of whom were in attendance, smiling on this special occasion. Evidently they had declared a temporary truce because I didn't see any wrestling matches or anybody sticking a foot out to trip each other on the way by. In fact, I couldn't tell how anyone may have voted in the big Migden Election, or who ate lunch together, or who was plotting to let the air out of each other's tires.

For the moment, it didn't matter. What did matter, was that this ceremony looked just like the ones I had experienced at Skyline School in Solana Beach. Children at Skyline left for seventh grade and eventually on to their Advanced Placement classes at Torrey Pines High School in Del Mar, one of America's top high schools. From there, they went to Stanford and Cornell and USC and pretty much wherever they wanted to go.

I wondered where these children would go. Same optimism. Same speeches. Same helium balloons. Same sense of having completed something important in their lives.

I was convinced in that moment, that parents in all communities have the same hopes and dreams for their children no matter how different their circumstances might be. We all want the best for our babies.

I felt blessed to attend this event and to have that message reinforced through my own observation. I resolved in that moment, that my mission at Mueller Charter School was not just to pick up the pieces and heal all of the wounds that were so fresh and present and thick in the air. I am not a healer. Many of those wounds were necessary to the transformation of this school. I resolved that I was not here for the adults at all. I was here for these children. And I resolved that one day children from Mueller Charter School would have the same academic success and attend the same universities as the children from Skyline School.

My conditioning from Race and Human Relations was coming back. My outrage at the number of children I saw every day in the

Juvenile Court and Community School was rekindled. They had all been dropped out of our schools just like this one and onto their heads. And it was all rooted in years of low expectations.

"Congratulations, Ms. Rodriguez, Emilio has finally graduated from elementary school."

"Thank you, but I need to know...has he learned anything? Is he ready for high school?"

"Don't worry about it, Ms. Rodriguez. They will have some kind of shop class that he can take in high school. And ya know, he might even get to play football. He might make a good lineman some day...if he can just remember the plays!" Chuckle, chuckle.

"Excuse me?"

"Well, I don't mean that he is...just that lineman aren't always...well, that in football the slower guys are...oh, never mind. He's graduating today. It is time for celebration!"

"Teacher...my question is, has Emilio *learned* anything?"

And how do we know?

At Skyline School in Solana Beach we knew that a lot more of the children were at grade level at the end of the school year than were not. When compared to other children of the same age and grade level in school, they could demonstrate mastery of the competencies that they were supposed to have mastered. And they could demonstrate it in any classroom project or any standardized test you wanted to give them.

When children are asked to demonstrate what they know and are able to do on a standardized test, the results are no longer subjective. It is a clear and definitive answer to the question: "Has my child learned anything? Has my child learned what he was supposed to have learned for his grade level?"

"Is my child *at grade level?*"

So, inspired by the 90-90-90 Schools, I resolved that the children at Mueller Charter School would be at grade level by end of the school year. A tall order. On this special day, only 18% of these graduating sixth-graders in their borrowed and baggy dinner jackets and quinceañera gowns were at grade level as they left for their celebration brunches at Denny's and local parks.

During the ceremony I had sat next to Libi Gil, our superintendent. I leaned over and shared my plan with her.

"90%, Libi, no excuses."

She smiled but she didn't say anything. So I continued.

"Would you like the three-year plan or the five-year plan?" I whispered.

She looked at me with a sardonic smile that I could have interpreted in one of many ways.

In either case, I waited for her to answer. Finally she said, "Do it as fast as you can, 'hot shot.' These children can't wait forever."

I sat back and quietly watched the end of the ceremony. While a graduating sixth-grader sang an off-key arrangement of "Wind Beneath My Wings," I actually had to fight back my emotions. In that moment, I knew why I was here, even if nobody else did. I learned it from the parents.

Not a bad lesson for my first day at Mueller Charter School.

FRESH PAINT

When the last pictures were taken and the balloons were popped, the graduating sixth-graders made their way out into the world. It was the last day of school and after a long and acrimonious year during which there were bruised egos derailed careers, most everyone just wanted to pack up their stuff and get out of there. Besides, Mueller Charter School was about to be the beneficiary of a local bond measure that had been passed in an effort to modernize the older schools in the district.

So just as the bell was ringing to send the last of our kids home for the summer, the heavy equipment rolled onto the campus like thick-necked dinosaurs in search of lunch. Children dodged the wrecking ball as steamrollers bulldozed fifty-year-old walls into a giant compost of stucco and graffiti and old homework assignments that would forever go unclaimed.

The district had set aside fifty days for a complete modernization effort. It called for, among others things, rebuilding walls and cabinetry, opening up the office space, and rewiring for the Internet and other new technologies that Colonel Sanders-Mueller never even dreamed of. And, of course, it called for fresh paint.

The transformation of the campus was phenomenal. What was once an ugly, barf-green and run-down old school pile, suddenly began to look and smell state of the art. The windows, carpets, bookshelves, playground structures…even the bathrooms were brand spanking new.

During the summer, while they were bulldozing windows and resurrecting old Mueller, I tried to meet one-on-one with as many teachers and parents as I could. That's when it started to become very clear to me that the good folks at Mueller had undergone some significant trauma.

For too long they had been waging their civil war. Initially, I didn't know who was aligned with whom. I knew only that the teachers union was driving the wedge between those who thought that they could operate a charter school without the influence or interference of the teachers union, and those who felt that their membership in the California Teachers Association was a birthright...charter or no charter.

And after a while, I even thought that I had the teams and the issues pretty well pegged. But then my wife and I joined one of the teacher leaders for a midsummer dinner and a glass of wine. At one point during the evening I asked the teacher: "So what is your expectation of me? And, what can I do to significantly improve Mueller Charter School?"

Her answer was immediate. "You can't save this school unless you get rid of all of *them*." The them she was referring to were the pro-union teachers who hated the last principal for meddling in union business. In her mind, they represented the dark side.

But I had invested in meeting with *them*, too. I discovered that they were generally good people with good hearts. They believed in the union. They believed that unions are a fundamentally American ideal and that unions were worth fighting for. The unions built America and they built our communities and they were over there bulldozing and resurrecting Mueller Charter School at this very moment. Mueller had operated for nearly ten years as a charter school, and for all that time, the teachers had belonged to the union. The pro-union teachers did not feel that charters and unions were mutually exclusive.

But the times they were a-changin'. The Migden vote was a declaration of independence.

And when I asked each of the pro-union teachers the same questions: "What is your expectation of me? And, what can I do to significantly improve Mueller?"

They each gave me the same answer: "You can't save this school unless you get rid of all of *them*." Stalemate. "And," they each added, "restore the union".

By late July, when we were all ready to report back to work, the new construction and modernization wasn't quite done. The crews wanted a few more days to detail the last of the projects and make sure they had all of their tools picked up.

I wanted to meet the staff and facilitate a discussion about how we were going to grow El Milagro from the bloody battlefields and the union wars. Since everybody was officially scheduled to report back, and we weren't permitted on the grounds of the school, we decided to hold an off-site at National University, which was directly across the freeway at the J Street Marina.

I wanted them all in the same room. For an entire day. This was going to be the staffs' only chance to talk me out of our mission.

SKYLINE

The cars pulled up at National University and the entire staff filled the room. There were teachers, classroom assistants, counselors, office staff, custodians—nearly ninety-five participants in all. Everybody employed by Mueller Charter School was required to attend. Everybody *wanted* to attend.

Perhaps not surprisingly, there was an upbeat and celebratory mood in the air. They had all driven past the new school and were excited about moving in. They were excited about a change in leadership, because nobody wanted to come to teach every day in the kind of ugly atmosphere that they had created last spring. Even those who were very close to the former principal were hopeful—though, on a personal level, they knew they would miss him dearly.

Like any first day back to work, there were lots of hugs and welcome back handshakes as familiar faces pressed into the room. They lined the walls and hovered near prime real estate: the tables where the doughnuts and bananas sat stacked next to chugging coffee pots and cartons of fruit juice.

And the banter rose, fueled by a spigot of new voices pouring into the room. "So how was your summer? Where did you go? You ready to be back? Have you seen the new school? Did you talk with the new guy? What did you think?"

And then we started our meeting.

During that long day I asked the teachers and support staff a lot of questions:

"Why are our students not among the highest-performing children in California? You know...like my former students up at Skyline School...

"Are the children at Skyline School somehow intellectually superior?"

"What are we really good at here? What are we known for?"

"What is the difference between our students at Mueller Charter School, and the children at Skyline School in Solana Beach?"

"What can possibly account for the fact that only 20% are at grade level at Mueller, and 90% are at grade level at Skyline?"

"Are their teachers that much better?"

"Do their parents love their children more?"

"Do they have resources that we don't have?"

"Do they have some secret strategy that we don't know about?"

"Are our children somehow incapable of high academic achievement?"

"What gives?"

I had lots of questions. None of us had answers.

I asked the school staff to list the variables that make the children at Mueller different from the children at Skyline. They wrote exactly the variables that you would expect:

- 60% of our students are second-language learners.
- 75% come from low-income families who qualify for the federally subsidized Free or Reduced Lunch Program.
- Many Mueller parents have very low levels of formal education.
- We have a 20% mobility rate.
- Few of our students come to school ready to learn...few have been to preschool, few know their letters or sounds, and many barely know their names!

By contrast, at Skyline School the children arrive from their accelerated, Montessori-type preschools already ahead of schedule. About 95% of the students are at grade level just by showing up. If they aren't, they work with a private tutor or go to the highly individualized *Score Higher* tutoring service located in the strip mall. It's never too early to prep for the SATs!

So, according to the voices of our staff members, that was the difference between Skyline School and Mueller Charter School. The difference in student achievement was attributable to the presence of:

- Second-language learners
- Low-income families
- Low parent education
- High family mobility
- Low levels of school readiness

Now we were getting somewhere. All we have to do is eliminate the influence of these variables on our students' learning and they will be at the same academic level as the students at Skyline School!

So now it was time to bury all the excuses. The message to the staff was simple. It was the same theme that I had whispered to Libi Gil during a long pause in the sixth-grade graduation ceremony this past June:

"Listen, you all *chose* to be at this charter school. We can organize our school any way we see fit. We control all of the resources: the budget, the calendar, the curriculum, the instructional minutes. We can even control the impact that some of these difficult life circumstances have on our students. But ultimately, your students have to be at grade level by the end of the school year. If they aren't, we need to do something different...because the kids have it in them. Besides, are these variables really insurmountable? Let me ask you: Do you think there is a teacher somewhere on this planet who could take over your class right now and get a full 90% of your kids to grade level?"

They were surprised by the question, but they all nodded yes.

"Chances are there are many teachers who could do it. You just need to know what they know. It can be done. It has been done. From this day forward, friends...No more excuses."

To their credit, no one argued with me. However, it would take a long time for them to grasp the implications: to get our students performing at grade level would require dramatic transformation of virtually every element of this school.

I had articulated a worthy mission, and our teachers felt it too.

In that moment, we eliminated all doubt about what we were going to accomplish together for children. We didn't just create a slogan or pipe dream or strategic plan...we defined our mission. Made it sky high. Made everybody swear a blood oath.

"Where do you want your own children?" I asked them while they were still weighing the portents of swearing a blood oath on a near-unattainable mission. "At Skyline School where the kids fall out of bed at grade level and the staff's expectations are sky high? Or Mueller Charter School, where teachers aren't even paying attention? Where kids are failing. Where kids are dying. Where our babies are falling on their heads!"

"Someone fell on their head?" asked a middle-aged teacher in the corner.

"No, Patti, he's just using that as a metaphor," her buddy whispered back.

"Oh, that's a relief. I knew Ms. Cook tripped on a first-grader but I didn't think any of our students fell on their heads..."

"Never mind...just keep listening..."

FROGS

The National University off-site wasn't the only place that our staff gathered to consider the future of Mueller Charter School. We also held a "Change of Leadership Workshop."

I learned how to run a Change of Leadership Workshop when I was in the Race and Human Relations Program of San Diego Unified School District. It was loosely based on a military model that was used when they changed out the command of ships or bases. It is an awesome process that promotes communication and optimism and gives the new leader some very tangible early targets to work on. It was invaluable in aligning the mission of Mueller Charter School with the organization's culture and with their infinite potential.

The Change of Leadership Workshop, when properly facilitated, features an intuitive formula that will ultimately answer some pretty important questions:

- What are our strengths as an organization?
- Who are our leaders?
- What do we collectively consider to be the non-negotiables?
- Where are we vulnerable?
- What must change for us to continue to improve?
- What is our mission?

The end result is a "state of the union" report as seen through the eyes of the stakeholders who live every day in the culture of a very imperfect human enterprise. The entire process is so nonthreatening and collaborative that solution strategies percolate constantly.

It is a valuable gift for an incoming principal to have the entire organization sliced open like a ninth-grade frog dissection. The wishes and dreams of kids and parents and teachers are all revealed—all pinned and labeled.

The Change of Principal Workshop at Mueller Charter School revealed the major organs and the heart and the digestive tract almost immediately. It even allowed us to see the very soul of the organization. And that is its purpose of the process if you can make it work.

The mission statement barely does justice to its extraordinarily complex function. But at least we all agree that it is there and we saw it—as we laid bare the thoracic cavity—and now we know where to go from here.

NINJAS

Inspiration for our mission came from other sources too, like our Charter Helpers. Over the past ten years, we have used charter funds to hire about twenty parents as instructional aides. We call them *Charter Helpers* and they are an integral part of the staff. They provide support for teachers in the classroom, help run special events, and provide playground supervision at recess so teachers don't have to. During a time when instructional aides are nearly extinct in many public schools, Charter Helpers have been tremendous lifesavers for our teachers. They are all mommies who care dearly about their children and cherish the opportunity to work and to be paid to be with their kids.

But they haven't always felt like a part of the team. Back in the days when the teachers were at war, parents were kept at a safe distance from the battlefields. They weren't invited to meetings, they were rarely asked for their opinion about things...in fact, they were treated as if they were invisible.

But they *weren't* invisible and Mueller was not only their child's school, it was also their place of employment. While many of them may have lacked the level of education of the teachers, and many struggled with their command of English, they had watched and listened and observed everything that the teachers and former principal were doing. They blended in with their eyes and ears wide open. They were like Ninjas. Chameleons. They had a ringside seat in the shadows at all of the boxing matches. They had heard the anger and threats and ugly language. They had quietly witnessed students treated as if they didn't matter. They had passed in and out of the lounge while teachers bitched and bellyached about parents and the principal, and the kids, and the crappy condition the school was in. They watched. And they waited.

Then I started to interview staff, including Charter Helpers, to learn more about the school. Then several others were invited to participate in the Change of Leadership Workshop. Then still others were invited to be active participants at the National University off-site.

"Won't the teachers be mad if we are there? They always say their meetings are closed to Charter Helpers because they are dealing with school business."

"The teachers might be mad...but they will get over it...and they will get used to it...because we need to hear your voices now."

And so they came in force, dressed for Sunday mass, and prepared to participate in whatever transformation they were needed for. And since they couldn't be sure that anyone would ever ask their opinion again, they thought it might not be a good idea to hold anything back. And so they didn't. And they said plenty.

"Parents aren't valued here."

"We love our teachers, but they are fighting with each other all the time."

"Parents are never asked for their opinions. And we have opinions. We have ideas."

"Some of our teachers are outstanding. But some are just not very good."

"I feel like I am standing outside of a house, looking through the window, wondering how my child is being treated inside."

"I live in this neighborhood in my parents' old house. My older brother went to Mueller School long before it was a charter; back when there was some white guy here who looked like the Colonel Sanders chicken guy."

"But sometimes the teachers treat me like I came over the border yesterday. I didn't. My family has been living here for sixty years!"

I asked the teachers at the off-site to consider where they would want their own children to go to school—a place where the teachers fight like alley cats and only 18% of the children reach a level of academic competency that will prepare them for lifelong learning,...or a school where the teachers and parents are collaborative partners. A school where the majority of students are at grade level?

It was not a rhetorical question. It was revolution starter.

"This school should be worthy of its children," I said. And our Charter Helpers led the applause.

Our Charter Helpers got the other message too. We were going to step up the pace. And the only way to do it was to articulate our mission, focus our intentions, and go to work. Together.

MOVING DAY

A first step toward achieving the ridiculously optimistic goal of getting 90% of our children to perform at grade level was saying it out loud. And so of course we did.

A second huge step was completed as one hundred construction workers unwrapped Mueller Charter School like a birthday surprise and revealed the impressive modernization of our campus.

It was the end of a long summer. The teachers and staff of Mueller

Charter School were moving into a brand new facility. It was time to appreciate the fresh new paint. It was a new beginning. But even a new facility could not sustain a "cease-fire agreement" indefinitely. So, inspired by the optimism of our Change of Leadership Workshop at National University, and fortified by all of my summer meetings with individual teachers and students and parents, I had a clear sense of my own guiding principles:

I resolved 1) to stay above the pettiness of the past—*to stay above the bullshit*, 2) to remain 100% focused on our mission—regardless of whatever missiles or explosions or small-arms fire we might be sustaining, 3) to inspire a unity of purpose, and 4) to transform a dangerously divided workforce into a high-functioning team.

And to help our teachers move their stuff back into their classrooms.

The mission was crystal clear. Our journey of a hundred miles began. This was our first dusty step.

NO DOUBT

If you want to engrave your mission on everyone's hearts you have to write it down. So we wrote it down in our Charter Petition. It is not squeezed into some subtle and secret passage that you can read only when you hold it up to the moonlight. We wrote it so you couldn't miss it. Then, to ensure our mission and our charter were one in the same, we rewrote our entire Charter Petition so that there could be no doubt what we stood for.

The turmoil caused by union wars, workplace politics, and the haggling for turf and authority had once sidetracked even the most committed teachers at Mueller Charter School. They routinely used the Charter Petition when they wanted to give some validity to an argument, no matter how goofy that argument might be. It was the obligatory preface: "Well, according to the Charter Petition..." or "Our Charter Petition does not permit us to..." or "Well, let's consult the Charter Petition to get the directions to the Emerald City..."

...and blah, blah, blah.

I don't know how many of those people actually read the Charter Petition. But I had. And I knew it backward and forward. I knew what it said and what it didn't say. I knew when people were playing wannabe lawyers and interpreting elements of the charter for their own advantage. So I decided to play wannabe lawyer and do some interpreting of my own. Since anybody can propose amendments or revisions to the charter, I peppered the Charter Petition with references to our children. Then, as always, we voted to accept the new language.

Nearly half of our teachers were still bristling over the outcome of the Migden vote and the subsequent departure of the teachers union. They knew there were lawsuits and grievances in the pipeline and assumed it would be a matter of time before the union came back. In their view, the union would trump anything in some Charter Petition anyway. So they voted to approve all the new language. How could they not? It was about how we could serve our children better. It was about getting results.

What they approved, among other things, was a bar so high it is guaranteed to consume the nonbelievers. It addressed eighteen charter goals—everything from academic achievement, to school participation, morale, attendance, behavior and the development of the multiple intelligences.

"That ought to do it," we said. Everyone voted. Everyone agreed. The mission was written. Once the Charter Petition institutionalized these goals as the only game we were playing, it became obvious that significant organizational change would be necessary.

We agreed that we could not continue to do what we had always done as a school that ended each academic year with only one-fifth of our students achieving at grade level. We knew that what *didn't* work for children was anything that resembled the status quo, and so virtually every system, policy, program, idea, and resource was on the table for discussion and analysis.

There was an immediate explosion of energy. Ideas came rushing into the room. Nonstop. Every day a new possibility. It was impossible for people to stand still and balance themselves.

TIJUANA LIGHTS

One morning we posted our mission on the marquis: "90% at grade level...by any measure!"

When parents dropped their kids off they read it. But talk is cheap and at first, they didn't get that it meant there was an enormous shift happening at their child's school.

And though it may be a tall order for any school, we are not asking for a miracle. Neither can we treat our daily responsibilities, or our mission, as if it will take a miracle to achieve. While this is God's work, it can't be all up to Him. We can't light candles and say novenas waiting for some divine intervention. Charter schools were created to pilot strategies that can be tested and replicated. Miracles can't be replicated.

Nevertheless, for an elementary school in a poor corner of the American Southwest, literally minutes from the flickering lights of Tijuana, this would require an Olympian effort. From the beginning, we saw our teachers and staff respond to the challenges in a variety of ways:

- Some teachers at first ignored the minimum 90% threshold, assuming (and hoping) that it was merely an exercise to get a new charter approved…then it would go away;
- Some teachers were so intimidated by the challenge that they packed up and moved away themselves;
- Some teachers quietly and even subconsciously tried to sabotage the whole effort;
- While other teachers vowed to move heaven and earth to achieve it.

There are vast and complex variables that impact our academic results from year to year: aside from all of the challenges of teaching and learning, there are the daily school operations, home life of students, the flow of resources, evolving legislation. And, of course, the inconsistency inherent in the testing system itself.

No organization has achieved greatness by investing emotional energy in excuses. In fact, quite the opposite. So we resolved to take all of the challenges associated with teaching impoverished, native Spanish-speaking children, and turn them into strengths. We resolved to utilize our own professional gifts in such a way that we could overcome poverty and its insidious and debilitating effects on children and their families. We resolved to become an anchor and to freeze the highly mobile segment of children who moved from school to school as if they were changing grocery stores.

And we resolved to do it as a team of educators unified by a common purpose and motivated by a shared belief not only in our own abilities, but also in the unlimited potential of our children.

We had a mission, but not a road map. It had been done in the 90-90-90 Schools, but, of course, every school is different. We could learn from them, and get clues from them, but ultimately Mueller Charter School would have to divine its own road map out of the deep mystery of its own unique make-up.

LONG SHOT

Some of the conspiracy theorists among the teachers initially doubted that we would ever get 90% of our students to grade level in this or any other lifetime. Not because they didn't think our kids could do it, and not because they lacked confidence in themselves. They just didn't know where this mandate for change was coming from.

Sure I was a new principal who talked a good game. But maybe I was a district plant. Maybe I was a secret operative who came here to expose Mueller as a patsy for the anti-charter movement. Maybe I was a covert spy for NCLB. There were lots of rumors about my intentions.

I had to be very clear:

"No...I didn't propose the mission just to comply with the NCLB laws or the State of California's testing program."

"No...I'm not trying to impress anyone in the board room or win favor with the superintendent."

"No...I'm not passing through Mueller on my way to some high-level administrative job at the Department of Education in Sacramento."

"No...I'm not an embedded journalist who has come here only long enough to ask questions and write a book!" (Okay, well...I might write a book.)

But as their new principal, their new leader, I was going live or die on the strength of my convictions that Mueller Charter School, and any child whom we were fortunate enough to serve, was part and parcel of El Milagro. I was here to drive the change.

The second revolutionary shift, after we cut the ribbon and unwrapped the wonders of our modernized campus, came when we committed to a mission that was rooted in the academic achievement of our children. And not only did we commit to it, we wrote it down and defined it in our charter petition.

In that moment we altered our genetic code:

- We changed the "fight" from contesting the philosophies and values of our colleagues to analyzing the circumstances that inhibit high achievement for our students;
- We changed our purpose: from using the petition to define employee rights to defining the rights and needs of children;
- We transcended a need to define the union's role and instead redefined each teacher's role in achieving academic results for our students;
- We fixed everyone's time, energy, and attention on a collective

challenge that would require intense focus;

- We created greater demands to identify and implement instructional strategies that actually work;
- We established a compelling mission for people that promised to one day define their careers;
- We made student work and academic outcomes actually matter;
- We made every child matter;
- We began to alter the way that children and families in underperforming Latino communities like Chula Vista, see themselves;
- And thus, we provided the impetus to change an entire community.

And, by the way...we sowed the seeds for a national model that could transform public education.

The politicians will come and go and so will their politically motivated initiatives. No Child Left Behind neither moves nor motivates us. With or without it we will transform Mueller Charter School.

OVERNIGHT

The easiest part of establishing our mission was to stand up in front of the room and say it.

Then there was the hard part: actually accomplishing the mission! From the beginning there were two enormous limitations:

First, too few teachers and staff members really believed it was possible. That has been remedied. The unbelievers have either all gone or they have had their professional awakening.

And second, we had no idea how to do it. That has not been remedied. We still don't know the path. But we are crystal clear on what the path *isn't*.

In the beginning I honestly thought we could achieve the mission within three to four years. Just like I told Libi Gil we would. But it didn't happen. Not even close. It took that long just to fully comprehend the scope of the challenge and begin to ask the right questions.

After several years of steady but modest results, we adopted a *Five-Year, Take-it-a-Step at-a-Time and Let's-Build-on-Our-Successes (Such-as-They-Are)* Plan.

We had to reluctantly accept that greatness just doesn't happen that fast. You draft, you trade, you develop your talent, a superstar blossoms, the winds blow in your favor...the stars align. It requires patience and persistence—to say nothing of a systematic building scheme.

In fact, one of the most important things we learned along the way, was that if we were really going inspire academic growth in our students, we were going to have to build and scaffold each level. Brick by brick. Innovation by innovation. No matter how badly we wanted to do it, we were not going to make it happen overnight.

Once we adopted the "Five-Year Plan," each grade level had a more achievable mark to shoot for. Not that we were in search of reasonableness. We still believe in audacious goals and vision. But a series of achievable annual goals would pace us to where we ultimately wanted to go. Without them, the mountain would be so steep that teachers would throw themselves off the side every year.

We saw it happening.

Each year our teachers would look at their class's final test results and say, "Oh, my God. I busted my ass all year and only 37% were at grade level? You gotta be kidding me! What more can I do? What the hell is it going to take? That was my best work. I must just suck as a teacher!!!"

And then, right off the edge they would leap.

We were either going to need a lot more safety nets around here or a better system to measure our progress.

THE PRIZE

Keep your eyes on the prize...
Keep your eyes on the prize...
Keep your eyes on the prize...

We all agreed on what the *prize* was now. No one could argue that the mission was not a noble one. They would have to persuade others that our students somehow didn't deserve to achieve at so high a level... or worse, that they were not capable of it. They would be forced to say out loud (what some may have privately accepted as truth), that Latino children from poor neighborhoods lacked the drive or the ability or the genes or the innate brainpower to read and compute!

Never mind the research from the 90-90-90 Schools. Never mind the inspirational efforts of Jaime Escalante and the high-achieving Latino students from Garfield High School in East LA. Never mind that there are plenty of other Garfield High Schools if you are willing to look for them. Never mind Erin Gruwell and her Freedom Writers.

Never mind that academic brilliance is in our students' blood! Didn't you know? Our Latino children descend from the very peoples that created the extraordinary temples and pyramids and observatories and celestial mapping systems still standing in the jungles of the Yucatan! They descend from the 7 Wonders!

Keep your eyes on the prize!

Never mind that we agreed on our mission at the National University off-site before we even moved into the modernized campus with new carpets and roofing nails still on the window sills.

Never mind that our Charter Helpers spoke truth to power.

Never mind the surveys and charts left over from the Change of Leadership Workshop.

Never mind the remarkable gains we have already seen.

Keep your eyes on the prize!

When people are driven by a common vision, when achieving the prize is important to them, they begin to act differently. They become more collaborative. They start to look for evidence that they are on the right trail in their common journey together. They seek signs of success. They loathe excuses. No matter how screwed up an organization might be, no matter how lost the people are, the transformation begins when they all step out together and begin that common journey.

I never asked that our teachers love or follow me. I only asked that they believe in the prize. To set aside their own personal agenda and to be a part the greatness of El Milagro.

Like Christopher Columbus, I knew only that I wanted to sail to a far-off land where people who looked like us had never visited before. I had no freakin' clue of how to get there. Columbus at least knew how to load the boats, yank up the barnacle-encrusted anchors and capture the wind in his sails. The ships he could lead to the open sea.

To capture the wind in our sails and at least get into some open water, I offered our teachers and staff a series of propositions...kind of "guiding truths":

First Truth: **"As a school, we cannot continue to do the same things we have always done, because we will continue to get the same results."** The quality and nature of the work we put in determines the results that come out. Garbage in—garbage out. Greatness in—greatness out. We have no idea what will make the difference between 20% of our students at grade level and 90%, but we know with 100% certainty, that what we are currently doing does not work! Every policy, practice, system, and structure is suspect because—

until all of our students are at grade level—there will be a demand for organizational growth. There will be a demand for new ideas. We will have to be innovative. We will have to be comfortable with a climate of experimentation, ambiguity, and creative initiatives. In short, we have to embrace change.

"Do you agree...in principle...with this First Truth?" I asked.

And they sort of nodded in agreement.

Second Truth: **"We must be prepared to change whatever doesn't work. And nothing works!"** This is our call to arms. A call for nothing short of anarchy. Challenge the authorities. Challenge the status quo. Leave no stone unturned. Just as they have razed the fifty-year-old buildings that old man Mueller built, we have to raze the elements that define a *school*, and rebuild it in the image of our children. Mohandas Gandhi said, "You must be the change you wish to see in the world." Gandhi said a lot of cool stuff that turned out to be right. This may have been the coolest. And it definitely fit for us.

"Do you agree...in principle...with this Second Truth?" I asked.

And though they may have been trying to formulate an alternative argument, perhaps it took more energy than imagination...so again, they reluctantly nodded.

Third Truth: When you internalize this mission, it will define your career and shape who you are as a professional and as a person...It is indeed bigger than any of us. It is bigger than all of us. It is El Milagro. It comes from a different spiritual source. If you trust in this mission, everything else you seek as a professional will fall into place. So we have no choice...we must **"Focus like a laser."** It will require every ounce of creative energy you have. It will take years. The journey will exhaust you. It will break your heart. It will test your resolve. But in the end, we will surely get there.

"Do you agree...in principle...with this Third Truth?" I asked.

And though this may have been more than they bargained for on an otherwise routine summery day in San Diego when they could have been at the beach...again, they reluctantly nodded.

Fourth Truth: **"We must get there together."** We have to have an understanding of the rules of engagement as a team. We have to accept as our creed that:

• Our charter mission is to get our kids to grade level. And that includes pretty much all of them;

• The effort of every teacher and every employee should be

devoted to this mission;

- Getting our students to grade level is a process…a journey— the mission is reflective of an organization that is committed to continuous improvement, experimentation, innovation and risk taking;
- There is no template or road map to tell us how to achieve the mission. There are only clues;
- Our mission demands that we challenge, question, research, rethink, and especially discontinue practices and strategies that result in only 20% of our students at grade level;
- The achievement of this mission may be more dependent on our *attitudes* regarding our students' academic potential and our own efficacy as educators—than on any other single factor;
- Our mission demands that we recognize, accept, and mitigate obstacles inherent in the population of children who attend Mueller Charter School;
- This is Mueller Charter School…these are our children…this is who we serve;
- Our mission demands that we make NO EXCUSES;
- Our results should be used to gauge our collective progress… not *your* worth as a teacher! It is not about YOU…and finally,
- To get 90% at grade level will require RIGOR, UNCOMMON FOCUS, and state-of-the-art, research-based INSTRUCTIONAL STRATEGIES.

"Do you agree…in principle…with this Fourth Truth?"

And though they may have been tempted to offer a few new bullets to the creed—like how people who want a union ought to get the hell out….or how teachers who are afraid of the union are turning their backs on a noble legacy for which they are the ungrateful beneficiaries—again, they nodded.

And the *Fifth and final Truth:* **No matter what…we must model the resiliency we seek in our students—Keep your eyes on the prize!**

"Do you agree…in principle…with this Fifth Truth?"

And though by now they may very well have been exhausted—they dutifully nodded.

So keep your eyes on the prize! And hang on tight.

CHAPTER EIGHT

Rainmakers

To achieve the mood of a warrior is not a simple matter. It is a revolution. To regard the lion and the water rats and our fellow men as equals is a magnificent act of a warrior's spirit. It takes power to do that.

— Carlos Castaneda

THE SECOND SYSTEM

We created processes and strategies to recruit, hire, train, and inspire the right people.

EXODUS

There are truths and consistencies at Mueller Charter School but none so true or consistent as this: We are always searching for the *right* teachers for El Milagro.

It seems to be always posted on the wall or website. Even in the rare moments when it doesn't apply, we keep our vacancies posted because as sure as the fog dissolves into another temperate San Diego morning...we will have a vacancy soon.

We are the ballpark turnstile. They check in, buy a hot dog and a soda, and borrow a chair until midway through the ninth inning when it occurs to them that the hometown team hasn't quite achieved it's potential and they sneak out a side gate to beat the traffic home. Our teachers leave their engines running. They back up their laptop files. They hang their keys by the door.

Some are called away to relocate with family to Las Vegas or Phoenix or Oregon or anyplace where a young family can afford to buy a home. Without lots of help, they cannot buy in San Diego where the median family housing is in the $225,000 range. Even in Chula Vista where families live below the poverty line and 75% of our children qualify for lunch on the government, the small, 1960-era tract homes with their tiny yards go for the mid-$300,000s!

Some are called away by their own children. Young teachers are young parents and many have chosen to stay home and invest their time and energy and passion and expertise into raising their own children. "Perhaps some day," they reckon, "when my children are old enough to go to school, I will come back to El Milagro."

But I notice, they never come back.

Some are called away because perhaps the grass really *is* greener in other schools. Perhaps it is not just an enticing illusion or sleight of hand that makes it seem like any place could be easier to teach than Mueller Charter School. For all of the challenges and joys, and rewards, and resources, and services, and relationships...for all of the children whose cause is irresistible...some must resist. So they transfer to a different school or a different district and find an unsettling peace there.

Some are called away because in between the reality of Mueller Charter School and the intoxicating spirit of El Milagro, there lies tough, tough work. Heartbreaking. Grinding. Infuriating. El Milagro exacts its toll in raw energy and emotion. It is a roller coaster and the ride goes on. And after hanging on, white-knuckled, your knees knock against the side car with such regularity that they are bruised and sometimes blood caked. And though it seems like you have barely been in your seat at all...your back and your backside are inexplicably sore. One more loop and high speed charge down the steep back track and you just want to crawl out of the coaster car and hurl. And so they do. Stopping only long enough to consult with a chiropractor, some limp away with necks so stiff from pushing against their own inertia, they can't even manage to turn back and gaze—even one last time—at the children they left standing on the platform.

"Tickets please!"

Some are called away because in *getting* El Milagro they got more than they bargained for. Be careful what you wish for. The work never ends. The mission, tantalizingly elusive. The solutions, the secrets, the answers, as if built on foundations of snow, seem so exactly right for a minute, then melt away in the midday sun. One day, on their way to work, as they stop to empty the buckets of ice water mysteriously pouring off of their daily lesson plans and ungraded homework projects, they realize that the dream is an illusion and they vote to simplify their lives by working at the school down the street.

Some are called away because they learn they have not learned enough. You can never learn enough. But the experience, for how ever long it lasts, parlayed into an advanced degree, can open doors for our former teachers well into the future. So they leave to get masters and doctoral degrees and know that having experienced the daily challenges of El Milagro, there is nothing in their lives they cannot do.

Some simply sneak away in the stillness and unsettling quiet of midnight—after they stand on the platform of the train station and experience that awkward realization that the train is never coming back. And they were never on board. There was no boarding pass with their name at "will call". They had been at the wrong station all along.

And occasionally, there are those who just have to move along.

FORTY TEACHERS

We were all fully aware back in 2000 that achieving our mission would call for a Herculean effort on the part of over one hundred people—many of whom at the time didn't belong here. Too many hurdles. Too much history. Still, we shouted: "Our children will change the world!" It was hard to argue with that kind of idealism.

We had all of the right clichés mounted on PowerPoints and embedded in our strategic plan: the "shared vision," the "unity of purpose," the "common mission" all created a beautiful and prosaic tapestry of unattainable goals. Unattainable not because our children weren't capable...and not because our teachers weren't capable. But rather, we didn't have that critical mass of believers that is so necessary to create a miracle. We didn't have the will.

"Give me any group of children in the United States," I said to Libi Gil when I was first hired, "but let me pick my own team of teachers and those children will achieve amazing things—regardless of facilities or resources."

"That's great," Libi Gil said in reply. "But in education you inherit your teachers."

Not even charter schools can stack the deck.

At the beginning of the journey toward El Milagro, I would describe our forty teachers this way:

- Some were at Mueller Charter School because it was the place to retire from. We offered an extended year, and thus, a much higher salary than any other school. Our senior teachers were making more money than most administrators in the state. When they retired, this high salary determined their monthly pension. They might have preferred to be at a school where 90% of the kids were already at grade level, but they were in no way equipped to make it happen here.

- Some were here because they applied in the Chula Vista Elementary School District and this is where the openings popped up. There was no compelling reason why they were at Mueller...they finished their credential and now they wanted a job to start making a dent in their school loans. This was their first teaching opportunity.
- Some were here by total chance.
- And some were here because they were drawn by a sense that something very special was about to happen. This was going to define their careers...maybe even define their lives.

They all signed on to the mission and even voted to approve it. But nobody envisioned that Mueller would soon demand more from them than they could ever possibly give. The long journey had begun. Our biggest obstacle was not the poverty, or family dysfunction, or language difficulties or even dwindling resources. It was that our team was not a *team* and some of our teachers had to find another place to work.

SKEPTICS

There are those who see only *Mueller School* while others who feel *El Milagro* in their bones. There are those whose professional lives merely hover—in a state of suspended animation—moving neither forward nor back; neither learning nor forgetting; feeling neither passion nor urgency. They are not inspired enough to even consider an alternative path. A different school.

For them El Milagro is merely an irritant. Talk to them. Ask them what it's like to be part of such a fast-paced, career-altering phenomenon and they will merely smile and roll their eyes as if to say, "If there is a miracle here, I sure as hell don't feel it. I'm not a part of it. Maybe my indifference is proof that El Milagro carries the tired, and the heartbroken, and the exhausted...and the jaded teachers too. Maybe that's the miracle. That I am still here at all."

We will nourish them back to life. For everyone, staying is a choice just as leaving is a choice. And if they stay long enough they will eventually breathe the air and find renewed hope that their professional dreams are still reachable. They will come to teach the children.

In the expectations and demands and rhythms of this place there is room for all forms of believing.

JOB FAIR

When we conduct job fairs and talk about the challenges of El Milagro, we tell candidates to be sure that they are okay on the high wire without safety nets below. We have good ropes. We have an eager audience. The smell of circus popcorn is in the air. But it is possible to fall off of the rope, and there is no guarantee we will be able to catch you.

Commitment is elusive. You feel it. You see it in people's actions. But there are no half measures. Like the great Wallenda, you get out on the rope and walk. You trust your feet. Carpe Diem!

Everything about teaching in the lights of El Milagro is difficult. It is hard to leave. It is hard to stay. And most of all, it is hard to get hired.

It is not as if candidates don't have plenty of opportunity to reflect on the worthiness of our mission. Ours is one of the most exhaustive interview processes you will find. After all, hiring a teacher is the most expensive decision we can make; expensive in terms of salary and benefits, and in terms of potential lost years for students if we don't do it right.

It takes weeks and multiple sessions. Prospective teacher candidates are wrung out by the time they reach the end of the interviews but at least they know they have been heard. They have had a fair chance. They also know that there are a heck of a lot easier ways to get a teaching job. They learn that if they are coming this way, they have to be dead serious about the risks they are taking. They have to examine their own soul and spirit and search for the match.

Then, if all goes right, and if they are feeling the bold and exhilarating call of a very wild ride, we assign them to their own car on the roller coaster.

BUS TOKENS

In his book *Good to Great*, Jim Collins suggests that to elevate any organization requires that you get the "right people on the bus." And you have to get them in the right seats.

In any endeavor, the right people are those who want to be there, who are there for the right reasons, and who are driven by a mission that is bigger than any one person. When you have the right people, it changes things.

Since the day that the first shots of the revolution were fired here a few years back, teachers have streamed out of El Milagro in droves. In the millions. Perhaps ten million teachers have now worked at El Milagro in the past seven years, and most of those are gone now.

Or maybe it just seems like a steady stream. Maybe it just seems like there have been ten million faces. We lose track of the casualties. When some left it was a huge gain for our mission, but others left and we felt sincere loss. In either case, they passed like shadows.

"Step right up, ladies and gentleman...try your hand at this fantastic miracle school, guaranteed to leave you curled up in exhaustion. Pay no attention to that line of former teachers going out the backdoor, stretching to the horizon. Step right up...bring your resume, your dreams, your innovative ideas, your magic tricks...just don't unpack your suitcase..."

We have had every kind of teacher over the years. They have been diverse in their talents and interests and skills and in their abilities to manage the daily rhythms of the ride. We have had imposters and misfits. We have had spoiled crybabies and selfish charlatans with no capacity for the mission or the march. We have had frontier schoolmarms born into their profession one hundred years too late.

But in the end, it's not the line out the backdoor that gets your attention. For all of those who stand with their backs in the doorway, there are those teachers who *didn't* leave. There are those who have—in the parlance of the astronauts—the right stuff. They have attributes that sustain them. They are uniquely gifted. They succeed where others have piled their losses in neat stacks of sea salt and feathers—like gulls crashed against the rocks.

Perhaps the greatest miracle that is El Milagro, is that in time, the right teachers came and the right teachers stayed. Today, they are nothing short of remarkable. On a parched desertscape...they are rainmakers.

There are attributes that steel teachers to the rigors of our mission. There are attributes that present themselves as gifts and talents that you have or you don't. To be a light, you must be a light.

So now when we search for the *right* people to put in newly vacated seats on the bus, we know exactly what we are looking for: the "Seven Gifts of El Milagro". We seek these seven attributes in our new teachers because we find them in abundance in the teachers who have stayed to grow Mueller Charter School. Those seven attributes include Commitment, Talent, Innovation, Collaboration, Intrinsic Motivation, Resilience, and Passion.

THE GIFT OF COMMITMENT

The first of the *Seven Gifts* is the Gift of **Commitment**; an ability and willingness to focus like a red laser on the battle at hand. A belief in the cause.

We look for *warriors*, and not just in the poetic sense of the term. True warriors are relentless in their pursuit of the mission. Even in the face of personal loss and harm, they give of themselves. No excuses. No compromise. And the warriors of Mueller Charter School are nothing if not tenacious, persistent, indomitable fighters.

To teach at El Milagro you have to have the gift.

HOW WARRIORS PRAY

Perhaps in the quiet moments of midnight exhaustion and bone-numbing fatigue, when every last fiber of creative energy has been spent, and when, in the silent shadows, they hear the haunting voices of children for whom they have committed their life's work...there is time to pray.

These private moments are punctuated sometimes with tears and sometimes with a random remembrance of the day that makes you chuckle one last time before being folded into a deeper sleep. Our warriors pray like this:

Dear God...

Tonight, give me a moment's rest. I am tired. I am overwhelmed with a sadness because no matter how much I teach, or how I plan, or care, or stretch, or invent...no matter how badly I want it for my students or for myself...I cannot find the answers that fit for everyone today. And I am drained.

Why do I bother?

I came into this profession to make a difference in the world...to make a contribution. So I work with children who need me. I could have taught anywhere but El Milagro.

There are so many other schools where children are already at grade level when they walk through the door. Where there is no heartbreaking, painful push up the mountain. Where the parents are savvy and supportive and send their children prepared for school every day.

I could have taught in schools of privilege: with stable families and stable homes and economic advantages. Shiny new schools...where awesome results are preordained and achievement levels are high.

Or I could have at least taught in a more stable school, where you connect the dots each day and pursue the tried and true approach. Where the results are predictable, even if they are unspectacular.

Or I could have taught in one of those low-achieving schools where the results don't matter! Where the salaries are structured as combat pay, and the tragic lives of children give their disconnected teachers something to talk about at dinner parties with their suburban friends. "You gotta be kidding! You teach there? In the barrios? Do you go through the metal detector? You are so brave!"

But I chose to be a warrior for El Milagro—a school of contradictions, of disappointments, of extreme highs and lows...of paradoxes. Where students achieve at levels no one ever thought possible.

Here...the children need me. I am their light. I am their hope. I am the difference between a lifetime of mediocrity, underachievement, poverty, crime, and dysfunction. My work will break that generational cycle of poverty for one child, one family, maybe even the whole neighborhood. And that matters to me.

I have been blessed with this terrible burden of a sincere and genuine commitment to children. I have been blessed with a good education, with pedagogical skills, with expertise and experience, and with a worldview that gives me a source of deep and sometimes mysterious power. And the strange thing is, I know that I can apply that gift anywhere I choose.

At El Milagro, I am blessed with the freedom to make my own way. Sometimes I curse that freedom...I resent the ambiguity...I just want the damn road map!

But I am in it now. The mission compels me. It defines me and gives my life meaning. I have to push beyond my capabilities and motivate children to push beyond theirs. I have to get up when I am pushed down. I have to bounce back. I have to be resilient.

I have to fight for the first time in my life...fight like someone else's life depends on it. And it does. And it scares the hell out of me that I am their champion. That if I quit...they quit. And if they quit...they die. Their lives depend on me.

So now I know my purpose for teaching, and for being in this world, is to make a difference for these children. And ultimately, the difference we make for the children of El Milagro, will have a profound effect—the ripple in a pond—on millions of other children across this country.

I am the butterfly, whose gently flapping wings create a chain reaction in the atmosphere...and ultimately trigger a monsoon on the other side of the world.

I am their warrior. And I will never give up on them. Amen.

Somehow warriors are restored through the faith of their prayers.

Oh yeah...one more thing, Lord. Please give me patience for even just one more day of Javier's nonsense. That boy pissed me off today...but I hope he knows I forgive him. Amen.

Sometimes commitment just prays like that.

LEAKING BOATS

When Lowell Billings served as the assistant superintendent of business services for the Chula Vista Elementary School District he mastered his craft. He left no rock unturned in his search for dough. He counted every nickel in California's largest elementary school district and he knew when and where the boats were leaking. And one place the boats were leaking was out in the district's charter schools. Lowell Billings is a very bright guy and he figured something out that lots of other bright folks failed to see: that if the teachers in the charter schools were hired by the charter schools to work in the charter schools for their entire lives, then the boat wouldn't leak. But that isn't what was happening.

The charters have their own budgets and they pay for their own teachers out of those budgets. But as of 2002, some 200 charter school teachers were still employed by the Chula Vista Elementary School District. They were "on loan" to the charter. They still had tenure as defined by the education code. And they had transfer rights because charter law states that a district cannot force a teacher to work at a charter school against his or her will.

So, if a district-employed teacher in a charter school decided to exercise his or her right to return to one of the thirty-seven other non-charter elementary schools in the district, the district would have to take them back. They would be obligated to assign them to another school. And they would have to place them before they placed any new teachers.

And here is what Lowell Billings realized about that arrangement:

- 200 teachers represented nearly $15,000,000 in salaries and benefits. And secondly...
- These teachers—many of whom were hired by the charter school and not the district—would be entitled to return to district schools whether they were a match for that school or not. And finally...
- If the teacher who is returning to the district is, for example, a ten-year veteran, the district would have to pick up that teacher's salary. The charter would then be free to replace the ten-year veteran with a brand new teacher who is at the lower end of the salary scale. Thus the district could be faced with constantly cycling in higher-priced teachers whom they didn't hire, while the charters got the pick of the litter for much cheaper teachers. So the district would bear the burden for 1) charter schools hiring the wrong teachers, and 2) for maintaining, as a benefit, a teacher's right to transfer back to the district whenever the spirit moved them to do so.

With six charters and 200 teachers in charter schools, Lowell Billings envisioned the disastrous scenario of multiple, bathtub-sized leaks springing in the bottom and sides of the district boat. And Lowell Billings determined that this was an unfair advantage for charters that needed to be reconciled. Lowell Billings had a great business mind and he was very adept at putting a price tag on the charter's cost of doing business with the school district. He determined that if charters were going to benefit from—let's say—the district's maintenance and landscaping services, or the HR department, or training offered by the curriculum division, or the testing office, or even the school board's oversight responsibilities—the charters would have to pay for those services in the form of *chargebacks*. Then he created a chargeback to offset the potential cost associated with the right of district teachers to transfer from charters back to district schools. He called this chargeback *reciprocity*.

The cost of reciprocity was steep. It was calculated as the district's average salary, minus Mueller Charter School's average salary. Then the difference was multiplied by the number of district teachers on the staff. The resulting chargeback was several hundreds of thousands of dollars, and as we lost senior teachers and hired young teachers, the cost grew exponentially. Suddenly Lowell Billings' boats weren't leaking anymore. But our boat was starting to flounder like a waffle-bottomed pontoon.

Besides, having an option to transfer back to the district if something went wrong gave the district teachers an out. Theirs was a lifeboat paid for by charter resources.

So we tapped out. "Uncle!!!" "No mas!!!" And then we made a deal.

We agreed that every teacher we hired after July 1, 2002, would be employed by the charter—with no transfer rights, no employment rights, and no tenure rights whatsoever with the Chula Vista Elementary School District. We would therefore no longer have to pay the nearly half million dollars a year in reciprocity costs to the district. In effect, we would no longer be paying for individuals to maintain the right or benefit of returning to a district school. It was a great solution because it shored the thin walls of Lowell Billings' fragile boats. But more importantly for us, it challenged every teacher to think about the commitment they were making to the charter school.

THE GIFT OF TALENT

Every so often there is an article in the newspaper that summarizes the results of still another national study that had concluded the obvious: Our children don't know beans about nutrition...or they don't know their geography, or they have never done a proper push-up, or they can't describe the scientific method or recite the periodic table of elements. As if they have been commissioned to publish in a never-ending series of sequels and prequels—a la Harry Potter—the latest episode of *How America's Public Schools Have Screwed Up Your Kid* is sure to be released in the morning paper. It will lament that American kids are spoiled and presumably brain dead because they can't name any of the founding fathers or any of their accomplishments; or that they are not conversant on how dollar bills get placed into circulation or why gray whales swim all the way to Mexico to have their babies or what keeps airplanes floating on air. And did you know that many schools have fired their music teachers and that most American students have never been to the Louvre? Nor could they spell it!

These are all, no doubt, things that an enlightened and educated citizen might someday learn. But I am not yet prepared to write off our children simply because they can recite Tu Pac's lyrics but have never heard of William Butler Yeats. Or that while they may not like the literature we assign to them, they are masters at *technical* reading and can navigate the

Internet, reprogram video games or drop ringtones into their cell phones from directions downloaded off of obscure Web sites.

The conclusion that trails every report will inevitably implicate the elementary school curriculum and recommend that we accelerate our science or our physical education or our advanced studies of global economies. Of course, it depends on which special interest group has woken up long enough to formulate new research designed to influence our schools' curricula and ultimately save America from itself.

While it would be nice to place a classic and complete teacher in every classroom, we have to settle for talented and inspiring and academically curious idealists. We learned from years of hiring teachers for El Milagro that they have to have a strong, strong foundation in literacy and writing and mathematical reasoning. They have to have that content knowledge for starters.

But math and language arts are not enough. We teach science, social studies, physical education, and the visual and performing arts. These are just curriculum labels. In between, who will make Yo-Yo Ma as real as Beyoncé? Who will inspire children to take a second microscopic look at a cricket's wing and marvel at the intricate similarities that exist among living things? Who will explain how the same people who gave us Babylon, now also give us Hamas? Who will teach children to sing with whatever voice God gave them...if not their teacher?

At El Milagro, our teachers must first be *talented* human beings if they are going to be talented teachers. And talent is formed from each individual's unique amalgam of interest and curiosity, their personalities, their life experiences, their natural gifts. And, of course, their ability to translate their excitement and love for learning to others: a prerequisite for mastering the components of Powerful Teaching.

To teach at El Milagro you have to have the gift.

TOROS

The University of San Diego is one of the most beautiful universities in America. It sits high on a mesa with an unobstructed view of the Pacific Ocean to the west, downtown San Diego to the south, and Mt. Soledad to the north. USD is a private Catholic university that seems to cater now to kids who are, for the most part, lifelong beneficiaries of their white privilege. That is not to say that USD is not diverse. It is. But certainly not in proportion to the rich ethnic mix of the population at large. They have a good law school at USD. They also have an outstanding baseball program and a pretty good School of Education.

I taught foundation classes—philosophy and psychology—for several years in the School of Education. I was considered an adjunct professor, which means I got paid next to nothing for the one class I taught but was assigned my own mailbox. I didn't teach at USD for the dough anyway. I did it partly for the view of the ocean, partly to challenge myself to continue to develop as a teacher, and partly to stay connected to the new, young teaching candidates coming into the profession. From my vantage point there on the mesa, I saw and recruited talented teachers before they could get too deep into the pool. And the staff at Mueller Charter School has been strengthened immeasurably by those teachers.

One thing I learned from teaching in the School of Education is that the students who are working on their teaching credentials are not much different from any other students working on a degree. Their main objective is to *get done!* They just aren't positioned to realize that what they are learning is critical to their success as a teacher. They don't have the context yet...any more than a thirteen-year-old can fathom why studying ancient history will somehow enrich his life.

Consequently, many new teaching candidates arrive woefully unprepared to step into their own classrooms. They will all get by if they are willing to learn from their mistakes and from the *right* veteran teachers around them. When our new teachers come to Mueller Charter School, they are three to five years behind the professional development of their colleagues. So we make them apprentices. We invest in their continued training. We pair them up with veterans. I remind them that, even after thirty years, I now know that I know next to nothing about teaching...and they know a lot less than me. And that the only way to keep current in this incredibly complex enterprise, is to be a career learner. Starting now.

While I was teaching at USD I opined that the teachers were not coming out to the schools with everything they needed to make a contribution in their first year of teaching. I suggested that they needed a lot less theory and a lot more practice in context. And that they needed to be connecting with schools that were creating significant change. Like Mueller Charter School. As usual, the message must have gotten obscured by the messenger because not long after my observations about teacher preparation, I lost my mailbox.

Graduates from USD spent five years enjoying one of the most breathtaking views of beautiful San Diego. They enjoyed their close proximity to the beaches and Old Town and margaritas at Tio Leos. They enjoyed the exquisite architecture and spiritual ambiance of the Immaculata Cathedral in the heart of the campus. And they enjoyed watching one of collegiate baseball's top twenty teams if they managed to find the stadium over behind the Jenny Craig Pavilion.

The teams at USD are called the *Toros* for reasons that no one can quite explain. There has never been bullfight here. There are no classes for matadors. But in the dance between university programs designed to prepare future teachers, and the schools where they are heading, sometimes sacred cows are gored.

BEND IT

No matter how talented teachers might be, we never let them forget that we have only one mission. We are all playing one game and you have to have the skills for the game that the rest of us are playing. To extend the metaphor, don't come to Mueller Charter School knowing that we are playing football, and then start complaining that you really prefer soccer.

It doesn't matter how good a soccer player you are, it won't do you any good in football unless you are the kicker. And we don't need a kicker. If you want to play soccer, go somewhere where they play soccer.

I don't care if you played goalie for Brazil in the World Cup. I don't care if you are money in soccer shoot-outs. I don't care if you can bend it like Beckham. This is football. Not European football. American football. You have to block and tackle and pass the ball sixty yards in the air or you can't win. The name of the game here is tackle football and sometimes it is rough catching in a crowd.

Welcome to the bold new world of El Milagro. We seek enormously talented teachers. No midfielders need apply.

WIZARD

Prior to coming to Mueller Charter School I had never worked with a Wizard before. I have had assistant principals and counselors and teachers. I have worked with the parent council, the chamber of commerce, the media, and every kind of social service and law enforcement agency. I worked with the juvenile court judges. I even worked with politicians. But never a Wizard. Until now.

The Wizard sets our bar for individual talent.

The Wizard knows technology and has wired El Milagro so tightly to the future that we are completely wireless. He is the chief architect of our customized database. The Wizard knows finances and where every penny of our budget is allocated. He moves accounts like chess pieces and you trust him to do it.

The Wizard knows change and expects it to happen.

The Wizard's real name is Don Mizock, but the kids all know him as the Wizard. He is magical and he makes things happen. Children may not know much about school finance or tethering a teacher to Bluetooth technology, but they know magic when they see it. They know there is wizardry in results.

And so do we. The Wizard is a big part of the magic of El Milagro. You don't see him much but his shadows can be trusted. He is a force for energy and ideas and metamorphosis. He is a force for transforming the lives of children by any means necessary. He reminds us that behind every successful leader—behind every group of people aspiring to greatness—there is a wizard.

When Dorothy was deceived by her nightmare balloon pilot, she was chided to pay no attention to the man behind the curtain.

"Pay no attention to that man behind the curtain...!!!"

There was no wizard there...only a traveling snake oil salesman from somewhere deep in Kansas. Not so at El Milagro, where the Wizard is real and speaks without shouting.

THE GIFT OF INNOVATION

The grand metaphors of life do not escape the creative observer. Life, in and of itself, may very well be the metaphor. In the meantime, however, there are those whose minds can bend and accept ambiguity and change and chaos and the long rough ride. There is a flexibility in their mental constructs. They solve problems with a sense of humor. They are confident in their own efficacy.

We used to say that we were looking for people who were capable of "thinking outside the box" until thinking outside the box became its own confining metaphor.

So now we are just looking for gifted innovators...people with imaginations, playful spirits, and an ability to create El Milagro from Mueller Charter School. We are looking for Picasso or George Lucas. We are looking for Andy Warhol to find something useful to do with a can of soup besides open it with a rusted kitchen tool. We are looking for Christo to drape Central Park in orange banners and photograph the tourists as they run through them—catching and consuming them as if they were snowflakes melting in their mouths for the first time.

To teach at El Milagro you have to have the gift.

A GIFT FOR COLLABORATION

We are not the passengers. We are the crew. We row together or die in irons.

There is no option for reclusive entrepreneurs concocting unilateral innovations in the broom closet. We share. We talk. We brainstorm and ask lots of questions that begin with "What if..."

Don't get me wrong. If we had an extraordinarily committed and talented teacher who was blowing up with innovative instructional methods, and whose children were benefiting from his or her reclusive nature, we would make it work. But we just haven't seen that happen. We have seen much more success from teachers who communicate about their students' progress on a regular basis. Our teachers collaborate with anyone that wants to play. And they all want to play.

To teach at El Milagro you have to have the gift.

APOLLO 13

I don't remember much about the actual Apollo 13 mission except what I saw in the movie. It was Tom Hanks spiraling through space like a wayward puck. No tracks, no brakes, no direction, no steering, no power, and no way home. Just when you think things couldn't get any worse, they do. The astronauts could look outside the window and see nothing but deep black space and the moon, close enough to spit on. So close. And so much more tantalizing than being stuck on a deserted island with only your wits and a volleyball named Wilson.

Apollo 13 was the perfect storm, and the perfect opportunity for NASA to enshrine its credo that "Failure is Not an Option." In the face of incredible adversity and time constraints, they pooled together their creative energy and egos and collective professional reputations as problem-solving pioneers, and they engineered a solution that brought three pretty good actors back home. Lives were saved on the strength of collaboration. Human beings, for all of their pettiness and minimal capacity for using their brain power, achieved a technological miracle, as they reached into the universe and retrieved NASA from the very steps of oblivion.

We learned too. There is no miracle beyond our reach when human beings harness their energy and imagination through collaborative effort.

Ex Luna, Scientia...says the Apollo 13 logo. "From the Moon... Knowledge."

THE GIFT OF INTRINSIC MOTIVATION

We are looking for teachers who have the rare ability to find inspiration in their own magic, teachers who are driven only by a compulsion to serve. Indeed, if people are *intrinsically* driven to achieve greatness on behalf of others, and to be a part of a passionate force of change, there is simply no more powerful source of motivation.

How far are you willing to go to guarantee the success of students in your care?

Would you stay late to help them?

Would you work without compensation for them?

Would you go to jail for them?

Are you willing to get fired to help them?

If we are an organization that is truly committed to the success of its clients...then nothing can motivate us but *their* success! Nothing. Not money, not fear of sanctions, not a manager's praise.

To teach at El Milagro you have to have the gift.

CORPORAL TILLMAN

I had taken a personal business day on the morning of September 11, 2001. Anne woke me up and told me to turn on the news and I did so, right as the first tower fell. There was fire and smoke and for a moment it was hard to see the building through the grainy debris. Then we could see nothing at all.

We had just returned from New York City a few weeks earlier. In August, we had taken a family trip to the East Coast to introduce Keenan and Kira to the wonders of Washington, DC, and the big city. Later, when our children were trying to process the horrific television footage shown over and over and over again—they kept coming back to the people whom they had met in the South Tower.

"What about the security guard that told us how to find the elevator?"

"We don't know, Kira...he may have taken the day off....like I did."

"What about the lady that sold the Statue of Liberty bears on the ground floor...do you think she made it out okay?"

"We don't know about her either. We don't know what time she comes to work."

"Remember the police officer who sat next to us in the deli? Wouldn't he have run straight to the building? He was so cool. Didn't he say he lived in San Diego when he was doing his Marine Corps training?"

"We'll try to find out, guys. There may be a way to track him down." (There was, by the way. During lunch I had taken his picture. When Anne went to New York on a business trip a year after 9-11, she returned the deli where we had met this burly Port Authority officer. Anne asked

at the counter and they recognized his picture. He was alive and well
and working at the Smithsonian in Battery Park.)

We remember what we are equipped to remember.

Impossible questions. Impossible confusion that only a child could
capture in elegant questions about the welfare of others.

Like you, I watched for the next few days, and weeks, and months,
and even years...the smoke-filled city, the ashen horror. I have visited
Ground Zero. I have touched the very spot of earth that has become
our nation's holiest shrine. I have prayed there. But I have yet to find
closure.

The heroic stories that emerged on that fateful morning will frame
our history books for as long as we exist as a nation. Perhaps Chapter 23
will be called something like *The Dawn of a New Millennium*. There will
be small shaded boxes amidst the crystal clear photographs of a Wall
Street fireball. The boxes will memorialize everyday working citizens,
in the right place at the wrong time, driven by sheer terror and a will
to live and help others live too. They will forever be heroes, somehow
symbolizing what we want generations of children to internalize as the
American Spirit.

And one shaded box will be reserved for one of the boldest among
the 9-11 heroes. Corporal Pat Tillman was not in New York that day. He
contributed later in the subsequent war to rout the Taliban out of the
mountains and caves of Afghanistan. After weeks of helplessly watching
television's account of an attack on America, Corporal Tillman felt
compelled to serve.

He could have just donated money to the cause and that would have
been sufficient. After all, he was a multimillionaire and there was plenty
more where that came from. He could have volunteered to help train
some army rangers. After all, as a free safety in the National Football
League he was among the strongest, the fastest, the most athletic, and
the most fit young men in the history of civilization. He could have just
popped in to visit on a USO tour. After all, he was famous, photogenic,
and tremendously marketable. He could have just joined the National
Guard or Knights of Columbus or Big Brothers or United Way, for
God's sake. After all, that too is real *service*.

Instead, Pat Tillman resigned his position with the Arizona Cardinals
of the NFL and joined the Army Rangers to avenge the attack on America
that took place on 9-11. He didn't need or ask for anything in return. He
refused all media interviews and requested that the Army conceal his
whereabouts. His brother, a professional baseball player, joined him in
the same unit. While the NFL went on playing Sunday football games,

Corporal Tillman, on a soldier's wages, followed his sense of mission to Afghanistan and the general public lost track of him.

I didn't though. I wondered what would drive someone to trade all the fame, fortune, adulation, and rare lifestyle of a professional American athlete to join the army and crawl through caves looking for shadows.

One night my family was enjoying ice cream at Ghirardelli in the Gaslamp Quarter of downtown San Diego. I was two spoons into a small sundae when Anne asked, "Did you hear about the football player that was killed in Afghanistan today?"

"What football player? I didn't hear any news today."

"I heard a report that a former NFL football player was killed in a battle in Afghanistan." And I felt the strangest chill. A cold wind on the back of my neck. A whisper of snow that falls from a tree branch and is trapped inside your collar.

"Please tell me that's not true."

Keenan picked up his cell phone and checked the news. "The soldier's name was Patrick Tillman."

For the next ten minutes I quietly finished my ice cream. I was numb. My tears filled the bowl. I could not look up and I could not speak. As my children sat quietly and finished their ice cream too, I felt their tiny hands on my back. "It's okay, Dad."

I wept even as I wrote this. Intrinsic motivation ought not to cost so much. But it often does.

EVALUATIONS

Our faith in the intrinsic motivation of *people* has led to perhaps the most radical and risky of our many innovations: the complete elimination of employee evaluations. After all, what is the point of employee evaluations when you have the right people?

After ten years of conducting mind-numbing teacher evaluations I learned a couple of things:

- Evaluations do not lead to the kind of significant performance improvement that we are seeking.
- Evaluations do not typically accelerate organizational momentum.
- Evaluations do not motivate people who are already *intrinsically motivated to do the right thing.*

The process, multiplied by all the teachers being evaluated, creates a system so labor intensive that a principal can be tied up all spring writing summary performance reports. Worse, there are no teeth in the process to leverage long-term gains for kids. It is a formality. It is all but meaningless. Tenured teachers could get a truckload of mediocre biennial evaluations but never go away.

Since we are our own employer we can create our own evaluation system. So we did. And the most significant feature of our evaluation system is that we don't have one! Instead, we create a context for teachers to develop their own internal drive to excel—to sustain collaborative relationships, and to maintain a constant state of professional reflection.

There is risk built into this process of self-reflection. We cannot fool ourselves. We know our own shadows and our own truths. And from such risk comes the ultimate reward as teachers improve in ways that are authentic.

EL PATIO

Down on Broadway, just a few short blocks from Mueller Charter School, there is a small Mexican Restaurant called El Patio. It has been there forever. Father Juniperro Serra stopped there for their famous "flying saucers" and a sack of tortas for the long road to Carmel.

Some things change...but not El Patio. It has the same juke box with some of the same songs that were in it when we came here in high school. It has the same red checkered table cloths that were pulled off in the middle of one of our late-night college brawls. It has the same bowl of carrots and hot sauce that I saw some drunken construction worker sleeping in just before closing.

One day before the beginning of the 2004 school year, the Wizard and I were eating tortilla chips and listening to some old-school Tejano *musica* from Roberto Pulido on the jukebox. We were discussing the need to shore up our *non*-evaluation procedures by creating a system for providing constructive and collegial feedback for our teachers.

"I am in the classrooms every week. Writing little notes on the yellow stickies doesn't work. I can never remember what I have said in previous visits. We can't build on anything."

"Why don't you keep a journal with each teacher?"

"A journal?"

"Yeah...just keep a journal of some sort in each room. Pick it up when you do your observation and write things there. Teachers can then journal back."

"A journal. Hmmmm."

"It will be like maintaining a simultaneous professional conversation with forty teachers at once."

"A journal."

Sometimes the Wizard has ideas that must marinate. But at El Patio, where annoying Tex Mex accordion rifts mix with hundred-proof jalapenos, the marinating of ideas is accelerated.

"What a great idea, Wizard. I think I'll do it." And so I did.

TEJANO

Inspired by the Wizard and the Tejano music at El Patio, I returned to school that afternoon and collected forty black composition books from our supply room. In our Friday afternoon staff meeting, I gave each teacher a journal and explained what I wanted to accomplish.

"You have often asked for feedback and you like the little blue notes I leave. But that practice has always been spotty and inconsistent. It seems judgmental and evaluative. I want to honor your expertise and—at best—be a neutral set of eyes in your classroom. So lets share a journal. Write whatever you want. Write what's on your mind. I'll write my questions and observations...you do the same." And they do.

Each year begins on page one. It is the same prompt for everyone. I ask them to write why they have returned to teach at Mueller Charter School. Why are they still compelled by the mission?

But then as the year gets under way, our forty journals immediately begin to take on their own appearances and personalities, especially for:

- The teacher who answers every question I ask with a lengthy narrative
- The teacher who rarely directly responds to anything
- The teacher who reflects on whether teaching is the right career for her
- The teacher who pours out her deep pain at not being able to have her own children
- The teacher who provides ongoing updates on her mother's recovery from cancer
- The teacher who is searching for his voice
- The teacher who earnestly asks exhaustive questions about improving his craft
- The teacher who writes first drafts of articles soon to be published

- The teacher whose loneliness is unmistakable while her husband serves in Iraq
- The teacher who's collecting journal entries and moving toward a doctoral dissertation on something like *"Journaling: A Progressive Alternative to Teacher Evaluation Systems"*
- The teacher who writes every entry on her computer, then prints it out and staples it to the next available page
- The teacher who argues with every suggestion
- The teacher whose stylized cursive is so clean she should create those little alphabet posters that teachers frame their whiteboards with
- The teacher who writes in icons and pictures
- The teacher who philosophizes about life's deepest mysteries and meanings
- The teacher who complains about the Republicans
- The teacher who always seems to have hastily scribbled a response to my last journal entry only when he saw me in the classroom next door and headed his way.

To mention just a few.

When I go into a classroom for my weekly observation, I pick up the journal. Each teacher keeps it just inside the door where I can find it—though there are many possible locations "just inside the door." In time, you learn where every journal is kept.

I read my last entry. Then I read their response. Then I write a new entry. The whole time, I observe the classroom, and the students observe me. They are used to seeing me curled up in the corner, reading, squinting to make out the undecipherable handwriting. They keep secrets though. I would guess their teacher has often complained that if her students' handwriting was a bad as mine, she would suspect them of holding the pencil with the wrong hand.

Sometimes I am in a hurry and have no idea what I write. Sometimes I'm tired or bored or unfocused. Sometimes, I reread an entry over and over—laughing quietly. Sometimes I leave, fighting back my emotions, overwhelmed by the tremendous sense of personal mission these teachers have.

We tried to create an anthology: *"The Best of the 2006 Professional Journal Entries."* Then the Best of 2007. But our teachers guard their treasures tightly. As it turns out, this process is deeply personal. Healing. Self-motivating.

I observed two students outside of your classroom today, who were doing nothing. They have been out there for most of the morning. They said you did not like the way they did their homework last night, and that you refused to accept it. You want them to sit outside and think about the quality of their work. I believe they will have a chance to make it up during recess this afternoon. Did I get it right?

Just a few wonderings...

I wondered what they are missing right now while they spend an hour outside "thinking" about the quality of their homework...

I wondered if they are thinking about anything or just enjoying playing outside all morning...

I wondered if I would want my own children to sit outside if their teacher didn't like their homework...

I wondered: what other strategies do you use to communicate high expectations for quality work...other than sending children outside...

I wondered why the homework assignment didn't inspire them to do better work.

Oh...one more wondering. We don't do recess in the afternoon...what happened to physical education?

Sometimes the wonderings drive people nuts, but it is their classroom and they make the decisions on how they will raise the achievement of their students. I do not tell them what to do. My job is to prompt deeper reflective thinking about their professional values and practices.

Sometimes they are just annoyed because I don't have a context for my observation. Those two students may have been warned twenty times about what would happen if they turned in sloppy work again. Perhaps they had plenty of time to complete the assignment in class the day before. Perhaps this is an agreement with the parents to motivate children to be more conscientious. Perhaps the homework was just the last straw and the two students failed to tell me the rest of the story. If the teachers choose to respond to my wonderings, or if they can address the underlying questions by providing the logical context, they often do.

And sometimes I strike a raw nerve.

Our journals have resulted in tremendous growth, professional trust, and healing conversations about teaching children.

Somehow the Wizard knew.

THE GIFT OF RESILIENCY

You have to be resilient. That's why we seek warriors who will not take "No" for an answer. Our teachers will not be denied. They fall and they rise up. They fall and they rise up. Their resilience is as much a part of El Milagro as anything else we do.

We can't promise much. But we can promise you will stumble and cuss and agonize over the challenges: the mobility, the poverty, the ambiguity. The never-ending meetings and demands when you are sick and tired and buried and when you just want to hide out in your classroom and catch your breath.

You must bounce back even when the daily events roll by with no regard for your personal and private life — marriage proposals and divorce proceedings; the birth of a child, the terminal illness of a parent.

You will become resilient because the one certainty is that the children keep marching by, like the waves that pound the shoreline relentlessly just a few miles from here. Sometimes when it is quiet in our classrooms, you can almost hear the waves. You can look up and see the deep and hopeful eyes of children who have no idea how long their journey will be. You realize how quickly their faces change. And you realize, it is indeed the waves you hear.

And just when you arrive at your breaking point, in that moment when you discover that you cannot succeed at El Milagro unless you are resilient...you rise yet again. Bouncing back. Modeling persistence. While children all around you notice that the mysterious strength that they are drawing from their teacher somehow carries them — and they discover in themselves the strength to overcome anything.

That is some Powerful Teaching.

To teach at El Milagro you have to have the gift.

THE GIFT OF COMPASSION

Heather Naddour is one of the forty—a first-grade teacher at El Milagro. She soaks up ideas like a blanket. She has big dark eyes and they are always open. She listens. She learns. She gets better by the minute. And when she writes in her journal, in response to my incessant questions or wonderings or observations, she thinks things through. Heather's journal is easy to read. She enjoys writing as much as she enjoys the opportunity for professional reflection. She has become more curious about the process and wants to know if it has benefited others as much as it has benefited her.

Heather is a poet and she is not afraid to perform at coffee shops or our own Mueller Charter School "Open Mic Night" for our resident student-poets. One day, in her professional reflection, she sent this poem-prayer, as if she too had somehow channeled every teacher of

El Milagro...channeled, in fact, every teacher who inspired us each to become teachers. And channeled our collective gifts of Commitment, Talent, Innovation, Collaboration, Intrinsic Motivation, Resilience, and Passion.

A Love Poem for My Students
by Heather Naddour

I live to learn how to teach
my young people how to reach
the stars.

By far—
they are the most blessed gift given to me.

I am...here for them.
Most days on a whim
I walk the halls and watch them grow...
into readers and future leaders—of us.

This poem is for them...My students.

Stay true to who you are...
Don't walk far from your ways,
let your gaze fall as far as your eyes can see.
'Cause that's where you'll be...after us.

You'll leave this place like a rocket ship, full blast
to your next destination,
But don't worry 'cause your home station
will always be here
near
me...
Where I taught you to read your way to the top.

Mark my words...
you have what it takes to wake and walk in your ambition.
You may stumble and fall, but walk tall
Towards your dreams.

Because...I want to meet you there.

I want a seat at your graduation.
And on the top of your mountain
I want a fountain
...of knowledge.

I want to be showered with your power and strength.

I want to see you reach out a hand and demand
more from me.

Because I can take and make the world yours.

But smile and take awhile to grow up.
I'll wait for you to bloom into a flower.
Your hour will come.

We'll wait here in the first grade
take our time and watch the sun fade into your glory!

Sit down next to me and let me admire
the fire that burns inside of you.

Let's relish in the time that we have together.

Tell me about the Berenstain Bears
and the wear and tear on the playground.

Tell me about how you found your best friend.

Teach me your ways and I'll stay by your side.
Because with pride I can say that you make me...
...a better teacher!

To teach at El Milagro you have to have the gift.

AMEN

It is not likely that the Book of Exodus was written with El Milagro in mind. Nevertheless, it speaks to our teachers all the same. *"You are blessed,"* it says. *"You are a blessing to others. You are a blessing to the world."*

At Mueller Charter School, we take our leave. We all, at some point in time, will do so. We are always leaving. Always passing through. And in our time, we will each leave El Milagro too. And if we are possessed of the Seven Gifts, we will leave more than we have taken.

CHAPTER NINE

Dancing with Our Own Shadows

We are here to awaken from the illusion of our separateness.

—Thich Naht Hanh

THE THIRD SYSTEM

We developed a democratic system of governance that distributes power, invites participation, and leads to the rapid implementation of impactful and creative ideas.

GETTYSBURG

On the morning of July 4, 1863, the horrible battle for Gettysburg had been decided. The human carnage smoked in faceless mounds, strewn now for miles in every direction. Every loss destroyed a piece of the human spirit, but you would not have known it given the destructive force of battle fury. As the sun rose to its place in a midmorning sky, occasional rifle shots could be heard punctuating the air. Sometimes a bird called, but they too were otherwise mute at this thing the people had done to one another. And days, or weeks, or years later, when the last wheelbarrow of awful debris had been carted away, and the land returned to normal, there was a permanent reminder that the terrible price of civil war could never be worth the reward. Nothing could be worth this. Nothing could justify it.

Except democracy.

The United States had a Constitution. Our forefathers had written it, voted for it, approved it, amended it, interpreted it, enshrined it, and bled for it. And by God, one day, we Americans were going to be worthy of it.

Ideals of justice, fairness, and equality were woven together with clearly articulated processes and rules of engagement that were sure to sustain our young nation against any threats from outside or from within. And they have.

If all organizations must come to the brink of Gettysburg before they achieve greatness, we had. And now it was time to rebuild.

A GOLDEN ERA

By the time the teachers of Mueller Charter School had scratched and clawed their way to near annihilation, there was nothing that resembled an innovative "break the mold" school. The union issue had posed an interesting challenge. Take away the politics and personalities associated with the Migden vote and what you were left with was a fundamental philosophical question that would determine whether this group of educators was capable of anything innovative at all. Essentially: "Do you have the courage to put the needs and rights of children ahead of the needs and rights of adults?" "Do kids come first?" "Do you have the strength of your convictions?" "Are you willing to sacrifice the union's version of job security for the sheer exhilaration of creating a one-of-a-kind institution so unique and so effective that it would one day be known as El Milagro?"

And, of course, you know by now these teachers did.

For all young democracies, the task at hand immediately after a revolution is to rebuild a system that people are willing to invest their future in—that they can have faith in. The Unites States was forever changed by Gettysburg and by the experience of the Civil War. In the years that followed, while it was by no means easy to grow a democratic nation, the American spirit was released unbridled into the air. It was as if the birds had found their throats again. The explosion of ideas fueled an industrial revolution. America began to reinvent itself and led the world out of sleepy agrarian fields and into the cities. We were modernizing.

Organizations may be far less complicated than nations to rebuild, but the need for infrastructure is no less urgent. At Mueller Charter School it required a structure of governance that could restore trust, collegiality, and unity of purpose—while at the same time stimulate crazy and creative ideas, unleash the flow of positive energy, and usher in a kind of golden era of innovation.

The governance structure that we created redistributed power because we redefined it. In schools, in governments, in law firms, in nonprofits, and in the board rooms of Fortune 500 companies—*power* is a commodity.

Who makes the decisions?
What is the scope of their authority?
What is the process used in decision making?
Who pays for bad decisions?
Who pays for good decisions poorly executed?
Who has a voice in decision making?
Who has a vote?
What works?
Who cares?
Is anybody listening?

CALLING THE SHOTS

We realized early on that rebuilding the governance structure of Mueller Charter School was a top priority. I had studied the minutes of old committee meetings, read the court documents, and interviewed the participants. I concluded that power at Mueller, as it is in so many schools and organizations, was merely an illusion. It belonged to the former principal and to no one else. He called the shots. If you were in his club, you liked the shots he called. If you weren't in the club, you waited for him to call another shot and then whacked him in the head with all of the reasons why whatever shot he called was never going to work. Compared to the complexities of actually teaching children, this was quite an entertaining game. It sustained them for several years until the teachers who were not in the club launched their final coup d'etat and they dragged the old bastard out by his boot heels.

In effect, Mueller was a "charter" school in name only. There were few innovations in place...and the ones that were there were not implemented to serve children or their families.

Moreover, Mueller was attracting lots of senior teachers who had one eye on retirement because their pension is based on the highest year's salary. It was as if the recruiting poster said:

"Come to Mueller. Make an extra $17,000 a year and build your retirement pension! Perfect working conditions: the kids can't learn, the parents don't care, and the principal ain't watching!"

So they came. In droves. Teachers worked a year or two and then retired on a fat pension that they could not have gotten anywhere else. And while they were there they pushed and bullied and agitated and wrapped themselves in the safe protection of the union flag.

This was not the vision of the authors of charter law in California. To his credit, the former principal also recruited a younger group of idealistic and hard-working teachers too. When the forces on both side reached the tipping point, the battle for control was on. Their Gettysburg was the election forced by Assemblywoman Carolyn Migden and her law that required charters to declare their allegiance to the status quo or unloosen the tethers and entrust your destiny to the laws of physics. In the summer of 2000, smack in the middle of the first five-year cycle of a new charter...the staff at Mueller was split exactly down the middle.

By then, the blood had been shed. The principal had been released. Some of the old guard immediately took the money and ran as soon as I appeared in the doorway. And there we stood at a fork in the road that could lead to only one of two extreme outcomes: the old garbage heap where they stack dead charter schools or El Milagro.

THE REAL POWER

We took the high road. I was aware that the school board had given serious consideration to pulling our charter—and they would have been justified. The staff and the community needed desperately to get excited about teaching children again. I was committed to using the charter law and the existing charter petition for the purpose of creating a better school. That idea resonated with enough people that they were willing to temporarily suspend hostilities and listen to what I had in mind.

"90% of our students at grade level," I proposed.

"Okay....we get that one. We agree. 90% at grade level. Ain't gonna happen in a thousand years but we'll play along. Is that really all you have? You came all the way to Chula Vista for a slogan? Come on new guy. Is that your whole vision?"

"No. We also need to rewrite our charter petition. Especially the part that defines our system of governance."

They agreed, even if they didn't see the connection.

I proposed that we rewrite the governance section of the charter to redefine our mission, our purpose, and every individual's role and responsibility in achieving our goals.

During that summer I had sat in on a few meetings and witnessed how they make decisions. The more vocal teachers bully the submissive teachers. The bulldogs batter away until they beat everybody into numb resignation. Out of pure frustration they capitulate: "Alright, fine, we'll move the money into the teachers' classroom budget. Jeezus, can we move on to something else?"

In the name of fairness they voted and voted and voted some more. These were the voting-est teachers I had ever encountered. And they kept score by who won the votes. There were winners and losers and they knew that score too.

All the while I noticed four important things:

First: For all of their meeting and voting and bullying and conspiring—it rarely had *anything* to do with teaching children.

Second: They often voted for the sake of voting. It created the illusion of democracy, but the aftermath of a divisive vote lingered for a long time. Like the casualties of Gettysburg.

Third: Parents were on the outside peering over the picket fence. They had no voice, no vote, and no recourse for goofy things that were happening in their children's school.

Finally: No one really read the charter petition. So they didn't follow the structure that had been approved with regard to governance. And since no one read the charter or knew what it said...individuals just made stuff up to advance their point of view.

The governance structure, as defined in the charter petition, had the right idea. It called for teachers to be involved in decision making at every level. But the structure for effective *government* was missing.

They had established committees to share the workload. One committee dealt with curriculum materials. Another was a personnel committee. Still another participated in writing the school's evacuation plan. In creating these committees, they had duplicated the role of a central office—without the service imperative. The kindergarten teachers were meeting the delivery trucks to inventory the latest shipments. Instead of focusing on why their five-year-olds were already two years behind the five-year-olds in Solana Beach, they were schlepping new text books out to the classrooms.

"I don't think we are stretching enough here, friends. If the teachers in Solana Beach are no more skilled than you, and if their parents don't love their children more than Mueller's parents love theirs, and if there is nothing genetically different about our students...then there should be no difference in achievement levels."

They agreed.

"Your charter petition says that stakeholders are to be involved in decision making. But making decisions about what? Right now, it looks like you are just shoving the furniture around the room. You're not making *significant* decisions. You are not designing the policies and routines and procedures to produce anything—let alone an accomplished charter school. So based on our new mission of getting our students to grade level...what do you think are now the most significant decisions we have to make?"

They knew the questions that had to be answered:

- What are the most effective instructional strategies we can use?
- What math text is going to create more continuity across all grade levels?
- How do we ensure that our campus is safe and our classrooms orderly?
- How can we help parents become better models and advocates for learning?
- How do we overcome our high mobility rate?
- How do we get children to come to school on time every day?
- How do we recruit, select, and train teachers who are equipped for our new mission?
- What is the best use of our budget in achieving high academic results?

It soon became clear that whoever had the answers to these questions...had authentic POWER!

"You have been bludgeoning each other to gain some sense of control. But none of you have ever been in control because you have been trying to control the wrong things. Going forward, our mission will define power, success, and influence if that is what is important to you. Because when you consistently get your students to grade level, we will listen. We will follow your lead. And you will have the keys to the kingdom."

SIX COMMITTEES

We had to align the critical process of decision making to our charter mission. We had to create a government. We were presented with an opportunity. In exchange for our freedom and independence as a charter school, we merely needed to redesign the delivery system so that children who were not beneficiaries of affluence, could get the same results as those who were. We all agreed on one thing: **to accomplish the mission of getting our students to grade level will require that we overcome poverty and the effect that poverty has on school performance.**

We had to transform the traditional, top-down elementary school model of government into a state-of-the-art organization that was worthy of a feature in *Fast Company*: democratic, agile, inclusive, and immensely successful in achieving results!

If we couldn't mitigate the effects of our environmental factors on teaching and learning, we could never elevate our students. And, by conventions of the charter, if we aren't making real process on the achievement levels of our students, we can't keep the charter. So all of the shenanigans about voting and posturing to be a committee chair were an empty sham. It was wasted energy. Rearranging the deck chairs.

So we agreed to suspend the existing committees and create six new ones:

- The Powerful Teaching and Learning Committee
- The Language and Culture Committee
- The Empowering Parents Committee
- The Safety and Caring Committee
- The Community Partnerships Committee
- The Committee for Creative and Talented Children

But creating more committees doesn't necessarily transform anything. They can drain an organization of valuable energy, morale and resources. If these were not high-functioning teams with a clear purpose—our teachers would be better off in their classrooms working with children and their parents. No more busy work. No more social networks to lobby and agitate. Teachers are free to do that on their own if the so choose.

We wanted committees that would energize every staff member. Those external environmental conditions that were once used as stock excuses for low performance—the conditions that schools historically cite as factors "beyond our control"—were now going to be central to our work. No more secrets. No more whispering. No more wringing of our hands as if we are powerless to change our students' destiny. If you want to teach at Mueller Charter School, these are our children, these are their parents, these are their life circumstances...and our potential together is limitless.

In developing our governance committees, we threw down the gauntlet for every staff member to be a force for dynamic change:

You want power? If you are the chair of the **Powerful Teaching and Learning Committee** you have the opportunity to lead your colleagues in significant action research efforts to identify best practices. Identify the most effective instructional methods, materials, and training and then make them happen. Advocate for children and for the funding you need to teach them. Don't take "no" for an answer. Make teaching at Mueller Charter School state of the art.

You want power? Serve on the **Language and Culture Committee**. Bilingual education is going through radical change in California where voters lost their will to preserve our children's native tongue. They even tie the language debate to the immigrant reform movement. Lay people can't separate the issues: driver's licenses for illegal immigrants versus the legitimate power of bilingualism in a child's cognitive development. This committee has tentacles all the way to Sacramento. All the way to Washington, DC! What do charter schools have to offer in the efforts to address our second-language learners? The stakes are sky high. We are at ground zero on this front. We are losing Latino children in droves. Why? *Because all of the achievement tests are in English!* You research and implement the most effective systems for English language acquisition. Find out how we accelerate their English *without* robbing them of their native language. You obtain the resources to train everybody. Including parents. The clock is ticking. We need results now!

You want power? Chair a committee that exists to educate our parents, like the **Empowering Parents Committee**. Bring those parents into the school. We have to engage them. We have to redefine what we mean by parent involvement. They have to be more effective in raising their children so we can be more effective in teaching them. If we are partners in this, we can make great things happen.

You want power? The **Safety and Caring Committee** will make or break our charter. Not by scheduling fire drills or designing disaster plans. This whole freakin' school is a disaster! If the evacuation routes worked we would have no students because they all would have left three years ago when the geezers were coming here to fatten their pensions. "Safety" is about *creating safety*—physical, emotional, psychological safety. It is about elevating our expectations so high that it will be impossible for children to fail. Where was our Safety and Caring Committee when you were stomping on each other in the hallways and plotting the demise of your last principal?

You want power? Serve as our liaison to Intuit and Sony and the land developers and local businesses...none of whom can afford to have schools continue to produce such woefully undereducated children.

Serve on the committee that fosters relationships with the community—the **Community Partnership Committee**. This is not the "adopt-a-school" campaign of the '90s. We don't need to be adopted. And we don't need their dough. We do need to learn from them, however. We need to connect with state-of-the-art concepts in organizational development. How does GE consistently make such good strategic decisions? How can we learn from the entrepreneurial leadership of Vitamin Water or MySpace or Yahoo? What is it about the culture of Apple that so consistently produces such inventive and innovative products? Why was Starbucks named one of Fortune Magazine's "100 Great Places to Work"? What would we have to do to earn the trust of Century 21 so that they start to list us in their marketing brochures as a primary benefit for buying a home down the street?

You want power? There is a way to unleash every child's full academic potential. It might not be by multiplying another page of mixed fractions or concocting fractured sentences from a generic word list. What if we could structure the multiple intelligences into everything we do? What if by discovering our dancers and artists and natural-born leaders, we give them permission to be uniquely talented. What if we give our children wings? Why not serve on the **ACT Committee** (Artistic-Creative-Talented Children) instead of replicating some central office process for distributing new cases of Charmin?

These six committees are where the power is. Period. They will propel us on our mission. Decision making and governance in any other context, for any other purpose, is an illusionary and distracting exercise.

THE COUNCIL

The teachers agreed. Again. We adopted and launched the six committees. We still needed another structure for school operations and process though.

So we re-designed our governing board in accordance with charter law. From the beginning we knew we did not want any traditional trappings of governing boards that might slow down progress. We didn't even want to imply the name governing board...so we created a fluid form of governance and called it the Leadership Council.

Our Leadership Council is a representative democracy. All stakeholders are included: every grade level and committee, classified staff and parents. We also have support staff to advise the Leadership Council, like our business manager and our secretary. My role is to chair the Council in its weekly meetings, and to keep everyone focused on the mission.

None of the support staff, myself included, are entitled to any kind of final vote or opinion. All decisions are made by the representatives. By the teachers. Get it?

The scope of authority of the Leadership Council is defined by the Charter Petition and it is a wide scope. Our Leadership Council members determine how to spend the school's $7 million budget. They manage and monitor programs, systems, services, operations, textbook selections, school supplies, landscape ideas, building maintenance and construction, and capital outlay. They design and approve schedules, calendars, special events, working conditions, safety features, student discipline, parent education programs, and school communications.

They even approve salaries. While our state has been conflicted over the application of conflict of interest laws in charter schools, we have not been. We don't negotiate. There is no collective bargaining with the public's money. Our teachers simply approve increases that allow them to keep pace with the salary schedule of the Chula Vista Elementary School District.

Any issue or decision—regardless of who makes it—that might impact the school budget or affect the charter or the mission, must be on the agenda for discussion and approval.

So teachers are managing. They are leading change.

There is only one area that the Leadership Council does not touch. "We ain't touching that," they said, as they looked toward me. "That's why you get paid the big bucks."

When it comes to supervisory responsibilities, the Leadership Council does not hire, evaluate, discipline, assign, or terminate other employees.

"Not with a ten-foot pole," they said. And they were adamant.

So who holds the principal accountable for the quality and humaneness of his or her supervisory decisions? The Leadership Council and the superintendent of the Chula Vista Elementary School District. There is a balance of authority. The principal is expected to lead the Council with responsibility, integrity, wisdom, and fairness.

As the principal, I don't participate in final council votes or decisions, but I am fully accountable for the quality of their work. If I have concerns about the direction they are going—about legal, ethical, educational, or financial issues—I am obligated to share those concerns and influence their thinking before they make a final decision. But I do not overrule them. No matter what. We all live with the decisions that are made by our Leadership Council. Or we die by them. If we screw it up, I lose my job and we all lose the charter. There is a *shared* risk...an element too often missing in models of *shared* decision making.

The Leadership Council has continued to evolve since its development in 2000.

Like all democratic bodies, it is at times slow and clumsy. Teachers and staff invest many hours in discussing issues that would have been decided in two minutes at the school down the street. But it would have been decided by the principal and proclaimed across the realm as the *truth*. And they will have placed the destiny of thousands of children in the hands of one.

LESSONS FROM JEFE

During the nascent rise and evolution of El Milagro, we learned many lessons about the power and unifying force of a compelling mission. The righteousness of our mission crushed the mighty teachers union and sent its most passionate apologists packing in early retirement. Were it not for the Leadership Council, however, and the doctrine of democracy and voice upon which it was built—Mueller would not have survived the transformation from a school that was structured to serve adults, to a school structured to serve children.

As if we had founded some new island nation, we experimented with processes that were more inclusive and democratic, while simultaneously, deflecting the voices that opposed anything unfamiliar. My advantage, as the chair of the council, was that I knew every word of the charter petition backward and forward. I had now authored major portions of it. I could defend it. And I knew we had created an remarkable model for decision making that was consistent with the charter spirit. We couldn't lose. This was no longer *Lord of the Flies*.

But we definitely had an opportunity to learn some things. And so we did. We learned, for example, twelve important lessons about nation building in a charter school:

Lesson One: **"There are many flavors of shared decision making."**

We learned that there are many models and philosophies that clumsily distribute decision making in schools. Many flavors.

The industry standard is "shared decision making" but that name is a misnomer because there really is no *shared* decision making if there aren't *shared* consequences for the decisions that are made! There is no *shared* risk. Besides, it's not practical to engage all the stakeholders when you need to make a decision.

At Mueller Charter School, our Leadership Council relies on the model of a representative democracy, constitutional precedent, and the balance of power. Democracy has to have a shape. It's got to be put in a box or a bottle or at least some kind of container or it will leak out all over the place and spill onto the floor.

For us, every decision takes us back to the mission. We simply do not waste energy on any issues or decisions that are not going to contribute to the mission. There are no other interests so the only conflict of interest is a decision that will not help us achieve the mission.

Do you have an idea on how we might overcome the effects of poverty on learning? We are all ears. Do you have a program idea or instructional strategy that can mitigate the double whammy of being a second-language learner on roller skates...moving from school to school to school seemingly every other month? We will try it. Is there an assessment model that can help teachers make better in-flight adjustments? Let's implement it.

We move quickly. We are inclusive. We involve anybody who has a dog in the fight. We consistently make good decisions about the right things.

Lesson Two: **"We are better at making some decisions than others."**

We learned that—no matter what their scope of authority might be—the most important decisions that teachers make are the decisions they make every day *in their classrooms!* They may have been on the Leadership Council when we decided to make a juice machine available for our students or when we approved this year's cost of living increase or when we decided to invest more funds in our literacy center: but those aren't the decisions that will really accomplish our mission.

It's the decisions from the classroom that add up.

In the classroom, teachers make thousands of decisions a day. Not just the big *strategic* decisions like which story to read at 9:40 or when to return a phone call to an inexplicably ticked-off parent or how to respond to David who has Maria trapped in a corner with a chair...but the many little *spontaneous* and even *subconscious* decisions: to check a student's work, to peek at the e-mail while students are reading independently, to finish an explanation even though the bell to recess just rang.

The cumulative quality of those myriad decisions, day after day, week after week, month after month—will determine a teacher's overall effectiveness through the course of the year. The difference between a teacher who gets 90% of his or her children to grade level and one who gets only 30% to grade level, inevitably comes down to the decisions that each teacher has made through the course of the entire year. When you consider the total number of teachers on a campus all making the same kinds of decisions, simultaneously, through the course of a day, it becomes evident that Camus was right: *We are the sum total of the decisions that we make.*

Lesson Three: **"I am the Lorax..."**
We learned that to grow El Milagro requires consistent, child-centered, decision making with results that can be measured and quantified in academic gains. We learned that it takes some fierce discipline as an organization to keep the focus there. In the decision-making equation, kids are definitely at a disadvantage because they are not there making the decision. Especially in elementary schools, if they have a voice at all, it is only symbolic, or only because there are enough enlightened advocates at the table reminding the others that their job is to speak for kids!
"I am the Lorax," wrote Dr. Seuss. *" I speak for the trees!"*
Our Leadership Council swears an oath to speak for the trees.

Lesson Four: **"We spray around power as if it comes from a hose."**
We learned that power at El Milagro must be distributed among those positioned to do "power-full" things.
We wondered what would happen in an organization that was perfectly balanced—where power was distributed in an authentic way that you could hear and taste and feel.
We wondered:

- What if every critical final decision was the teachers' to make?
- What if we didn't have to ask permission from anybody?
- What if we *refused* to ask permission from anybody?
- What if the teachers hired and fired and evaluated the principal who was hired to evaluate them?
- What if teachers were as powerful as the board president?
- What if teachers were the board president? .

- What if we left the trivial decisions to the traditional bureaucrats in the basement of the power pyramid?
- What if we devoted our intellectual and creative energy to deciding only things of significance to children: how to spend the dough, what texts to purchase (if any); how to organize the school day, the calendar, the salaries, and the policies and procedures and programs that make a school a school?

And in those wonderings, we concluded that power is a relative thing. The superintendent, the mayor, the governor, and the president all have *positional* power. But they don't know our children by name. The further away they are the fewer the students they actually know and the less influence they have to get real academic results. The power and promise of El Milagro lies in the Leadership Council and in the Charter Petition. So we spray power around in hopes that all of the furniture and all of the carpets get soaked.

Lesson Five: **"Parents come with stuff."**

We want to believe in the capacity of our parents to participate in school governance. We want them to advise and advocate. We want them to be more than a tall version of the children for whom we have all committed our professional allegiance. We want them to peer at us from the end of the table, their glasses pushed down on the edge of their noses, like the wise old shareholders in a company that is as old as electric power.

But we learned that parents come in all types and stages of readiness. They come with stuff. It's not all bad. And it's not all good.

The system that inspires parent engagement at Mueller Charter School is clumsy and impractical. We know it is relatively important to engage our parents at school, and yet, for all the systems we create, this one is fragile as a spider web. Parents have better things to do. Like raise their children. And that's the way it ought to be.

When it comes to governance and shared decision making, we created a transparent process at Mueller Charter School. We extend an open invitation to any parent who wants to serve on the Leadership Council. And sometimes they do. But the hard truth is that we seek the expertise required to lift our children toward grade level. We need more than opinions. More than input. We need parents to be parents first. Then if there is anything left in the tank, and if there is any magic or untapped brilliance, there is room to contribute to the energy of El

Milagro. Our children may have to get to grade level with or without their parents driving on field trips.

Our parents come with stuff. Some of it we can use. Some of it we can do without.

Lesson Six: **"Ambition is paradoxical."**

We learned that our leaders must lead with humility...but at the same time, they need to inspire organizations to audacious vision. We need a push toward *greatness*!

It is just not like educators to strive for greatness. It is a profession that survives on anonymity, compliance, and conformity. We seek greatness not for ourselves, but for our work. We seek greatness manifest in our collective creativity, in the quality of our craft, in the depth of our commitment, and ultimately, in the achievement of children.

The difference between magic and a miracle is that when miracles occur in our world, they are owed not to the wizardry of human brilliance, but rather, to the very hand of God. And God seems so busy sometimes. After all, we live in a universe that is infinitely large and, ever expanding. Or so the astronomers tell us. How can He possibly have the time or the interest in our affairs? In what little spiritual energy we can identify in the humble evolution of the human intelligence, we have at least developed the sense to leave all explanation of miracles to Him. As if the message is to simply: "let them flow."

Mueller Charter School is an example of what happens when immensely talented, creative, and tireless people work together in a common mission. Compared to most human organizations we have a tremendous advantage: our universe favors children. And though a lot of organizations serve children, we sense a difference here.

Perhaps it is because—while we have pursued tangible academic results, and while we have tried to be an innovative laboratory for nontraditional strategies and structures and processes—we have also consciously pursued excellence on a spiritual level as well.

El Milagro is the perfect and perfectly contained storm. It is combustible energy harnessed to serve our planet, when for a moment there, it could just as easily have destroyed it. It is for profit—when the currency of value is not defined in gold, but rather, in the degree to which we can be a light to others. Where a day's wages are calculated in the small gains that are only illuminated when our gift is nurturing the gift in others.

El Milagro is what happens when every day, we collectively decide to strive for greatness. "To whom much is given, much is required."

Or so they say. El Milagro is the sum total of decisions made—in all humility—to better serve those others.

Lesson Seven: **"Learning is paradoxical too."**

In developing a democratic and inclusive model of governance at Mueller Charter School, we learned that the more we know…the more we realize that we don't know squat!

Lesson Eight: Lesson Eight: **"We borrow and loan power like lawn tools."**

We learned still another paradox about the fluid nature of power.

We learned, for instance, that the more power you give a way, the more powerful you become. So we distribute it freely.

And sometimes power is returned to your doorstep like a lawn tool lent to a neighbor—perhaps a tool that fits neatly into the hedges and edging that define your lawn, but never quite does the trick across the street. At least they left a note:

Thanks for letting me use your lawn tool. I am returning it exactly as I borrowed it in light of the fact that I could not get it to work. Perhaps it is broken. Hope you enjoy these tomatoes from our yard. Your friend, Julius.

We learned that it is often just too hard to find *truth* in decision making and that it is easier to return the package of opportunity… unopened. Regardless of how power is structured or how it is laid out on party trays for people to pick up and sample, according to their moods or tastes, the *truth* is that sometimes teachers just want you to give them the answers. Even when they have absolute power…sometimes they are too afraid, too distracted, too impatient, too malleable, too paralyzed to move themselves or others forward.

Sometimes teachers just want to go back to their classrooms and leave the decisions to someone else. And so the world turns on the strength of its leaders.

Lesson Nine: **"Leadership is more than being Jefe."**

We learned that for all of the democratic and inclusive systems of governance, there must still be one strong person in whom the people trust. Even if only for the blink of an eye. There has to be a leader.

In Spanish, the boss is *Jefe*. And if you took Spanish you know the "j" is pronounced like an "h". So *Jefe* is "Hef—ay".

But regardless of how you pronounce it, Jefe is in charge. In a traditional, top-down, hierarchical organization, the Jefe is the top of the rock. You go to the Jefe when you have questions or when you need something; or when you want to bitch about Jefe's latest edict or when you want to unload your personal frustrations and let Jefe fix them.

Jefe is the fix-it guy. Jefe is Dad and Mom and big brother all in one. He is older than all the other kids on the block so he can even kick the neighborhood bully's ass. "Go tell Jefe. He'll kick his ass for you." Jefe takes requests.

Jefe is everywhere. He is omniscient. He is wise. He is unflappable. Jefe can jump rope and he does long division and he carries heavy boxes and sets them down exactly where you want them. And he'll move them if you change your mind to wherever you want them next. Jefe can write and sew and turn flapjacks at the pancake breakfast. Jefe is the first to volunteer because Jefe knows that there is power in leading by example.

Jefe knows all about symbolic leadership. Jefe has a bookshelf filled with books about symbolic leadership. Jefe tells jokes and brings Krispy Kreme donuts. Jefe rolls up his sleeves and builds the haunted house for the Halloween carnival. Jefe has jumper cables and starts dead batteries. He used them on old lady Cochrane when we all thought she was dead. He jump-started her teaching career long enough for her to idle her way down the road and retire somewhere else. We were all grateful because no one else would even walk into her classroom for fear that she might have been dead in there for weeks and stinking up the joint.

Jefe can talk up a storm. Jefe goes to Kiwanis meetings. Jefe doesn't rest or eat or gather air. Jefe can Jefe in his sleep. He can Jefe standing on his freakin' head.

Some day they'll all give Jefe a golden apple lapel pin and a plaque declaring that "Jefe Made A Difference" and he'll be a step behind old lady Cochrane headed for whatever it is that retired people do all day. Then a new Jefe will come to the door and move the furniture and we can all sit in the lounge and confess his sins or articulate her obvious weaknesses and shortcomings. And we will wish we had the old Jefe back even though just a year ago we were sitting around complaining that Jefe had lost a step or two and maybe he's a little burned out and "maybe Jefe oughta think about calling it a career."

And we are reminded that in a world where you leave leadership to others, you get what you pay for. Nothing.

I am reminded that at Mueller Charter School I am Jefe by position only. And though by convention of organizational structure we need a single Jefe, at El Milagro, we are, in fact, all one. *E pluribus uno*. Somos Jefe. Never forget it.

We are *all* Jefe.

Lesson Ten: **"We ride the wave...and paddle back out."**

We learned that sometimes you just have to ride the wave and paddle back out.

When Dr. Libi Gil decided to move to another professional challenge she suggested to the district's governing board that Lowell Billings would be a logical choice as her successor. He had, after all, repaired many of the district's leaking boats. And the governing board agreed. So Lowell Billings became the new superintendent of the Chula Vista Elementary School District.

Lowell Billings is a superintendent who knows what is happening in the forty-three schools for which he is responsible. He knows teachers by name. All 2,000 of them! And if that isn't impressive enough he knows their spouses and where their kids go to school and what kind of food their pets eat. Lowell Billings is a man blessed with many gifts. And being able to cram information into his head and store it on neat synaptic shelves for easy retrieval is one of them.

And he can surf. San Diego's beaches are filled with old grey-haired rascals who couldn't get out of the water even after they grew up, and Lowell Billings is one of them. The salt water is evidently good for memory storage. Or perhaps sitting out on the edge of the ocean, feet dangling with the fin-backed denizens of Sunset Cliffs gives one time to think about stuff before the next wave crashes over you.

So one morning while surfing Lowell Billings thought about how valuable it would be to visit every classroom of every school in the district—twice a year. He thought about how hard it is to influence the lives of children when you don't know any of their names. And how, being stuck in a district office—surrounded by samples of student work and silver shovels from ground-breaking ceremonies—just isn't the same when it comes to changing children's lives.

He also thought about the time and logistics associated with that commitment, and about how much crap he would have to take from teachers and principals whining about him snooping in their schools. And then, just as he picked up a rare eight-foot swell, the sun glistened off the lip of a wave and Lowell Billings rose up like Neptune. "Heck with 'em," he thought. "I'm gonna walk through every classroom and the principals that don't like it can transfer to Alpine." And he rode the wave to shore. Lowell Billings knew he could influence the direction of his forty-three schools if he could stand in every classroom and ask questions that didn't have any one right answer.

And so, of course, he did. And after each wave crashed, the momentum and fury and roiling gallons of holy water thrust him toward land. Ride the wave. Paddle back out. Ride the wave. Paddle back out.

"Why do you keep coming to check up on us? We hate your goddamn walk-throughs!" some of them said.

Ride the wave. Paddle back out.

"That freakin' Lowell Billings keeps asking me questions I can't answer. And every time he does...we get better. Why can't he just tell us what we are all supposed to do and save the drama." Ride the wave. Paddle back out.

When the superintendent and his cabinet buddies come to Mueller Charter School to do their classroom walk-throughs they always want to know what our current curricular focus is and what they should be looking for. Walk-throughs are, by design, collaborative. They are opportunities for coaching. The cabinet assumes the role, not of experts, but rather, of "critical friends." They do not dispense advice, criticism, or mandates. Instead, they ask questions. Lots of questions. Often in the form of "wonderings"—like, "I wonder what writing strategies are consistent across all grade levels." Or, "I wonder if these children are really being challenged." Sometimes there are "what-ifs." "What if Ms. Johnson relied more on manipulatives to teach the mathematic thinking behind the addition of fractions?" Hmm.

The last time Lowell Billings and his cabinet buddies came through Mueller Charter School they indeed came as our critical friends. So I reminded our staff:

"You are a charter school...this is not an evaluative visit. So, do what you do. Ignore them. No dog and pony shows." No eleventh-hour bulletin board displays. No dressing up like a Sunday wedding. No prompting kids to be on their very best behavior.

"Just do your thing," said the advisory. And so they did.

"What did Lowell Billings have to say?" they all asked at the end of the day.

"He said Mueller Charter School is as focused as he has ever seen it. That the teaching is rigorous. That the kids are dead serious about their learning. That there is something very exciting happening here."

"Well we knew that. Did he have any constructive criticism for us? Anything we could do to improve?"

God bless 'em. Our teachers are always interested in constructive feedback and ways to improve. Or at least that is what they say.

So I gave them some. "Well he did wonder whether there was seventy-five minutes of writing instruction happening every day?"

"Seventy-five minutes of writing instruction!!! Is he freakin' nuts? He's been swallowing too much salt water! There is only so much time in a day! How can we possibly squeeze in another minute of writing time?"

...and blah, blah, blah.

Within three weeks, however, I noticed that virtually every teacher had figured out how to structure more sustained writing time across the curriculum, and that our students were writing well in excess of seventy-five minutes a day. Walk-throughs had brought fresh eyes and those eyes saw our work in a different light. Lowell Billings *wondered*. He did not criticize or dictate how we, as a charter school, should teach writing. He did not define rigor. He did not offer a secret or magical solution to the riddles of high achievement. But Lowell Billings made a profound impact on our teaching that day. Then he left in a rush for the next school.

Ride the Wave. Paddle back out.

Lesson Eleven: **"You roll the dice...make no excuses."**

We learned that no organization can discover the Holy Grail by making excuses for why previous missions failed. We fail. It is what humans do well. What we do not do so well is accept the wisdom inherent in our failing moments. The teaching is evident: "This path is not the path this time." Making excuses, however blinds us to the teachings inherent in our failures. Making excuses is who we are when we are pathetically cowering and trying to protect our jobs.

"It wasn't my fault."

"It's their fault."

"I never had a good feeling about that program but the primary teachers have been using it for a long time...so they got their way."

"The kids didn't do what I asked them to do."

"The parents were asleep at the wheel."

"Jefe didn't Jefe enough in my classroom. It's Jefe's fault."

"The wind was blowing too hard."

"The sun got in my eyes."

Excuses. Excuses are momentum killers.

Lesson Twelve: **"Leaders have to stretch...and then stretch some more."**

We learned that those universal qualities of Vision, Alignment, Execution, Courage, and Communication are as important as all of the leadership books at Borders say they are. They are components of a skill set that you simply cannot lead without. It's just not enough. Especially in an organization that cultivates leadership. So I had to learn some things about leadership too.

To lead in charter schools, at any level, you have to have that revolutionary warrior's mentality that someday they are going to capture you and send you to the gallows...but before they do, you are going to turn everything you touch inside out. You are going to loosen all of the rusted and barnacle-encrusted bolts that have held the foundation in place for centuries, and topple over a few useless towers.

That is intimidating.

School leaders tend to be former school teachers. They must go against their own conditioning. They have to emerge from an organizational structure that is absolutely paralyzed by adherence to the status quo. Change is anathema. The wild wheels that have a chance to track with speed and certainty are mired in deep, deep mud. Leaders must come with a giant winch to get the wheels out of the mud. They must be hyper-focused on what is possible, with an absolute conviction that greatness is achievable. And it helps if they are a little naïve to the forces that conspire to temper their revolutionary spirit.

Change leaders seem to make everybody uncomfortable, including the very people who hired them because they wisely adjudged some characteristic in them that suggested they would be "the breath of fresh air we have been looking for." Then they change stuff and everybody becomes indignant. You can fire them, but you can never undo the forces of change that they initiated. Those forces will roll on through that school or district or community for decades.

Causing people to think and reexamine their values and attitudes and systems and services and strategies for serving children is a righteous thing. If you are leading in that way, you don't have to make excuses. You don't have to be defensive. You don't need a scapegoat. Some ideas work and some don't. If you were a better leader you would have already known that your latest initiative wasn't going to work and you would have done something different. Now you know. So now you are a better leader.

To lead change you have to be more creative and fuel your subversive side. You must be willing to visit a pawn shop, to volunteer in Tijuana, to drive a strange vehicle, to go to Spanish Harlem instead of Rockefeller Center, to write a poem in line at the DMV.

You must be willing to ask questions, to push back, to create a new path, to explore, to step up and incite a revolt! Leaders cannot accept "no" for an answer, and must not misinterpret failure as a sign that the answer is "NO!" Leaders fail. Often. Celebrate your new learnings. Be resilient. And strive to fail some more

This is, after all, the alluring unpredictability of leadership.

And these are just twelve of the many lessons that we have learned together at Mueller Charter School.

SWORD FROM STONE

To lead a school to greatness requires the courage, the confidence, and the magic to pull a sword from the stone.

The whole point of courageous action is that it is hard to take. The more courage that is required for an action, the fewer and fewer are the available candidates to step up.

Why were there only twelve Knights of the Round Table? In a land of lawless warriors, there were only a dozen or so who possessed the skills, the courage, the devotion to others, and the vision to seek the Holy Grail. Or maybe there were more that we just never read about.

In either case there were Knights worthy of the Round Table. The rest flailed around and knocked each other off their horses.

CHAPTER TEN

The Gospel

To see things in the seed, that is genius.

—Lao Tzu

THE FOURTH SYSTEM

We researched, modeled, and promoted the most powerful instructional strategies.

THE PYRAMIDS

Somewhere between Indiana Jones and King Tut, there lay all the millennia's ancient pyramids...all shadows and intrigue...where history itself cannot be sure. But of this even the by-gone philosophers agreed: within the pyramid...there is a mysterious power.

Great Power.

And so a pyramid is the schema we use to describe our components of *Powerful Teaching*. There are no dead pharaohs or boy-kings hidden in the vaults of this pyramid. But there are treasures of sorts.

To achieve our charter mission requires that every teacher be highly skilled in the craft of Powerful Teaching. What is Powerful Teaching? It is a combination of knowledge, skills, values, magic and passion. It is professional expertise that results in authentic learning by every child entrusted into that teacher's care.

Powerful Teaching is neither arbitrary nor experimental. It is grounded in decades, even centuries, of scientific research. The research has grown in fat volumes of sometimes conflicting findings. It fills entire wings of university libraries. It is stuffed into the Internet like quantum particles of infinite weight. And yet, for most teachers, the research findings are elusive—a patchwork tapestry of a thousand threads.

So we created this framework and defined our craft as it relates to Mueller Charter School. It is a lens through which to identify the most effective instructional strategies. It allows us to pinpoint teachers' training needs and themes for staff development. It also provides a common language around daily effective teaching practices. It codifies our collective knowledge and experience into a tangible and manageable system.

But while this system enables us to articulate the components of Powerful Teaching, it still has to be acted on. It is hard to do consistently. It is exhausting. It is, for us, non-negotiable. For all of our innovation, there is simply no variable more important than our teachers. The path to greatness, the road to our mission promise, runs through the heart of this inescapable truth: that the difference between mediocrity and 90% of our children performing at grade level is *the quality of our daily teaching*!

This is *The Way* of El Milagro. This is the gospel.

TRUE NORTH

These are at least six important elements of Powerful Teaching, but they are not the only elements. There are more. This is merely our starting point. This is how we do things at El Milagro. It is how we grow.

It might be helpful to think of these six elements layered on top of one another like a pyramid. They are, at least for discussion sake, hierarchical.

• Assessment
• Instructional Strategies
• Curriculum: Our "Critical Few"
• Classroom Management and Leadership
• School and Classroom Climate of Expectations
• Child Centered Core Values – Every Student Matters

The first three levels form a Base for everything we do to help children excel. This Base defines our belief in children as well as the behaviors great teachers exhibit every day in support of those beliefs. No one gets hired to teach at El Milagro without this Base, because it isn't something we can will to someone else. We can't teach it. It is an internal fire. It is the magnetic energy created when common core values fuse together around the organization's deepest internal orbit. It is our "true north." It's where the compass needle points even when we get knocked on our ass and end up lying upside down in the weeds.

The Base demands:

- Child-centered **core values**;
- The ability to create a **classroom climate** that generates energy, high expectations, personal effort and mutual support; and
- The skillful, democratic, and humane **management** of daily classroom life—coupled with the inspiration to **lead** the learning for every child.

These first three elements—the Base—must be present before even considering the more technical skills associated with curriculum, instruction, lesson design and assessment. The craft of teaching is built on this foundation.

THE BASE

Element One: Every Classroom is Child Centered.

To be successful at El Milagro, every classroom is designed around a student-centered philosophy and attitude. Every activity, system, and decision, is made with children in mind. Every conversation and idea. Every teaching act is filtered through the simple guiding question: "Will *this activity* benefit my students...will *this decision* make it more likely that my students can get to grade level and their full academic potential?"

This is the foundation of Powerful Teaching. If teachers do not have strong, student-centered values, if they don't believe their students are capable (or worthy) of academic excellence, their expertise in the rest of the components is irrelevant. This model of Powerful Teaching requires an absolute belief in children and commitment to their success. No excuses. No exceptions.

This component is secured by a moral imperative to serve every student. It is our Hippocratic oath. But we are compelled by more than just a moral obligation. No country on the planet has ever pursued free, public education for its citizens as aggressively as we have in America. But there are still many who have determined that the right to be educated belongs to only a few. They have decided—even subconsciously—that being educated is a birthright only if you are in the club that they are in. And their "club" is usually defined by some arbitrary characteristic that is difficult or impossible to change: like race, or social class, or gender, or the language spoken at home or maybe even the location of a child's house across the river, or the boulevard or the railroad tracks.

To successfully teach all children, regardless of their backgrounds and life circumstances, requires an uncommon passion along with the other *Seven Gifts*. Powerful Teaching is, after all, the focused application of the Seven Gifts of El Milagro.

We can teach people to teach, but we cannot give them heart transplants. They must approach their work with a missionary's zeal. They are all here by choice, knowing that there are plenty of other places that they could teach. Easier schools. Better neighborhoods. Less obsession with overcoming variables like poverty.

The prospects of getting such a high percentage of students to grade level appear daunting at first. When teachers look at their class roster at the beginning of the year, they may find that out of thirty students only six are currently at grade level, and of those, four are hanging on by a thread. Six students at grade level will not be nearly enough. There has to be significant, two- and even three-year gains—within *one* year—for the remaining twenty-two students!

To do so requires a student-centered philosophy, a deep core belief that:

- Children are capable of amazing achievement; that
- A child's achievement level is determined more by the skill, attitudes, and expectations of the classroom teacher than by any other variable; that
- Extraordinary "outcomes" require extraordinary "input"; that
- Extraordinary "outcomes" also demand focused energy—every minute of every day; and perhaps most importantly, that
- Every child is morally and legally *entitled to academic success.*

At Mueller Charter School, Powerful Teaching is built on this child-centered foundation and on our beliefs about human capacity for excellence. The next level seeks to align our *behaviors* with these beliefs.

OPENING DAY

Element Two: Educators and Staff Intentionally Cultivate a Healthy Classroom and School Climate.

You know the climate is right when it feels like opening day at a major league baseball park. It's like walking your small child by the hand to the entrance of the stadium...down the long tunnel to the seating area and out into the dusk for the very first time. Stadium lights are on and the music is bumping. Players are warming up. Barbecue aromas; popcorn, beer, garlic fries all laced with the smell of the fresh-cut grass. And the outfield seems to roll across the distance like a great green lake.

There is an electric energy that is unmistakable. The anticipation is as thick as mesquite. "Baseball is about going home," said A. Bartlett Giamatti, the former commissioner. "And how hard it is to get there... and how driven is our need."

On the foundation of a child-centered philosophy, we create an atmosphere that wraps around our students like a sticky cocoon.

Just like opening day at the ballpark.

Like going home.

We invest tremendous energy into creating a school environment that consistently communicates to every student that he or she is worthy of high expectations, of our constant caring and support, and of endless opportunities to successfully participate in school life.

Every interaction communicates these expectations that we have for our students. We simply *expect* them to excel. Every child. Sooner or later. We will not concede. We will not give up on a single one of them.

Those expectations and beliefs are reflected in at least a dozen different ways in our classrooms:

- Personal relationships
- Communication strategies and styles
- Levels of guidance, challenge, stimulus and support
- Respect for individual strengths, talents and abilities
- Curricula and learning experiences
- Respect for learning styles
- Opportunities to think creatively and critically
- Opportunities for developing social and civic literacy
- Opportunities for developing habits of mind as a learner
- Opportunities for developing character as a person

- Learning in an inclusive and multicultural context
- Cooperative and fluid grouping strategies
- Strategic use of evaluation methods
- Conscientious and strategic use of time as a resource

And so on.

Like chameleons, children turn the shape and hue of their environment. For purposes of protection and self-defense, they so often internalize the expectations of others, wear their foliage like desert camouflage, and blend into the scenery. They *become* those expectations. For better or for not so good. If a child is expected to achieve greatness, he or she will likely do so. And likewise, if a child is expected to achieve little, he or she is likely to sink to that level of expectation.

Classroom climate is fixed around expectations. But just as important, our teachers communicate a sense of caring—like the hopes and dreams and lives of our students matter. And they do. We make Mueller Charter School a safe place in every way: physically, emotionally, psychologically. Caring and support make our expectations real.

In this environment, children are less afraid to try new things and to expose themselves to what they do not know.

A cornerstone of our instructional philosophy is that all children are gifted and that it is our responsibility to help them discover *how* they are gifted. Most educators accept this philosophy. Most parents do too. But it has to be more than a nice slogan. In fact, if it is only a slogan, you can do more harm than good by pretending to believe it.

Our elementary schools typically define giftedness in terms of what children know and are able to perform in language arts and math. It is what is tested. By high school, students are afforded opportunities to express their giftedness through music, drama, visual arts, athletics, student leadership, speech, science, politics, and community involvement. In college, students are eligible for scholarships that pay for their entire education while they continue to develop and share their gifts with others. And then, of course, every individual has an opportunity to make a living on the talents and gifts that they have fully developed.

When people discover and develop their gifts and their talents, they really will be positioned to influence and even change their world. At our school that opportunity begins now. In the process they also develop the character, and the critical *habits of mind*—like goal setting and self-monitoring—that produce successful citizens.

But it doesn't come easy. Children must sometimes be shown

a window to the future that does not align with their own beliefs or experience. The most gifted teachers are those who can throw the window open, and let the sunlight in. Who else is so uniquely positioned to inspire and motivate children to learn?

So we create a positive climate in every classroom, and across the entire school campus; one in which children feel a sense of purpose. There is an urgency. There is a structure that guides them. It is influenced by the presence of high expectations, caring and support, and opportunities to participate fully in their own development as students and as people. There is a palpable sense of anticipation, day by day, that achievement is as inevitable as it is glorious.

Every day is Opening Day.

FENG SHUI

Element Three: We Diligently Cultivate the Companion Skills of Both Classroom Management and Classroom Leadership.

Classroom management is its own discipline. There are experts and consultants and books and workshops to help teachers develop their expertise in classroom management. And there should be because classroom management is pretty important.

Effective classroom managers *manage* their resources. They create appropriate tools and strategies. They know their students and their styles of learning. They have polished routines. They weigh and portion time as if it were gold. They manage the gold. They strategically move the furniture and re-design props like a movie set: seating charts, posters, artwork, aquariums, bulletin boards, incentive displays, classroom libraries, toys, and visuals. They study the lighting and traffic patterns in the room. They experiment with genres of music during quiet times. They exploit the ambiguous resources of silence and space. They fuss with the thermostats and know when to prop open the door.

Teachers at Mueller Charter School are expected to be masters of office management. Their classroom is their domain. They must juggle and dance. And they must weave resources together in a seamless tapestry that somehow hangs beautifully from the wall without getting in the way.

To be sure, teachers everywhere work to improve their classroom management strategies—as they should. It is a necessary component of Powerful Teaching. But at Mueller Charter School, effective classroom management has to also foster classroom *leadership*.

TEACHER LEADERS

There are professional libraries and publications filled with articles and research on effective classroom management. There is, by contrast, very little written about classroom *leadership*. But classroom management, no matter how polished or practiced, is not enough to inspire children to the greatness that is their birthright. For that, they need leadership. In fact, if there is no leadership—no vision or fire to excel beyond what students think they are capable of—then those *management* strategies will be no more effective than reorganizing the deck chairs on some famously wounded and sinking cruise liner.

Good managers can build a bridge across the river. They can establish and communicate clear project goals. They can acquire and monitor appropriate resources. They can motivate the troops, teach them to use the tools, supervise progress of the construction, and make the strategic decisions to work toward completion of the task.

Leadership isn't about just building the bridge...it is about crossing the river!

One of the great debilitating myths in the literature of public education is that the principal must be the sole instructional leader on the campus. Perhaps embedded in this notion is the very reason why we have not had significant academic gains across the country. We are waiting for the brilliance of *principals*—as instructional leaders—to translate into children learning.

But the instructional leader should also be the one providing the instruction—and that's the teacher!

In any organization, strong leaders communicate the organizational vision, they develop a plan, they provide support and encouragement, they keep up the drumbeat so that no matter how tired everybody gets—they never lose sight of the mission. They never quit. Strong leaders help others establish lofty individual goals and the path toward achieving them. They begin, as Covey says, with "the end in mind." They are tireless champions of "the cause." Every effort, every resource, every unit of organizational energy is expended to achieve the mission.

El Milagro grows on the strength of its leaders. Not just one. Not just the principal. Our teachers have to lead, too.

So at El Milagro, our teachers lead.

PEDAGOGY

When applied in the classroom, these first three elements of the Powerful Teaching Pyramid come together around the prerequisite foundation of classroom leadership: *the Base*. The next three elements define *what* we teach, *how* we teach, and *how we measure* the extent to which our students are learning. These components represent the art and science of effective teaching: the essential curriculum, the use of research-based instructional strategies, and a comprehensive approach to assessment.

FREEZE DRIED

Element Four: We Define and Prioritize the Essential Curriculum.

The curriculum represents *what* we teach. It defines what every learner should know and be able to do or value or appreciate. The curriculum communicates our belief in children's capacity to learn and aligns what we teach with what they must know in order to be successful citizens in an age of information technology and global competition. Identifying exactly what children must learn is fundamental to the art and sweet science of teaching. Author and futurist Alvin Toffler once wrote: "It is not enough just to prepare children for the future...we have to prepare them for the *right* future!"

One day, twenty years from now, educators may look back on this era of manic hyperallegiance toward basic skills and ask us all, rhetorically, just what had gotten into us:

"What the hell has gotten got into you? What about the other stuff? The Ancient ruins of Machu Picchu. The Boston Pops. The Great Books. The wonder of space flight. The power of life's metaphors. Crazy Van Gogh and all the other people and places that give children a reason to read. What about that stuff, too?"

At Mueller Charter School, we are fussy about what we teach. The curriculum cannot be determined by political expediency, or religious zealots, or software fads, or video games, or teacher whim, or a Ouija board, or a roll of the die. Nor can it be determined by text books. We can't rely on a for-profit textbook company in Texas to determine what our children need to learn. Not in any subject. When the wonders of Ancient Greece are reduced to a twenty-two-pound written text with a handful of art photos and comprehension questions...you know that we have sucked ever fiber of vitality and breath from the learning. Not even Diogenes can resurrect magic in a freeze-dried school.

TOO MANY STANDARDS

Though charter schools are free to establish their own curriculum, ultimately they are held accountable for how their students perform on the state and local school district tests. These tests amount to an assessment of basic skills in math and reading. They reflect a year's teaching toward the state standards. So the curriculum for charter schools is not as radical as critics of the movement would have you think.

Throughout the '70s, '80s and '90s...the first three decades of my teaching career, schools created their own curricula and defined their own standards. There were plenty of similarities. But the only really consistent feature was the lack of consistency and the degree to which children of color and poor children suffered in the absence of accountability. This was true throughout California, and all across the United States.

Accountability has long since returned.

And it's not all bad. In fact one by-product of the school accountability movement has been the codification of statewide curriculum standards. Teachers, students, and parents now have a published list of content standards for each subject area and each grade level. Everybody should know those target goals. Better yet, the daily lesson plan is no longer determined by text books, the weather, the resources, the district office, or how a teacher is feeling. Rather, it is, by necessity, a function of careful long-term and strategic planning to address all critical standards.

In California, each curriculum area also has a published framework that addresses the big ideas and standards for that discipline. It doesn't tell teachers *how* to teach, but rather, it identifies the key concepts that are essential for mastering each core subject

If there is a downside to the body of work now known as curriculum content standards, it is that there are too damn many of them. Each curriculum area has hundreds of standards that some interest group or another would argue establish the very foundation and essence of an educated citizen. There literally is not enough time in the day, the month, or even a school year to teach all of these standards. In fact, there isn't enough time in a child's entire school *career* to teach them all. To do that would require another ten grade levels!

In places like Mueller Charter School with high numbers of low-achieving students, the curriculum is, by necessity, rooted in basic skill development. However, we refuse to become fundamentalists. Children still need to think and problem solve, to appreciate others, to develop a sense of character, and to explore their unique learning gifts. And perhaps even more than the privileged children of Solana Beach, they deserve an enriched curriculum that makes learning meaningful and engaging.

So each year we develop our own *Essential Curriculum* that is unique to each grade level. It is balanced between the facts and skills that are sure to be tested and the big ideas and rich learning that we all want for our own children. We analyze the full range of the ten billion content standards for each curriculum area and organize them—at least for discussion purposes—in one of five prioritized sets:

- The Critical Few (aka Essential Standards)
- The Foundation Standards
- The Advanced Standards
- The Enrichment Standards
- The Habits of Mind (The Behavioral Standards)

The **Critical Few** include the skills or facts that *must* be mastered if a child is to perform at grade level on the California Standards Test. At the beginning of the year our teachers collaborate to identify their critical few by looking at all of the standards for that grade level and then identifying the most essential 20% on which they will invest 80% of their time, energy, attention, and resources. These standards are nonnegotiable. Like memorizing the multiplication tables in third grade, for instance.

The content standards included in the critical few are identified by consulting with colleagues and by reviewing the state frameworks. They are further pared down by reviewing released test items from the state assessments and determining the specific knowledge and skills that are required for a student to answer each test item correctly. We also conduct an item analysis of our local school district assessments and identify the skills and knowledge required to answer each of these questions correctly.

The State of California wants these skills taught...that's why they appear on the assessments. To ignore them is to miss the entire point of the system of accountability. So this is our one concession to the conventions of modern schooling and education law!

Next are the **Foundation Standards**—the remaining critical competencies and academic skills that are essential if students are going to continue to develop as learners. These form the gateway to academic success across all curriculum areas and may have been missed in prior grade levels. Whereas the critical few are essential for performing at grade level on the California Standards Test, the foundation standards make it possible for students to access all curricula through basic literacy and mathematics competency.

For example, conducting scientific investigations at the eighth-grade level, may require that a student reacquaint herself with the foundations principles of mathematical measurement that were introduced the fifth-grade level. These competencies may not be within the critical few for eighth-grade science. But they are essential tools for the students to go forward and excel in the science curriculum. They are among the foundation standards to be mastered by successful students.

The *Advanced Standards* are *next* year's critical few.

Some percentage of our students will master their grade-level standards during the course of the school year, and they must continue to be challenged. Our advanced standards are likely the critical few for the next grade level and beyond. We start to accelerate children's learning and introduce them to the skill sets that they will have to master during the next school year. It does not require that they be exposed to the materials or teaching activities that will be used in the next grade. Rather, by introducing advanced skills, their learning program can be individualized and they can begin to form a foundation for future learning.

Our *Enrichment Standards* address the curriculum areas that are too often pushed aside to make room for the basic skills. Here, our teachers integrate the standards and the "big ideas" from the arts and humanities to science and physical education.

Through thematic units, our teachers bring balance to classrooms otherwise preoccupied with test performance. They inspire and cultivate students' interests, abilities, gifts and experiences. In fact, in the name of our enrichment standards, we occasionally teach stuff that might not be part of the state standards at all. We exalt academic freedom.

This is how we integrate the arts and value kids for their ability to sing or play the guitar. It is how we teach them about the stock market when no one is looking. We celebrate the multiple intelligences and provide children with authentic opportunities to discover what they are really, *really* good at.

And sometimes they discover it.

Finally, the *Habits of Mind* represent our collective study skills, attitudes, efforts, and expectations. They contribute to a student's character and ability to learn. They emphasize personal organization and goal setting. These are the habits of mind that address learning and study skills and that inspire effort from engaged learners.

Ours is not a linear curriculum. It is not defined by a textbook, nor is it solely defined by a test. Rather, the sum total of all the billions of separate state standards are reviewed, prioritized, and woven together—even if inadvertently—in a tapestry designed by teachers for real learning.

CHALLENGER

Element Five: We Identify and Share the Most Effective Research-based Instructional Strategies.

A few minutes before noon on January 28, 1986, some of my students casually walked through the door at the beginning of my fourth period creative writing class at Muirlands Junior High School and told me the space shuttle had just exploded.

"That's not funny, guys," I said. "There are astronauts on that thing."

"No, we aren't joking. We watched it in Mr. Anderson's class. It exploded when it took off."

"Oh, my God. Isn't this the flight that had the teacher on it?"

"Yeah...Christa McAuliffe. They all died."

And I swallowed hard and tried to teach that day as a tribute to Christa McAuliffe, even though my heart wasn't in it. Later I went home and watched the images on television...over and over and over. I wanted to write her students a note...or the whole world a note. I wanted to write Christa McAuliffe a note but I knew she wouldn't get it now. So I did the next best thing and encouraged my class to write a reflective, free verse poem about the event. It was our therapy and our collective release. In lieu of a card, we sent one that we liked to Christa McAuliffe's students in Massachusetts. It is called "We Look Up Like Children":

> *We chase the stars and planets-*
> *but we cannot catch them.*
>
> *We look up like children,*
> *Ride primitive rocketry*
> *into the void of distant worlds-*
> *but we cannot reach them.*
>
> *We dream like Ponce de Leon and Columbus*

and Sir Francis Drake,
but for them the worlds were flat...
and they couldn't change them.

We grow and prosper and
train new generations to try and touch the stars-
but we cannot own them.

So we rode God's silver promise,
chased by walls of flame
that pushed us nearer to His light.

We had barely pierced the dark mystery
of a sky Galileo mapped,
And in reaching for the stars...
America exploded into an angry ball of hydrogen.

In reaching for the stars...
we became one;
—a bursting supernova—

and white crystal trails of spent rocket fuel,
like streaming tentacles,
formed a giant scorpion in the Florida sky

And the world watched in wonder as
a hundred thousand television replays answered nothing—

Except that the earth and sky ARE flat
when God slams the door.

It was the best we could do by way of tribute to this crazy teacher who agreed to ride a rocket for Ronald Reagan's contribution to our work in public education.

"Hey, cowboys...I've got an idea that could really inject some life into public education and the space shuttle program at the same time. Let's send a teacher up on the next Challenger flight!"

We've all had teachers who we can't quite imagine strapped into an astronaut suit. And we've had teachers we wished they would send into space. But mostly it was a bizarre idea that Reagan seemed to have gotten away with, even after the disastrous results. Maybe because it had so much potential.

Maybe because the real lesson was this:

If you want to teach well...and you want to have a deep and life-long impact on your students...and you want to affect real change in children...and you want to inspire and motivate even the most distracted learners...have some courage. Take a different path. Take everything you have ever learned about teaching methodology and flush it. Flush your seating charts and lesson plans and quizzes. Flush those sorry stinkin' textbooks. Be willing to engage your students, even if you have to do so from the depths of outer space.

Christa McAuliffe did. There were many cool ideas and lessons designed to be delivered from the rocket as she hurtled through the universe. The kids would have listened, too. Even the ones screwing around in the back of the room would have gone home that night and looked up into the heavens to try and see if they could see their teacher. Aside from the spectacular explosion that caused Ronald Reagan and NASA to scrap Christa's lesson plans for the day, her legacy to the teaching profession is rooted in her courage. Not just the courage and blind faith required to ride a rocket filled with enough hydrogen fuel to blow up a small country, but the courage to engender powerful *learning* by any means necessary.

The end justifies the means. Teaching becomes a little more scientific when the learning outcomes matter.

So twenty years later Barbara Morgan collected all of Christa McAuliffe's cool lesson ideas and a few of her own and headed back into space. It seems like President George W. Bush has always wanted to be just like Ronald Reagan so he was all for launching America's first intergalactic substitute teacher on a rocket. Even if they did launch in mid-August.

I wondered if President George W. Bush knew that most of the kids would have paid attention to a teacher-astronaut providing lessons via shuttle-cam if only they had not been right in the middle of their summer vacation. They were at the freakin' beach while Professor Morgan was hard at work. But like all courageous teachers she will still leave her legacy and her students will experience their deepest learnings precisely when they are ready.

The rest they'll find on YouTube.

BLACK BELT

When I was forty-five years old I earned a black belt in Tae Kwon

Do. My children and my wife are black belts too. We took our final test for the black belt on the same day, and that was by design. We wanted to share a common goal as a family...work together, push one another, and model an attribute called *determination*. It took five years, a colorful assortment of different belts and injuries and lot of patience and perseverance, but we achieved the goal together.

One thing about the martial arts that has always fascinated me is that you can teach all sorts of people how to defend themselves. One minute they're slinking around afraid of their houseplants and the next thing you know they're chopping holes in the side of brick buildings with an elbow strike. I saw a lot of students come through our studio, and in time, they each began to evince a transformation from a total dork to something resembling an athlete.

There are many forms of martial arts with origins in all parts of the world. Some are centuries old. Some are new hybrid fighting events sanctioned for the octagon on late-night television. But the great secret of teaching the martial arts is that they are taught according to *how people learn*! And since human beings all learn in different and unique ways, it helps that the instructional methodology is varied. It is constructive, experiential, kinesthetic, and multimodal. Students learn a rich and relevant curriculum. They learn through discipline, focused study, and effort.

One additional feature of the martial arts is that they are goal-driven. Students aspire to learn the curriculum that will get them to the next belt. They know the learning objectives that correspond to each belt color, master the curriculum competencies, demonstrate that mastery in a performance-based demonstration, and then move to the next level. In the process, the idea of the black belt and all it represents, begins to have meaning.

One compelling incentive for me as we gradually became more skilled in Tae Kwon Do, was envisioning a family portrait with all of us in our black belts and crisp new *do boks*. Not long after our black belt ceremony and celebration, we scheduled an appointment at a photography studio and had some fantastic family shots taken. One of the photographs is on my office wall. There is another in our living room. And we each carry a wallet-sized picture with us to commemorate the power of a family goal.

You cannot earn a black belt through a freeze-dried curriculum. There must be sweat and blood and deep, deep fatigue in every muscle and bone. The black belt is only a symbol of the learning. It shaped our lives together as a family. It drew us closer. But in the bright and vibrant family portraits...the black belts are merely a prop. They did not bind us as much as the love and common experience of learning together binds us. And they did not motivate us as much as the vision of some day sitting as a family, cinched in ancient black warrior belts, all together for a cheesy portrait studio.

The learning was on such an intensely spiritual level, it will forever shape and filter the way we each experience our world and one another. And it changed the way I think about Powerful Teaching: it must be personalized, rigorous, and focused on the skills that matter.

BREAKING BREAD

Ultimately, our teachers have the freedom to teach anything they choose, any way they want to teach it. They can ignore the standards, the critical few, the curriculum frameworks and the giant state assessments looming on the horizon. They can ignore the volumes of research that identify the most effective instructional strategies. Academic freedom and individual autonomy are the essence of the charter movement. At least at Mueller Charter School.

Of course, so is the demand for academic results. We have all discovered that the more skilled our teachers are in utilizing effective instructional strategies, the higher the achievement of our students will be.

So even before we knew what the most effective instructional strategies were for Mueller Charter School, we developed a system for training our teachers. We declared that every Friday was a modified day for students, and we send them home at 12:15. Knowing that sending 1000 students out into the mid-day is a huge inconvenience for our parents, we promised that we would use every Friday afternoon as an opportunity to contribute to the professional competence of our teachers. And so we do.

We tap into our charter budget and cater lunch for every meeting. Our sessions begin with informal, relaxed time for teachers and staff to unwind at the end of a challenging week, to sit down and break bread together. It is quality time. There is always laughter and conversation. Always music.

We use the opportunity to celebrate the week. We celebrate our students and we celebrate each other. We acknowledge the birthdays, the engagements, the marriages, the births of new babies. We occasionally share in the loss of a parent or loved one and offer support for our colleagues who may be experiencing difficulties outside of El Milagro.

And we keep pounding the drums to sustain our momentum on the march toward our mission. Every Friday features opportunities for teachers to share promising practices, to collaborate on ways to improve student work, or to set short-term grade-level goals. But the main focus is on sharing effective instructional strategies.

Over the past few years we have incorporated extensive, ongoing training in multiple disciplines:

- Balancing our approach to literacy;
- Developing a strong school-wide writing program;
- Balancing math instruction;
- Integrating the multiple intelligences into daily lessons;
- Developing more effective strategies for English language learners;
- Integrating strategies for promoting critical thinking across all curricula;
- Understanding brain-based learning theory;
- Learning Marzano's nine most effective instructional methods;
- Teaching to children's unique learning styles; and
- Infusing cooperative learning strategies as a method for building student engagement.

And the training continues. Every week. Without exception. We literally set the agenda for how we incorporate Powerful Teaching methodology into our classrooms. It is highly effective for several reasons:

- Everyone contributes to the topics;
- Our teachers lead the sessions;
- We immediately implement new strategies;
- We expedite the learning curve for brand-new teachers;
- We see immediate results; and
- The confidence and competence of our teachers continues to grow.

That's just one feature of the ongoing effort to enhance the competency of our teachers. They also work in grade-level teams to improve their instructional methods. They work in vertical teams—teams with representatives from every grade level—to share learnings and ideas that are not necessarily a function of the grade or age of students. They visit each other's classrooms and other schools. They attend workshops and conferences of their own choosing. They pursue National Board Certification status and advanced degrees. It all adds up. We know that great education comes from great teaching so we invest heavily in their skills.

We can't take for granted that our teachers learned any of these things during their student teaching or while they were taking classes in preparation to be teachers. So at Mueller Charter School we build on the foundation that our new teachers come with. We cultivate the Seven Gifts. It is a work in progress. Whether someone has taught for a week or for twenty years, our students are depending on their teachers to be lifelong learners. They expect them to show up on Friday, have a few cheese enchiladas, and relax a little. But then they expect them to get to work on their bag of tricks and improve their instructional skills in time for class on Monday!

Along with the specific strategies for improving teaching practice, there are some other consistent themes that weave through our work on Fridays. They have accumulated over time. We seem to absorb them as each school year plays out and our mission continues to elude us. Those themes, which ultimately shape the instructional strategies used at Mueller Charter School, include these:

Differentiated Instruction. We continue to explore new strategies for differentiating and personalizing instruction for our students. We know how diverse our classrooms are. We also recognize the difficulty inherent in managing thirty different learners who have thirty unique sets of needs. It can be daunting. But it can be done.

Our formative assessments quantified the wide range of skills and abilities that are present in every one of our classrooms. Every child is a unique learner. One size does not fit all. The data lead us to an inescapable conclusion: our instructional methodology has to be designed around *differentiation*. And mastering strategies for differentiation will be *the most significant and impactful innovation that Mueller Charter School has experienced to date*! For all our innovation, there is virtually nothing that compares with a system designed to revolutionize *how teachers teach*. It is more complicated, more difficult, more exhausting. But nothing we do will push us closer to getting 90% of our students to grade level. So it is our highest priority in our training.

Technology. We continue to weave in state of the art solutions in education software and tools for better assessments. We now have hundreds of laptops, high speed wireless Internet, iPods, document cameras, and access to computers beyond the school day. In low income communities there is a technology divide and we are compelled to fill the gap. Our teachers are resourceful. They write grants. They experiment. They bring the world into the classroom and enrich our students' lives...by any means necessary.

Teacher Efficacy. Teachers have to believe in their students but they have to believe in each other too. They have to have confidence in their expertise and in their ability to get their children to grade level. We never let our teachers forget that we believe in them and that we believe they are in the right place. We cannot be successful with teachers who lack the skills or the confidence to compete in a system that demands excellence...especially a system that does not prescribe the way.

Rigor. We never stop talking about RIGOR. It is difficult to ramp up the RIGOR in a school that has spent decades resigned to mediocrity...because it is easier to be easier. And it is easier to be onerous.

So we reinforce the notion that instruction has to be RIGOROUS in every classroom, every day. We define RIGOR as challenging children just beyond what they (or anyone else) believe is possible for them to do. But more specifically, a RIGOROUS curriculum features at least four characteristics: 1) the depth and integrity of inquiry, 2) sustained focus and persistence, 3) critical thinking at all levels of the taxonomy, and 4) and a willingness to test and re-test hypotheses.

We use the term *RIGOR* so often, it becomes a lens through which teachers design virtually every learning activity and experience during the course of the day.

Focus. The Pareto Principle, borrowed from the business world, states that you should spend 80% of your time on 20% of the tasks that will yield the greatest results toward achieving your organizational mission. The 20% is known as the *critical few*.

Our *critical few* include the standards, skills, and competencies that our students must learn to achieve at grade level. They are nonnegotiable. We align all of our systems around teaching and assessing the degree to which our students master their critical few. They are so urgent that they define for us what it means to focus.

Research-based Strategies. We constantly reflect on our instruction:

What works? Who says?

Why do we use those word walls?

What does the research say about homework in third grade?

Why did you decide to put these samples of student work on the wall?

What are the best computer applications to infuse into your learning centers?

We keep asking questions, even when there are no answers. Even when we don't really care what the answer is. We want to stimulate professional reflection and an insistence that everything we do in the classroom is proven to be effective in reliable research.

As a result, our instructional program reflects the state of the art:

- Some classrooms "loop" and stay with the same teacher for multiple years.
- We maintain an extended year with over 200 instructional days.
- Parents have an option to place their children in an "ungraded" multiage program where student groupings are not based on artificial grade distinctions.
- We created a middle school designed to give young teens an opportunity to stay at Mueller Charter School instead of going on to the junior high. We combine the personal relationships and skills at integrating around curricular themes that elementary teachers are known for, with the deeper content expertise of secondary teachers. It is a leadership academy designed to prepare students for advanced placement courses when they reach high school.
- Our middle school classrooms are gender-based so that students can learn without the dynamics that so often influence behaviors among adolescent boys and girls.
- When our sixth-graders go off to a one-week Outdoor Education camp, our seventh-graders spend the week touring the campuses of each of the major colleges in San Diego: University of San Diego, San Diego State University, UC San Diego, Point Loma College, Cal State San Marcos.
- During the same week, our eighth-graders visit universities in Los Angeles, including USC and UCLA.

- We have a school-wide writing focus featuring seventy-five minutes of writing every day.
- Every week begins with a Monday assembly where we celebrate students' birthdays, students' perfect attendance, and students' performances.
- We designed a "wheel" schedule that provides every teacher with prep time while outstanding intern teachers conduct lessons in theater, visual arts, and physical education.
- Our students have access to the very latest technology from classroom computers, to iPods, document cameras, laptops and high-speed wireless Internet.
- We provide students with the opportunity to extend learning after school and on Saturdays through computer-based instructional systems.
- We even conduct our own action research on everything from use of instructional time, to learning styles, and homework. If we don't know the answers, we look 'em up. We ask. We consult. And we find wisdom in the strangest places.

So when we struggled with coherence on the issue of homework, we found Yogi.

YOGI ON HOMEWORK

Yogi Berra is now known more for the goofy things he says than he is for playing baseball. His Bronx Bomber malapropos and post-WWII philosophy is Norman Rockwell in a can of Copenhagen. It's baseball. And baseball players aren't often real bright.

But when asked about what the Yankees could do to increase fan attendance at their home games he shrugged and said, "If the people ain't gonna come out to the ballpark...you can't stop 'em."

I don't know what he did next. My guess? He smoked a cigarette, ate a few hoagies, and went out that afternoon and hit two doubles in another Yankee win.

Fifty years before Sports Center and twenty-four-hour new services, Yogi's comments somehow grew wings and flew above us. They were passed down from generation to generation for no good reason other than to punctuate otherwise meaningless dialogue...as in..."*You know what Yogi says...*"

Then the other person is supposed to nod as if to confirm that he knew what Yogi said. But actually not even Yogi knew what he said half the time, even right after he said it. So Yogi-isms were born and you have to think it was a pure accident of baseball history that arrogant New York baseball writers went back to the office after picking up the fragments of another tortured Yogi comment and twisted them into the evening's news line. And pretty soon Yogi's language was bigger than what he really said about the game...and what he *said* about the game became bigger than the game.

So Yogi said, "I want to thank you for making this day necessary," and he said, "It ain't over till it's over"...and he said, "The future ain't what it used to be"...and he said, "When you come to a fork in the road—take it." And by saying those things he endeared himself to generations of baseball fans who still stand in line and ask him to sign their pictures and baseballs and old yellow *New York Times* articles where they had circled some other silly thing he said.

In the meantime, many years later at Mueller Charter School, we came to a fork in the road. So we took it. On the logic and twisted wisdom about people coming to the ballpark, we solved a homework dilemma that was older than Yogi himself.

We struggle with homework, with all of its forms and any of its relevance. We struggle with getting it back, with giving too much, with not giving enough, with students who have no structure or help at home. We struggle interpreting the academicians who say it is essential for independent learners and others who say it is a waste of children's time when they could be doing things that are more productive with heir families.

When it comes to homework, it is as if everybody is right, and everybody is wrong.

So after Maureen DeLuca had tried everything else to get her fifth-graders to consistently do the homework she assigned, she applied Yogi's thinking: "If they ain't gonna do their homework...you can't stop 'em."

Oh. That explains it. It is no wonder that warnings, lectures, phone calls home, detentions, loss of privileges, loss of recess, and public floggings were no deterrent.

So Maureen DeLuca tried another equally illogical strategy: "If the kids won't do their homework...I won't let them!" And that solved a problem that is as old as organized schools. She stopped badgering and punishing children for not doing their homework, and simply *forbid* them from doing it.

"Tonight's homework is explained here in the packet. Jorge,

Angela, and Saul...you missed several assignments so I will not accept yours...you may do whatever you want with the packet."

"What do you mean I can't do it?"

"You didn't do the activity on integers...so you are not eligible for this assignment."

"That's not fair. I want to do it."

"Well, you can do it. I didn't say you couldn't. You just won't be eligible to submit it. It is like being declared ineligible for the game Friday. You can go. You just aren't gonna play."

"Well, I'm gonna do it anyway."

Such is Powerful Teaching, where even the most sacred cows of pedagogy are sometimes led into the veterinarian's office for an occasional rectal exam. Even homework.

Two things had to happen: First, Maureen DeLuca had to change the nature of her homework assignments. She had to think deeply about the purpose of homework as an exercise in independent practice. What motivates children to learn independently? What kinds of assignments lead to creative and critical thinking? What compels children to engage passionately in meaningful activities that influence their learning?

We all know: the most learning takes place when children are presented with activities that are relevant, rigorous, challenging, fun, interesting, and that appeal to the multiple intelligences and learning modalities. There are significantly higher levels of motivation and work completion when children are offered choices.

Like most teachers, when Maureen DeLuca analyzed what she was asking her students to do for homework at night, she realized it didn't fit any of these descriptions. It sometimes included boring, repetitious, mindless math operations, vocabulary sentences, and questions at the end of a textbook chapter—the kind of crap we have asked kids to do because someone made us do it when we were their age. And we didn't learn much from it either...except perhaps some lessons, by indirection, on how to organize your time and complete mindless and mundane tasks in the face of far better alternatives.

So our own action research, by way of Yogi Berra, recommends that you analyze what you ask your students to do for homework. That's what Maureen DeLuca did. Present activities that are even more interesting than video games and music videos. Compete with the technology. Use the technology. Be mindful of their time. Model creativity. They can't be good problem solvers if they aren't provided with good problems to solve.

And if you finally come to a fork in the road...take it.

THE GAME

Element Six: Teachers Use Integrated Assessment Systems to Leverage Change

In public education we used to keep score and pretend that winning wasn't important. Just like in Little League baseball where there is the illusion of inclusiveness and sportsmanship and opportunity; where the rules are watered down just enough to allow total dorks to play on the same field with virtual progenies. We pretend that the season is all about participation and the spirit of teamwork. But at the same time, league officials are already grinding the rosters looking for a core of elite twelve-year-olds who can take them all the way to Williamsburg.

It is about winning!!!

Just not for everybody.

And so it is with schools. For decades we have celebrated American public schools as the paragon of democracy and opportunity. Meanwhile kids were failing in droves. Kids were getting pushed out of our classrooms and standing in the streets with their book bags in hand, wondering what in the hell happened and why school didn't work for them. We have always been led to believe that the difference between the winners and losers is a function of those who *want* to succeed and those who don't. Children have been sifted and sorted along lines of race and social class and lineage so consistently, that pretty soon generations of new teachers begin to think that some kids can learn and some can't. They begin to believe that entire racial or ethnic groups are limited in their capacity to think and create and excel academically.

Now we know better. And now we know that the difference between the winners and losers lies as much in the quality of the teachers as in any other factor. The demand for the *Seven Gifts* keeps coming back. And while most teachers may enter the profession with a decent foundation in the elements of Powerful Teaching that have been presented in this chapter, it is the rare skill set required by this last element that will truly engender academic excellence for children and their schools. Our teachers must be masters at generating and using data through an assessment system that is simultaneously summative, formative, and diagnostic.

Chapter 11 will describe our integrated system of summative and formative assessments while Chapter 12 presents the extraordinarily effective diagnostic model called the "Resiliency Quadrant System."

These are the *Six Elements of Powerful Teaching*: Core values.

Classroom climate and a culture of high expectations. Classroom leadership. Engaging curricula delivered by way of skillful instructional design. Multi-dimensional assessment models that allow us to constantly monitor and adjust children's learning.

There is plenty that we don't know, too.

But for now there is mysterious power in this pyramid.

It's more than a road map. It is the gospel.

CHAPTER ELEVEN

How We Know We're Winning

Test fast, fail fast, adjust fast.

—Tom Peters

THE FIFTH SYSTEM

We grew our capacity to measure progress, to make midcourse adjustments, and to harness organizational momentum in pursuit of the mission.

WILLIAMSPORT

I've been conditioned to win. It's been in me since I was a young athlete growing up in San Diego: if they are going to keep score...I want to win.

There are all kinds of axioms and mindsets designed to help us all feel better about NOT winning. Like "It doesn't matter whether you win or lose...it's how you play the game."

Really? What would Yogi say?

My rule of thumb is that if we are keeping score, I intend to win. If we are playing baseball, shooting pool, throwing darts, or laughing through a game of Pictionary with Grandma...I am going to do everything I can to get the best score and the best outcome.

I coached my son's Little League team for four years and was under constant criticism and scrutiny because I coached our boys to win. We didn't cheat. We didn't place our athletes at risk. We didn't yell or pressure them....but we played hard and we played to win. Moreover, we taught them *how* to win because to an eleven-year-old, knowing how to win is rarely self-evident. They had to learn how to compete, how to rise above adversity, how to come from behind and how to hold a lead.

Most of the criticism came from the parents whose children were never on my team. Somehow, we were violating the spirit of Little League by playing each game like it mattered.

At the same time, the league was investing in a bigger scoreboard and trying to figure out how we could get our all stars all the way to Williamsport and the Little League Baseball World Series. They kept the standings and the statistics, had an elaborate play-off format, and crowned the winning team as champions. And we were the champions. But our players were confused because it seemed like winning was only important to the adults whose children played on the winning team. Everyone else criticized us for trying too hard.

Ironically our team lost a lot of games during the regular season. We lost a lot of games we should have won and then used those games to continue the lessons on how to win. The last regular game of the season was against a team that beat us on opening day and then thrashed us two more times during the season. We managed to win in the bottom of the sixth inning and squeaked into the playoffs to face three other teams—against whom we had a combined record of one win and eleven losses! But in the play-offs, we beat each team, one by one, and were crowned the league champions. Later I learned that we had the worst regular season win-loss record of any league champion in the history of Tierrasanta Little League baseball. But it didn't matter...because we won the games that mattered.

Our kids learned many critical lessons for competing in sports and in life. Just to send me a message, I was passed over as the all-star coach and only two of our players made the all-star team. Politics or no politics, in America, we consistently love athletes who win...almost as much as we love to see them defeated.

I am so conditioned to win that when the State of California first implemented its assessment system designed to pit schools against one another and publicly hold them all accountable...I was okay with it. In fact I thought it was pretty exciting. I was on board when most other administrators were convinced it was just another in a long line of passing whims from Sacramento. Others felt the whole plan would get tied up in the courts because it was so patently unfair. Some were totally oblivious to its portents. Most educators just didn't know what to do because they didn't know how to compete.

I was in my first year as director of the Juvenile Court and Community Schools when we were told that our kids—as fragile, and freaked out, and distracted, and damaged as they were—were no exception and they would have to take the standardized tests too.

They would have to demonstrate that they were actually learning something.

"Fine with me," I said. "Just don't complain if we play to win. Don't complain if we qualify to go to Williamsport with a bunch of overachievers who never quit, who scrap with the best of them, and who seem to win the games that matter."

BASS ACKWARD

The Stanford Achievement Test (SAT-9) was designated as the test du jour by the California Legislature in 1998, even against the advice of educators who complained that the assessment was norm referenced, and that the national norm group did not resemble the children of California. It was a prepackaged, off-the-shelf product that was found in the frozen food section of the state department commissary. And although it looked like stuff that wouldn't hurt you, it bore only a faint resemblance to the content standards that had only recently become the main diet of California schools.

No matter, all children in grades two through eleven were required to take it. In the meantime, additional content standards were developed and educators genuinely sought to align the assessments with what was actually being taught in their classrooms. In former Governor Wilson's zeal to get some kind of testing system off the ground, we launched a rocket into orbit ass backwards!

It would have made much more sense to first develop curriculum standards, then create the frameworks that assisted teachers and parents in understanding how those standards should be addressed. Then, once everyone became familiar with the standards, a statewide assessment system could be developed that would measure the degree to which children at each grade level were developing competency in those standards. But maybe Wilson knew what, deep down, we all knew.

For too long in California, we could not tell with certainty whether our students were learning, or if they were learning what they were supposed to be learning. That was by design. Without target standards, without a system to measure students' progress toward the standards, and without a common metric to compare schools...no one really knew who was learning and who wasn't. In fact, learning was optional...so teaching was optional. It was an enterprise with no accountability, and we were using the public's money to do it.

For decades, in fact, assessments were only used to sift and sort, stuff the bell curve in the middle, and ultimately provide a rationale for why some kids go through the gates and on to higher education and others join the military or look for employment in the fence and tile department at Home Depot. As a result, there was no common comparison—no way to determine if our kids were learning on par with students in Ogden, Utah, or Providence, Rhode Island. During that time, California public schools were ridiculed as flakey and unchallenging. Fair or not, they were the real life models for *Fast Times at Ridgemont High*, when Spicoli falls out of his van and into the parking lot, enshrouded in a thick blanket of smoke from his morning bong—ready for school!

Not anymore.

Even a rocket spinning bass ackwards into space is an improvement over an otherwise moribund system where there was no accountability and no metrics at all. And maybe it took a wild rocket to light up the darkness.

The SAT-9 was the placeholder for five years until it gave way to the California Standards Test in 2002. By now, an aggressive accountability system called STAR (still another acronym for California's Standardized Testing and Reporting Program) was in full flight and educators knew it was not going away.

As both a teaching tool, and as a means of keeping score, the California Standards Test has proven to be far more useful than the SAT-9. Children are no longer compared to a national norm group, but rather, to clear performance criteria. Upon taking the test in language arts and math, students are designated as:

- Far Below Basic
- Below Basic
- Basic
- Proficient, or
- Advanced

The very definition of "at grade level" is now universally accepted as students who scored *Proficient* or *Advanced*. At least in California. Now there is a target.

Each year, the STAR assessment system has steadily evolved. There are now additional writing tests for fourth and seventh grade; science tests for fifth grade and eighth grade, additional norm-referenced components for third and seventh grade, and modified test versions for special education students and English-language learners.

Simultaneously, the state's Department of Education improved its own systems for delivering reliable and timely results back to the schools.

In the initial years of the STAR system, the objective was not to provide data to schools but to hold them accountable for the academic achievement of their students. On the theory that California's schools needed a massive kick right in the ass, politicians, state school board members, and legislators were in search of a method for sorting between schools that got academic results and schools that merely housed children as a precondition for generating the necessary ADA to cover teachers' salaries. They knew they would get resistance from the powerful teachers union and from the critics who thought our kids were pansies and that testing them all would constitute an assault on their collective psyches.

California had been through these testing wars before. There was always somebody who thought the assessment system was too invasive or too liberal or too cosmic or too hard or just too damn inconvenient to administer. And they were coming out of the woodwork now. There were advocates for virtually every group of kids on the planet lobbying to have them excluded from the STAR testing system: GATE kids, special ed kids, immigrant kids, new kids, fundamentalist kids, fat kids, poor kids, dumb kids, foster kids, incarcerated kids, vegetarian kids, alcoholic kids, kids of alcoholics, crack kids, kids of kids...kids that fit into multiple categories and kids that didn't fit anywhere.

The ground rules of the STAR system addressed all of these advocates once and for all when they said: EVERY CHILD GETS TESTED! No exceptions. No excuses. No "yeah-buts." So quit asking.

"Excuse me but I represent children born to unwed software developers who don't come home from work until late at night and..."

"They all get tested."

"But my clients are a little different; they are children whose parents are in the service and..."

"They get tested too."

"What about my clients? They are part-time circus performers and some have trouble waking up when..."

"Are they enrolled in a public school in California?"

"Yeah-but..."

"No yeah-buts. They all get tested."

THE HALL

And the excuses rolled.

I was the director of the Juvenile Court and Community Schools in the first year of implementation of the SAT-9. I had teachers and administrators who couldn't even *spell* the word accountability much less survive a system that would now demand results. When we saw that the rules of the game required that "everybody plays," we would have been justified in launching our sanctimonious outrage toward Sacramento.

And the court school leaders complained in one unified and timorous voice:

"It is 'educational malpractice' to force our students to take this test. They are only temporarily assigned to our schools. Most of them will be in our programs for less than three months. Some will be here for a week. They are going be included in our data by pure chance and timing. And they're so damn fragile! They're kids who have been expelled by other schools, or taken from their parents and placed in protective custody, or children in detox, or fifteen-year-olds raising babies, or child-aged murderers waiting in *the hole* to be tried as adults. How focused can these kids really be? And, anyway, what could the data possibly tell us? What adjustments would we make in our schools, knowing that they are leaving tomorrow?"

Compelling arguments.

Nevertheless, the official reply from the State of California was uncompromising and consistent for all of the Juvenile Court and Community School educators who tried to lobby for exclusion from the assessment process: "Tough. They all get tested."

Schools all across America have similar horror stories. They all have kids who should not be tested and they all have kids whose test results cannot be attributed to anything their teachers have done or not done. And they all have kids they just can't reach for one legitimate reason or another.

The concern and even angry indignation of court school administrators, teachers unions, and lobbyists was palpable. But educators are nothing if not compliant. They dutifully administered the tests to everybody and prepared their excuses for the results that were inevitable.

And the bureaucrats in Sacramento did something they had not done in recent memory. In the face of very understandable, well-intentioned, and articulate resistance...they stood their ground.

"Every student. Every year," they said. "Even in Juvenile Hall. Results matter."

The folks in Sacramento conceded that there would be problems with the data from the SAT-9 because it doesn't align with the state's emerging set of academic standards. They were doing the whole assessment thing backwards and they knew it.

"Hang in there," they said. "Let the system evolve." And so we did.

We tested kids who desperately didn't want to be tested. And likewise, we desperately didn't want their results associated with us.

But while the Juvenile Court and Community School directors from throughout the state of California convened to develop an alternative system, I had a different idea.

I had the notion that perhaps this testing system could actually help us develop a stronger and more responsive program for high-risk youth who needed us the most. Of course our data sucked. We tested over 2,500 kids in some eighty-five different programs that we were operating at the time. We had entire grade levels scoring in single digits. We had kids in the hall carving their initials into the answer sheets. They were spitting on them, tearing them up, staring at them, or just defiantly writing "fuck you" in the unmistakable Old English calligraphy of Latino street gangs.

When the data did come back, I analyzed it backward and forward. I created tables and graphs. I made hypotheses and recommendations. We had forums and group discussions and brainstorming sessions with teachers, judges, probation officers, business leaders—anybody who had a theory on why our students' test scores were so shockingly low.

We found some interesting trends that got people's attention too. We were able to demonstrate through the data that the longer students were with us the better they did on this test. We were able to demonstrate that kids in San Diego's Juvenile Court Schools outperformed the kids in the Juvenile Court Schools of LA, Oakland, Bakersfield, and twenty other counties. Apples to apples. We pointed to our glaring weaknesses and glaring strengths and at least had some serious discussion about what the numbers said about our programs and the quality of our teaching. Maybe the data was flawed but it opened the discussion about the quality of our services and how our students respond to those services for the first time. And how we can improve.

"What does this data tell us about the quality of our teaching?"

We were a perfect example of how you could grow a slow and lumbering organization—even one as fragmented and atypical as the Juvenile Court and Community Schools—if you had the right attitude, some imagination, a few colorful overhead slides, and if you knew just enough about statistics to be dangerous.

KAIZEN

STAR is not just a dipstick. It is an accountability *system*. Test results are made public in local papers and on the Internet. There is the threat of sanctions for schools that fail to show progress. The goal is continuous improvement—or as they say in Total Quality Management movement: Kaizen! Reputations, and funding and even jobs are at stake! So much is at stake they call them *high-stakes* tests. Given the emerging importance of the test results, it was evident that both educators and the general public needed help in digesting all the new data and using it to improve their schools.

So statisticians of the STAR system cleverly concocted the *Academic Performance Index*, known as the API. By feeding each school's test results into a kind of computerized results compactor, they can spew out a little three-digit number that actually quantifies the degree to which teaching and learning are improving at any given school. The API measures more than just *who* is at grade level. It reveals trends in performance improvement from school to school.

With the API, we could now compare all schools in California, or schools with similar demographics, or those critical subgroups within the same school. If we were so inclined, we could determine whether the API of Latinas who were in the country for less than twelve months was higher than African-American boys' whose parents had at least a high school education.

With more consistent metrics like the API, performance goals could be established...and so they were. The rules of the STAR game say that every school in California has to eventually get to the API promised land of 800. And in the meantime, any school that has not yet hit 800, has to achieve a higher API than the one that was achieved the year before. Continuous improvement. Kaizen.

The Total Quality Management trend that had briefly blown through schools like a soft fish sneeze back in the 1990s—had come back by with a vengeance. And this time it blew fences and trees over. It lifted small barnyard animals and deposited them in the next county.

TEXAS DUST

In January of 2002, President George W. Bush decided to be the next in a very long line of politicians who wanted to improve, change, embarrass or dismantle the free public school system in America. So he authorized the law called "No Child Left Behind".

No one could disagree with the mission or the metaphor to leave no child behind. And on a national scale, centering educators on that mission may have been the one significant contribution of this federal act. But ultimately, as a method of eliminating the achievement gap in our country, it has not worked.

As midterm elections rolled forward in the fall of 2006, many communities no longer trusted President George W. Bush or his appointees or his ideas or his intentions. Iraq was a disaster. New Orleans, a city that symbolized the very soul of America, was still entombed in caked delta mud from the day the rivers of incompetence and blatant racism broke down the levee. Some of the leaders of George W. Bush's Republican Party who had made their bones on their claim to family values—turned out to be as morally corrupt as any group of politicians in our nation's history. And in San Diego, gas was so expensive, it cost our teachers a day's wages just to drive to school.

More to the issue, after four years of implementing NCLB, our students had not demonstrated any significant academic gains. Not in math, not in reading. In fact, when the academic growth of school children in the U.S. was measured over that period of time, an alarming statistic surfaced. While white children may have shown modest gains, African-American children and Latino children showed much less. The achievement gap persisted. If NCLB inspired any academic achievement, it worked only for white kids. Hmmmmmm.

Iraq? Katrina? Unemployment? Border fences? Hypocrisy and corruption? Racial profiling?

No child left behind?

"Excuse me, Mr. President. When you say NO child left behind... did you mean to say no *white* child left behind? Because it seems that the NCLB Act merely perpetuates the achievement gap."

By the 2006-07 school year, President George W. Bush's No Child Left Behind legislation was under major scrutiny. The complaints had steadily grown. Early dissent from the likes of California's Juvenile Court and Community School leaders had long since been eclipsed by the class action law suits coming from school systems and states all across the country. Schools simply didn't have the resources to accomplish the goals of NCLB. No amount of cajoling or bullying or public humiliation could change that fact. Besides, the root causes of the achievement gap are far more complex than any school district could ever hope to overcome on their own.

Much of the inspiration for President George W. Bush's federal intrusion into public education law came from his experience in Texas where, according to the pre-election profile, the schools had excelled under his leadership as governor. President George W. Bush fancied that the Texas public school success story could be replicated all over the country. We just had to get tough. NCLB created threats and sanctions for schools that could cause them to lose federal dollars if they don't get Texas-sized results. So they sort of had the schools by the nads.

What most people didn't know was that states are afforded the prerogative to determine the best way to educate their own children. NCLB allows each state to create or utilize its own accountability and assessment system to measure students' progress. And *individual states determine their own criteria for being at grade level.*

When the researchers at the Northwest Evaluation Association analyzed each state's threshold for grade-level proficiency, they found that to be *at grade level* in South Carolina required third-grade children to score in the top 33% of students in that state—or the 67th percentile. That is the highest threshold in America. The second highest threshold is in California where students must score among the top 39% of children in the state to be considered *at grade level*—the 61st percentile.

In President George W. Bush's home state of Texas, where we were told that schools once thrived as paradigms of educational excellence under Governor George W. Bush, the threshold for being *at grade level* is the 13th percentile! In other words, a child at a school in San Antonio who takes the Texas state assessment merely needs to score on par with 87% of the children in the state to be considered *at grade level*. If they move to San Francisco the next week and the child takes the STAR and remains at the 13th percentile, they will drop like a Texas dust clod from a level called "proficient" in Austin, Texas, to "far below basic" in California.

Not to impugn the accomplishments of hard-working educators and students in the state of Texas, but the lack of a consistent measure begs the question: who is leaving whom behind? There are no common national standards for children in our schools and no common agreement on what it means to be *at grade level*. Since the threshold for being *at grade level* is higher in states like South Carolina and California, more schools appear to be failing under NCLB in those states. If the NWEA research is correct, it looks like some states have sandbagged their own teachers and kids by setting the thresholds lower. And even worse, the real target for significantly elevating the level of academic competency and achievement for all children has been obscured.

So they still get left behind. Like they did in New Orleans. And like a lot of schools are getting left behind today.

One of the features of NCLB is its schedule of unreachable benchmarks that have to be met by every school in America. Each state is required to ensure that all schools make *Adequate Yearly Progress* (AYP) as defined by NCLB. In the beginning, the bar was so low schools would trip over it as they fumbled for the light switch. They needed to get only 13.6% of their students to grade level to comply. Then the bar started to go up. By 2005 it was 24.4%. It goes to 35.2% in 2008, 56.8% in 2010, 89% in 2013 and 100% in 2014.

If a school fails to meet a threshold for any critical group (like their English-language learners for instance), they are labeled a *Program Improvement School*. In spite of whatever variables or demographics or challenges they face, they are regarded as "underperforming." Parents are informed that their child's school is a *Program Improvement School* and they can leave if they want to. There are also some ambiguous and somewhat toothless sanctions and interventions that go along with becoming a *Program Improvement School*. Eventually, a state could even take over a *Program Improvement School*.

Since the AYP threshold rises continuously higher, over time more schools will be labeled as a *Program Improvement School*. By the year 2014, just about everybody will be a *Program Improvement School*. Then opponents of public education will be able to paint all schools with a broad and ugly brush. We will all be failures by definition of President George W. Bush's unfunded mandate called No Child Left Behind. And, perhaps not so ironically, by its own definition, every child will be left behind!

In the meantime, we presume that public schools will get more kids to grade level by calling them names: "You...you...freakin'...*Program Improvement School!*" Ouch.

As if the kids and the teachers and the parents should all feel a sense of common community shame. Like they all stepped in the same big pile of crap in the yard and tracked it onto the living room rug. "Melvin! Check your shoes. Somebody just brought an ugly mess into the house!" Something about the whole Program Improvement motive just doesn't smell right.

It is the equivalent of trying to teach kids to dunk a basketball by yelling at them to jump higher. There is more to dunking a basketball than that. You have to be about 6'4", have a good vertical jump, and master the technique of slamming the ball through the hoop in mid flight. If kids don't have these characteristics they might still be able to dunk, but it is unlikely. In either case, they don't need to be yelled at. They just need the proper tools.

Schools that remain as *Program Improvement Schools* are compelled to implement interventions that nobody really knows will work. If they knew they would work, they should have told the *Program Improvement School* before they became a *Program Improvement School*.

It makes you wonder.

You think at El Milagro we don't want our kids at grade level? You think it doesn't pain us to the core to see them struggle year after year against circumstances that would bring most people to their knees? You think we are motivated by name-calling?

Remember, we see our students' faces every day. We know their names. We wipe their tears and their noses and sometimes their butts. And—with all due respect—when the president of the United States has had that experience, perhaps he will be better equipped to demand schools that can overcome the socio-economic factors that are at the root of the achievement gap; the very life conditions that his administration has so consistently ignored.

BENCH PRESS

The STAR Program is a rigorous system that places far greater demands on educators and children in California than the assessment programs in most other states. But it is far from a perfect system. The limitations are many. All schools experience the limitations in their own way, but at Mueller Charter School, we accept these limitations as ground rules and conditions of the game:

LIMITATION ONE: The assessments are almost totally focused on **language arts and math**. These are clearly not the only disciplines that define an educated person. One can be a good reader...but not well read. Children can excel on multiple choice exams, in fact, without any imagination or capacity for creative and critical thinking at all.

As schools have become more manic about achieving the artificial goals of NCLB, good teaching sometimes flies out the window in the talons of bad judgment. What gets tested gets taught...and nothing more. The curriculum becomes more fragmented and exclusionary. It becomes basic. American children deserve more than "basic."

LIMITATION TWO: The singular focus on language arts and math precludes the full celebration and development of the many **talents, interests, gifts, and skills** that children innately possess. For example: at Mueller Charter School, we are witness to children blossoming in their ability...

- To acquire and speak a foreign language
- To sing

- To compose original music
- To consistently compete and excel athletically
- To compose and deliver persuasive speeches
- To debate
- To think in a critical, creative, innovative, playful, flexible, or inventive ways
- To influence and lead others
- To effectively work in a team setting
- To design, draw, and sculpt original works
- To perform on stage in a theatrical presentation
- To inspire others
- To design a business
- To trade stocks on NASDAQ
- To explore the world through scientific methods and reasoning
- To teach others

Surely these are attributes of learned individuals as well. These are talents and interests that we seek in our own children, that we invest in and that we cultivate. What if the assessments could really measure innate talent as valued by our modern culture?

What if there was an assessment based on the student's ability to build a to-scale model of the Roman Coliseum using only Legos?

What if the task was to shoot a plastic hockey puck into a net while on rollerblades?

What if the "test" was to create an original musical score?

What if the challenge was to create intuitive computer software that could capture the essence of a Langston Hughes poem in a watercolor painting?

We know this much—if these were the assessments a very different group of students would emerge at grade level.

LIMITATION THREE: Our assessment systems reward schools that have already moved kids over the bar. They do not reward schools that are making significant progress in moving students *toward* that bar.

LIMITATION FOUR: There are still too many logistical rough spots in the implementation of California's assessment system. For example, by the time the data comes back, the students are long gone. If educators are going to be judged on their results, those results should come back immediately. If the large number of students and their mind-boggling diversity cannot be an excuse for their academic results, it should not be an excuse for Sacramento either. Develop the technology.

Turn the results around in a week so that schools can counsel their parents and students and make appropriate adjustments with teachers and curriculum. No excuses.

LIMITATION FIVE: Standardized tests are fundamentally flawed, and not necessarily reliable in the high-stakes effort to measure academic achievement.

We value athleticism and the most elite levels of talent. We invest millions of dollars every year in salaries, stadiums, and season tickets. Otherwise healthy adults leverage their middle-class lives gambling on their games. We wink as college athletes bring in millions of dollars from post-season bowl games and tournaments...and the inestimable prestige associated with being national champions. We even forgive their crimes against society. We cannot, however, abide their inability to pass standardized tests. So all athletes have to take the math and reading portions of the SAT or ACT to determine their fitness for competing in interscholastic athletics.

If we require our athletes to demonstrate a level of competence in math and reading on the SAT's, shouldn't we expect the same from literature and engineering majors? Before the university even considers them for grants or scholarships (let alone admission), English majors should have to demonstrate that they can bench press their body weight. Music and business majors should prove that they can run the forty under five seconds. Fat-assed engineering and computer science majors should have a minimum expectation of completing the mile in under six minutes. These are better predictors of health and fitness than the SAT is of college success!

LIMITATION SIX: The assessments are all in English. In spite of the fact that nearly 35% of the children in California are learning English as a second language, and in spite of the NCLB mandate that children be assessed "in their native language" to determine what they know and can do, California has stubbornly adhered to tests that determine each child's proficiency in math, reading and the ability to read and understand English. Several other states, (including President George W. Bush's home state of Texas) assess their Spanish speakers *in Spanish*. If California school children were assessed in Spanish, there would be a significant increase in the number of children adjudged to be at grade level and there would be a significant decrease in the number of schools who have been labeled "Program Improvement" schools.

LIMITATION SEVEN: The politicization of state and national testing systems may ultimately benefit everyone except the children who were supposed to be helped in the first place.

Summative data can be packaged and spun and politicized. It can be marketed so that it is digestible by the average layperson who hated math in high school and whose sole understanding of statistics is reflected in his or her fantasy baseball teams. But if the words "summative data" are used in the same sentence as statewide tests or No Child Left Behind, you can assume the motive is more political than instructional.

"Since I have been governor, our schools have improved twenty-two points on statewide tests"...and..."if you elect me I will make sure our schools are NCLB compliant and narrowing the achievement gap"...and "my opponent says he is the education senator but during his tenure, academic achievement has declined in our state!"

LIMITATION EIGHT: By conventions of the California Standards Test and its rules of administration, children are assigned tests according to their *grade level*—regardless of their *achievement level.*

The California Standards Test is designed around the presumption of competency and the expectation that children have advanced to their current grade level because they have demonstrated mastery of state standards at their previous grade. In fact, according to California Education Code, children are not supposed to advance to the next grade level unless they have demonstrated proficiency on the California Standards Test. But of course, that is not how we really organize students into grade levels nor is it how we promote them.

Students are organized into grade levels on the basis of only two factors: **the grade level they last completed and their chronological age.** Even though we know that a child's chronological age is not a predictor of academic accomplishment, readiness, motivation or capacity to learn; and even though we know that children simply learn at different rates for many different reasons—the practice persists. And even though children sometimes miss significant blocks of school or their year has been fragmented by family crises or they refuse to comply with the demands of their teachers or they are just chronically disengaged—they are promoted anyway and the practice persists.

In fact, it is evidently so important to organize students by their chronological age, that they remain with their peer group even after they have been swallowed by academic holes so deep and so dark that they can never climb out of them.

Each year, all over America, hundreds of thousands of children fail to demonstrate mastery or competence or even a degree of awareness regarding the skills and standards required for their grade level. Yet we promote them merely because they have survived to June 15. It is called *social promotion* and in picking your poison it is deemed more palatable than *retaining* kids. The preponderance of industry research warns that retention destroys children's confidence and sense of efficacy. The effects linger. Sometimes they manifest themselves in later grades, long after some 2nd grade teacher's decision that Junior just wasn't prepared to go forward with his classmates. The language of retention is ominous: we say that a child "failed" third grade, or that they were "held back", or they "had to repeat" an entire year. It is destructive.

Or so we are told.

So we just promote them. The lesser of twin evils. In so doing we perpetuate the whole "grade level paradigm"—now one of the most entrenched structures of public schooling. And in so doing, we ignore the avalanche of new research generated by a very different set of variables, namely, those unique to a **standards-based** system of teaching and learning. In fact, the practice of social promotion conflicts in every way with the data now generated by state accountability and assessment systems. That data reveals that a student who performs at a level deemed *Far Below Basic* on the California Standards Test will go on to the next grade level likely to score *Far Below Basic* again. And then on to the next. In the process, he will bring with him all of the undiagnosed learning needs and unaddressed academic gaps that he had the year before. The only variables that will have increased are his chronological age and his portfolio of failures.

Perhaps that explains why some 6.7% of California's children failed the High School Exit Exam in 2007 when they were held to a performance standard. These children are not eligible for a high school diploma. Whatever uphill battles they may have fought in the K-12 system when they were growing up, are about to become even tougher.

High schools are not always positioned to affect these outcomes because their students spend their first nine years developing an academic foundation in K-8 schools. The holes become cumulative. And they are truly proving to be catastrophic.

There is a better way.

Organize children into classrooms according to their current *academic level of mastery*—regardless of their age.

In such a system, they would remain at the same level until they *test* to the next level. Just like in the martial arts. There would be no chronological age group to chase. There would be no stigma associated with taking more time to master the standards. Nor would there be barriers to prevent students from moving ahead faster than their classmates...they wouldn't have to wait until the next school year to be challenged.

Ungraded, fluid, differentiated, performance-based classrooms.

And since there are so many standards and competencies to master at each grade level, the continuum of learning would be arranged in smaller, sequential segments.

Some kids might progress faster in math than they do in reading and, of course, that is ok. They would be challenged on the level that they need to be challenged on. Educators would be accountable for continuously moving students up to the next academic level in the sequence. No holding kids in lower levels year after year. No tracking.

Changes in the culture of learning would be immediate if children had to work toward mastery as a precondition of promotion every year. It would be noticed in improved attendance, homework production, motivation, student engagement, teacher accountability, family support, and classroom behavior.

In such a system, students would be naturally driven to rise to the next level and take greater responsibility for their own learning. Teachers would be driven to carefully analyze and diagnose every student's needs and create a plan to accelerate them. Parents would know exactly where children were on their learning continuum and would have no expectation of an automatic pass to the next grade level.

How do I know?

Because this is how we organize our students in grades two through five at Mueller Charter School. Our summative, formative and diagnostic data tells us that children are very unique as learners and that the old method of organizing them into large, age-driven grade levels is an anachronism that may have worked for old man Mueller back in the 1920's, but it doesn't work now.

Grouping children according to their level of academic proficiency, as described in California's very own education code, requires no additional expense. It is the kind of systemic innovation that you would expect to spin directly out of the STAR assessment game and the demands of No Child Left Behind. We are accelerating academic growth on the strength of our own emergent action research. That research challenges even the most entrenched practices that may have once been thought to be sacrosanct. It demonstrates that we are looking beyond just programs and methods and services. We are not just tweaking the clockworks. We're yanking out gears that are as old as time.

Nevertheless, we still have a high percentage of students who are not yet ready to move on to the next grade level. Maybe 50%. If we assign 50% of our students, some 500 of them, to continue learning for another year in the same grade, the criticism and suspicion would be relentless! Not from our students or our parents who see the same data that we see and who collaborate with us on student action plans year after year—but from those who would question our motive. If the objective is really to dramatically improve teaching and learning, and in the process, to improve the public education system as a whole, such innovations would be welcomed. But if No Child Left Behind and the STAR assessment system and all of the political posturing really has nothing to do with our children and the achievement gap, then such innovations would be considered cheating! Gaming the system for higher test scores.

And that is the irony. The most formidable safeguard of social promotion is the current culture of the extreme accountability movement itself, where the chronological age of a student is the one variable that is held as a constant and where the system is designed to produce winners and inevitable losers.

As a charter school, we might independently *organize* students for instruction at their level of mastery, but we still *assess* them according to their declared grade level. Fifth graders are sent the fifth grade test... whether they are developmentally ready or not. And a fifth grader takes the fifth grade test for *both* math and reading, even if they happen to be at a fifth grade level for one subject and a third grade level for the other.

Why? Because if children started to take state assessments on the basis of their academic proficiency level instead of their chronological grade level, they would always perform *at grade level.* By definition. The API would be obsolete. Every school would have an API in the mid-950's. There would be no Program Improvement Schools. No political capital for being the legislator or governor or president who inspired school reform even though this one innovation—grade promotion based on proficiency—could be one of the most dramatic reforms in the history of public education. The apologists for NCLB and school accountability systems would have to develop all new metrics that *really* determine whether our children are learning.

These are eight limitations that are characteristic of California's STAR assessment system, and they are likely limitations of the assessment models used all across America. Their effectiveness is a function of motive. If accountability in public education has been engineered for political or financial purposes, and if the intention never really was to eliminate the achievement gap, then, by all means, keep score with summative data while rushing kids through schools on some endless conveyor belt left over from the industrial revolution. At the end of day, the children who are least likely to benefit from such politically-motivated systems are the very children who have been left behind for generations. We reap what we sow.

The winners will be the same winners we have always had. The losers will be the poor, the disenfranchised, the children of color trapped in horrible neighborhoods with frightening schools.

And perhaps that is the biggest limitation of them all: it takes more than assessment and accountability systems designed by bureaucrats to create quality schools. It takes a village. It takes child-centered public policies and a will to do better by our kids.

BOOTSTRAPS

For forty years we have known that there is a direct correlation between a child's socioeconomic level and academic achievement. The relationship between family income and academic gains are obvious: in wealthier families, children have access to more printed reading materials, more technology, more community-based learning opportunities, more travel experiences. Furthermore, they are likely to be exposed to more highly educated adults than children who come from poorer families.

All of those factors contribute to learning readiness, worldview, and the general knowledge that a child brings in to the classroom. These are the strengths that *proficient* and *advanced* children build on. It is certainly not to say that a child from a less affluent family cannot be at grade level, but the data paints a vivid picture. At Skyline School in affluent Solana Beach, more than 90% of the children are at grade level. In western Chula Vista, where 75% of the children qualify for the federal lunch program, less than 40% are at grade level.

The achievement gap is no myth. Neither is the correlation between family income and academic achievement. So if President George W. Bush is serious about leaving no child behind, he should address the fundamental, root causes of that academic achievement gap—that is, the presence of poverty and its devastating effect on children's ability to learn.

For example, President George W. Bush could:

- Provide health care for all of my students to address the scourge of childhood obesity, diabetes, and poor nutrition;
- Ensure that every child has access to comprehensive eye exams and appropriate interventions when they are struggling just to see well enough to read;
- Ensure that every child has regular dental checkups and access to highly qualified dentists so that my students' baby teeth aren't rotting in their heads;
- Provide the funding support and infrastructure so that all of my students can attend preschool like the affluent kids at Skyline do;
- Create a way for every child in America to have a laptop and access to the Internet so that poor children aren't pushed further behind by the technology divide that favors their more affluent counterparts;
- Invest in the modernization and construction of state-of-the-art school buildings in every community in America;
- Guarantee a college education of the highest quality for all children so they are motivated to apply themselves academically;
- Eliminate unemployment so that the parents of my students can properly provide the basic necessities for their children— food, clothing shelter;
- Significantly raise the minimum wage so that our parents are not forever struggling against the tide...fighting the unwinnable battle to stay ahead of a runaway economy and its stunning indifference to the working poor.

There are probably a hundred more public policy initiatives that would have an enormous impact on the quality of children's lives and, ultimately, their level of academic achievement. We could debate the potential effect of each initiative, but of course, it ain't gonna happen anyway. Not in this America.

It is easier to put the responsibility on the schools and threaten them with sanctions if they can't close the academic gap on their own. We have the means and the resources but people like President George W. Bush believe that every person ought to pull themselves up by the bootstraps and get on with it. Even though they themselves have never lived hand to mouth they romanticize it as the American Dream:

"All kids have challenges they have to overcome as they make their way through the school system. So what if some kids have to climb an entire freakin' mountain just to get to the same place on the starting line. Life ain't always fair. Shut up and start climbing!"

So the achievement gap persists.

THE LAW OF UNINTENDED CONSEQUENCES

And then there is the *Law of Unintended Consequences.*

Perhaps no one realized when the STAR system was conceived that human intelligence is too complex to develop by prescriptions or threats of sanction. Raising children is hard enough without whacking them over the head with stupefying concentrations of math and language arts. Notwithstanding the "great books" and the Pythagorean theorem, there is, forgive me, far more to the constitution of a truly educated human being.

No one can argue that basic literacy and math skills are not important—even critical. They just aren't enough! In our relentless obsession over the basics we are ignoring the full range of children's potential gifts and talents, and by doing so, no amount of laser-like focus will get us what we want. Learning, after all, is also about intrinsic motivation, joy, personal interests and passions. For deep learning to occur, there must be an appeal to the learner. Being good at taking the tests created by the test making empire, leads only to the arrogance of privilege.... that is there for the taking anyway.

So perhaps it is an unintended consequence that:

Educational decisions are now made about individual children on the basis of these test scores. Professional reputations and perceptions of competence and caring—personified in entire school districts and communities—are made on the basis of these test scores. Federal, state, and local funding sources are sometimes parceled out on the basis of these test scores, like a parent poring over her children's report cards and handing out dollars for A's and punishments for F's.

And perhaps it is an unintended consequence that:

As the demand for accountability has increased, the external pressures from the state and federal government have caused many educators to focus their efforts on simply preparing students to perform better on the annual assessments.

What else would you expect? Continuous improvement is the battle cry for every public school in America, and failure to engender incremental improvements over time can be costly in terms of state or federal dollars, autonomy, professional reputations, and jobs! As the pressure increases, teachers narrow their curricular focus, so much so that instructional minutes are devoted to only those subjects and skills that are tested.

We once claimed to teach the "whole child." But now we don't have time to. It's not really a system designed to inspire better teaching and learning. It is designed to engender higher test scores.

So perhaps it is an unintended consequence that:

NCLB and systems like STAR greatly influence children's eligibility for some of the very programs that make the school experience meaningful for older students: from Advanced Placement courses and athletics to marching band and drama. And when the scores aren't as high they can lead to required participation in summer school and inter-sessions and mandated remedial reading courses on Saturday mornings. Children's entire educational career will be tracked on the basis of these test scores. Even though, under the best circumstances, the testing system may have been designed to shine a bright light on the inequities and inefficiencies of public education *as a system*, the actual effect will be to exacerbate the differences in performances of kids, drive a wedge between the children who perform and those who do not, and ultimately push children prematurely out of the system!

Think not? *Perhaps it is merely an unintended consequence that:*

Some schools and entire schools districts find any way they can to eliminate those students whose performance on the STAR test will compromise overall school results and the API. It is no coincidence that the peak enrollment for the Juvenile Court and Community School districts across the state of California is just before the testing cycle, when low-performing students are often dropped from rolls or even expelled from their home schools for violations of "zero tolerance" laws, or poor attendance, or bad attitudes, or being chronically unproductive. Schools trim the fat. Like the track team that leaves the slow kids at home for the big meet, schools consciously or unconsciously play the averages by *selecting* the students who will excel on the test and flushing the ones who won't.

That applies to new kids, too. When a child goes to a new school to enroll, the office staff carefully sifts through prior school records for evidence of achievement. If they are *Far Below Basic* the school suddenly is at capacity. "Sorry, no room at the inn. Perhaps the school down the street has space." Of course, if the child is *Advanced*, he or she will be in a seat before Mom can even provide the residency verification.

Well-meaning, otherwise caring professionals are squeezed by the unintended consequences of a system out of balance.

So perhaps it is also an unintended consequence that:

The Academic Performance Index, the API, can literally influence the economic rise or decline of an entire community.

Homes are bought and sold on the basis of these test scores. School comparisons that are published in the newspaper and on the Internet are used as selling points for real estate agents...particularly in older communities. In new communities, the housing development with all of its amenities will often sell itself. But real estate agents still use district data to tout the advantages of living in one area of the county versus another. Web sites like *www.greatschools.net* are devoted to aligning test results with the real estate market. Find the best schools in a geographic region, then find available houses for sale within that school's boundaries—all on the same screen!

This definitely works in San Diego where the community has sprawled in an explosion of housing developments with their iconic strip malls and Red Robin Restaurants. Here the schools will be brand new. And who moves into new suburban developments? Families with higher incomes and greater earning potential. They tend to be younger. And they tend to be white. The very population that many teachers typically migrate toward.

So the scores become an influential force in the migration of families and thus, in the distribution of resources within and among communities. Lower scores mean less affluent families and less affluent families lack the means to live wherever they want. They also have less access to medical and dental care, less disposable income to contribute to the school "foundation," less time to contribute to PTA and other school functions, less faith in the end product, and less resources to relocate. People of means, on the other hand, track the schools that have the highest API scores and move next door to them. It is America's socio-economic/socio-educational diaspora. It's a brain drain!

Perhaps it is an unintended consequence that the cycle of achievement is all but preordained. And that:

Most teacher unions now have embedded in their boilerplate contract language some provision that allows senior teachers first dibs on job openings within a school district. A new school gets built out in the predominantly white, professional, upwardly mobile, school-savvy, teacher-supportive, gated enclave...and who are the first teachers to transfer there? The teachers with the seniority to compete for the openings.

The pattern in most districts also reveals that, in low-achieving schools with greater concentrations of poor students and children of color, the staff tends to feature less-experienced teachers. Meaning younger teachers. Teachers more likely to be of an age to have their own babies. Teachers who may, during the course of a school year, be out three to six months on pregnancy leave, leaving a less prepared substitute teacher to fill in until she returns. Teachers whose priorities are torn between their own responsibilities and instincts as a parent—and their responsibilities for raising other people's children. Teachers who tend to move with their spouses and their young families to other states and locations where they can afford to own their own home—a phenomenon that creates new openings for more new teachers and a continued cycle of inexperience in schools that serve the very population that needs superior teaching the most. The larger the pool of young teachers, the more frequently these circumstances disrupt the school's flow.

But it's even bigger than that. *So perhaps it is an unintended consequence that:*

The STAR test scores are directly affecting the lives of children, the careers of teachers, the funding for schools, the economic development of communities, the tenure of superintendents, the election of board members, and the campaign platforms of governors and presidents.

When President George W. Bush began his second term, he cited No Child Left Behind as perhaps the one and only issue that could get bipartisan support during reauthorization. But alas, there was plenty of disagreement—much of it from his own party—on the real value of the law and the damage created by its many unintended consequences...for which, as always, our children pay.

VOODOO

Even without President George W. Bush and his illusionary show horse called No Child Left Behind; even without California's STAR system and its threats of public ridicule and sanctions; even absent the culture of constant fear and confusion about how to stay ahead of the pace of expected academic growth—*we would still be El Milagro!*

We would still have identified the most rigorous standards for our students. We would still have set a sky-high threshold of student achievement. We would still demand professional excellence from each other and absolute parental accountability at home. But without STAR, our success and the unlimited capacity of our students to perform might be far harder to quantify in credible ways. So notwithstanding the limitations and failings and unintended consequences of STAR, we harness the data and create our own momentum.

We track data on attendance, parent participation, extracurricular activities, referrals to family services, grants, and any number of other variables that can quantify the health of any service-oriented school organization. But like the dashboard of a Land Cruiser, where the quality of the ride is measured by speed, odometer, engine heat, cabin temperature, oil levels, window washing fluid, and battery strength— these are only indicators. They can't tell you that you've arrived at your destination. "Are we there yet?" You need a GPS for that.

Are our children learning?

Are they learning everything that they are supposed to be learning?

How do we know?

Prior to the STAR assessment system we knew that the answers to these questions were:

No...

No...and,

Well, we just don't know!

And now we KNOW.

There is much debate about charter schools in general and whether they have lived up to their potential. There is no shortage of reports that contrast the achievement of students in charters with their counterparts in traditional public schools. Those comparisons are essential and are more valid now because we have common metrics with which to analyze results from very different kinds of schools. Not apples to kumquats.

Now at least everyone has been issued the same rule book to a very odd game. When children begin to rise to our expectations, we no longer have to attribute their learning to luck or magic or statistical wizardry or its voodoo cousin.

NEW TOOLS

The STAR assessment system with its California Standards Test is possessed of a thousand holes—yet lets in too little light.

Two weeks into the 2005-06 school year, I heard a loud voice speaking to me from some spooky corner of my imagination. Like the voices we all hear, it was not so much a *voice* as an *idea*, apparently not unlike the one that many educators had had long before me. The gist of the idea was that "summative data is not rigorous enough to leverage intense academic growth for individual students."

And not unlike many educators who had experienced this epiphany long before me, I couldn't quite decipher the message.

"Huh? What's that? Could you speak a little louder? I don't get what you are saying…I can't understand…"

Then, thankfully, the little voice leaned forward and blasted my ear drums the way stereo speakers do when you have the volume turned up and finally hit the right combination of dial settings to release the "mute" button:

"I SAID…YOU ARE USING THE WRONG TOOLS, DUMB ASS!!!"

"Ohhhhhhhhhhhhhhhhhhh. Now I get it."

Summative data systems, like STAR, are excellent for deciphering classroom or organizational trends and patterns *after* the teaching is all complete. But summative data does not allow you to make adjustments that will ultimately influence the learning outcomes while there is still time to influence those learning outcomes.

The STAR system gives us tools to conduct an autopsy. It is a post-mortem. We want to treat the patient while he is still alive! We want growth. We want healing.

BLUE BINDERS

Interestingly enough, the summative testing tools are all provided by departments of education within each state. They are part of the landscape of public education. There is no shortage of assessments that can be used to compare the achievement level of kids and subgroups of kids and schools to one another. They fit the old paradigm of "mass education." The one that says every child moves along at a standard pace and learns things in a standard sequence and matures on a standard continuum. The one that assumes all children can be compared against a common benchmark.

Monitoring growth, however, comes from the expert application of *formative assessment* systems, even if schools have to discover and devise them on their own. Using formative data is so transformational for schools, you might think that it is fundamental to the standard of care provided every child everywhere. It's not. I would venture to guess most educators—including teachers and their principals—not only lack robust formative tools, they don't even know that they need them!

We were determined to create our own assessment system that would integrate the state's STAR program, our school district's end-of-the-year summative tests, formative assessments, and other diagnostic information that comes from living with our students every day.

So we designed what we called a **student-centered** assessment system with three essential components:

- Summative Data
- Formative Data
- Diagnostic Data

Together, these processes and systems provide data and information that inspire revolutionary new approaches to instruction. The triangulation of data from summative, formative and diagnostic systems drives the achievement levels of students who might otherwise languish in distracted schools. We had *summative* data from STAR and we had already created our own innovative process for *diagnosing* the needs of our most high-risk children. (The Resiliency Quadrants System will be presented in the next chapter).

So we turned our energies toward the task of delivering reliable *formative* data to our teachers. We created our initial formative assessments by accident of discovery and by pure trial and error. Our instincts carried us as we made five significant program adjustments during the 2005-06 school year:

THE FIRST ADJUSTMENT: **We changed our mission timeline from "getting kids to grade level *by the end of the year*" to "getting kids to grade level *before we test* to see if they are at grade level!"**

We realized that our mission goal was fatally flawed because each year our time frame was misdirecting our efforts. We were aiming at the wrong target. We had always talked about getting our students to grade level by the end of the year. But the end of the year is too late. We test our students in early May! For them to demonstrate that they are at grade level requires that they master the competencies for their grade level and have the confidence and ability to demonstrate that mastery in any context, including the California Standards Test—*before* they take the test. Like law schools that provide the curriculum before students sit for the bar exam or flight schools teach their students to land the airplane before they are certified.

THE SECOND ADJUSTMENT: **We changed from a 200-day calendar of three trimesters to a 200-day calendar of four quarters.**

We realized almost immediately that our entire school calendar was structured around this flawed notion of preparing kids to be at grade level by the end of the year. We had created a calendar based on trimesters. And while we had created an excellent standards-based report card, and an expectation that 100% of our parents would meet and conference with their child's teacher at the end of each trimester, the system clearly didn't take into account the need for students to be academically prepared for a May testing date. In fact, every year, our students are tested in the middle of our third trimester. We couldn't alter those testing windows because they are established by the California Department of Education. But we could alter our grading periods and parent conferences so they time out better with the tests.

So we did what only a charter school could do—we changed our calendar in mid-flight! We went from a trimester system to a quarter system in one inspired meeting of our Leadership Council.

We proposed to use the extra twenty days in August as the beginning of the instructional year. And why could this have happened only in a charter school? Because school calendars are subject to negotiation with the teachers unions. Once a settlement is reached, and the calendar is part of the package, it cannot be changed without going back into the contract language. Even if it is good for kids. At Mueller Charter School, our teachers turned the entire program on a dime and changed the calendar.

THE THIRD ADJUSTMENT: **We identified benchmark tests to pace instruction from quarter to quarter.**

After we changed to a quarter system, we realized we needed quarter "benchmarks" to determine how are students were progressing. We had to be able to monitor our students' growth and find new and more reliable methods for determining who was learning and who wasn't. The third program change we made in the development of a formative evaluation system, was the identification of tools to assess each child's progress in math, reading, and writing.

We were already conducting frequent writing assessments and analyzing the development of our students' writing skills. But we struggled to find reliable measures for reading and math. In this first year of chasing our hunch about the potential power of formative assessments, we used a district math test and an off-the-shelf reading benchmark and started to gather quarterly data on each student. We improvised. We relied on our teachers' ingenuity and a mounting awareness that they needed far more reliable data than what some textbook publisher from Texas could provide.

THE FOURTH ADJUSTMENT: **We devised a tool to organize our data in every single classroom.**

As the data began to flow, we created our fourth significant systemic change: the development of a tool to organize and maintain the mountain of data that each teacher was generating. Our teachers are creative and resourceful and they began almost immediately to devise methods for keeping track of each student's growth. As a school, we needed some common tools to facilitate discussions among and between grade levels. The data is useless if we don't analyze, discuss, and make adjustments according to the trends.

We designed student data pages and organized them so that it was easier to see those growth trends at a glance. The growth pages were collected and organized in a blue, three-ring binder. Every teacher had one. Every classroom. Every student's real time record was accessible. The blue, three-ring binder became more than a three-ring binder. We referred to them as the "Blue Binders" when we wanted teachers to bring them to meetings or when we wanted to mine the data for new insights.

"Teachers...remember that we will be analyzing grade-level trends in your math data today. Please remember to bring your Blue Binders." It was our bible and our BlackBerry and our Thomas Brothers all rolled into one.

The Blue Binders evolved and they held clues to the mysteries of children's learning. There were solutions, often trapped within the pages as if written in secret code. Moon letters. We held our Blue Binders up at midnight and hoped that some lunar magic would reveal a new path for Carlos who still struggled to decode. We plugged our iPod headphones into our Blue Binders, hoping that Carlissa's troubling resistance to learning her math facts would be illuminated. We fell asleep on the couch at midnight on Saturdays...our Blue Binders splayed open across our chests, suppressing our breathing under the weight of the numbers and the consequence of our inability to decipher them.

The Blue Binders simultaneously annoyed and intimidated us, summoned and called us, frustrated and drove us, enlightened and inspired us.

And they led us to the fifth program change as we developed an integrated system for using formative assessments to engender results: a change in attitude. A kind of collective wisdom.

THE FIFTH ADJUSTMENT: **We taught our teachers to analyze the data and then make adjustments.**

We don't always know what the numbers really mean or where to go from here. However, we know this: "if we keep doing what we keep doing, we are sure to get the same results". We need to make adjustments close to kids. In the classroom. Mid-flight. Just like we have done as an organization. Leave the illusionary comfort of the lesson plan and curriculum map and realize that different kids are at different places on the learning continuum and sometimes we don't realize exactly where that place is until the school year is well underway.

We were in the beginning, primitive stages in the development of a comprehensive system for integrating the summative, diagnostic, and formative data. We were on the right path. The Blue Binders had been somewhat transforming even if the assessments we used weren't perfect. So we kept searching. We needed to make *better* adjustments on the basis of *better* data that was generated by *better* benchmarks.

Then I found another critical piece to the puzzle—or perhaps it was revealed to me—in the middle of OMBAC's quest for a thirteenth National Rugby Championship.

HUNTER S. THOMPSON

Justin Cunningham has to wear a hat because the sun is harmful to his skin. He is prone to skin cancers so his white-brimmed Hunter S. Thompson hat was appropriate in section 37 of Qualcomm Stadium where we sat next to one another and watched OMBAC Rugby Club beat the Old Blues from New York. This was Old Mission Beach Athletic Club's thirteenth National Championship, establishing them as America's premier rugby program.

Justin Cunningham and I had played for OMBAC when the club first started to tour and play teams from around the world. We were serious about our rugby. But beyond that, in those wild days, Justin Cunningham was not serious about much of anything else. Except having fun.

I first met him when I was fifteen at Marian Catholic High School. My family had just moved back to San Diego in February of my sophomore year. On my first day of school as the new kid, I dutifully stood up with everyone else at the beginning of English class to recite the Lord's Prayer. It was a Catholic high school, for God's sake, and the teachers believed that prayer was their competitive edge when it came to jamming Chaucer into our gullets. I was deep into the meditative "deliver us from evil" part when I heard the thunderous commotion of two large boys bursting into the room, laughing and knocking desks over as they wrestled and pawed at one another like playful cats.

Justin Cunningham got into big trouble that day but he didn't seem to care too much. He was a strong, tow-headed Irish kid who grinned like he knew something you didn't. 'Cause he did. He was the consummate California teenager. He loved life. He loved to read as much as he loved to argue or to punch someone in the face or to chase girls or pitch horseshoes or to play guitars or to surf. For as long as I have known Justin Cunningham, he has lived every day to the fullest.

Our lives have spiraled back and forth, constantly crossing into and out of each other's orbit. Like all childhood friends, we have passed through various stages of mutual respect and periodic aversion. But our friendship always survives to one degree or another.

We followed a similar path: coaching, teaching, and eventually school administration. He earned his doctorate in education not long after me and today he works with the small school districts of San Diego County as a consultant. He could have been a superintendent by now but the way he sees it...what would be the point? What does running a school district have to do with surfing every morning at 5:00 am?

As a consultant with the San Diego County Office of Education, Justin Cunningham has developed expertise in lots of areas. He was the first to teach me about the research on resiliency when it was starting to emerge. He has also developed enough expertise on brain theory and its application to learning that his book on the subject may very well precede this one in print. And he has become knowledgeable about formative assessments.

So while OMBAC was beating the New York Old Blues we caught up on what old friends catch up on when they haven't seen each other for a year or two. And we talked about our work. We talked about the struggle of pushing organizations toward greatness and the need for the tools to leverage change. We talked about the need for better assessments. It was an odd conversation for two old friends who used to camp in the back mountains and talk about one day playing in the NFL.

"Have you heard of MAPS?" he asked.

"You mean the GPS kind?"

"No, douche bag...the MAPS kind! It's a formative assessment system. MAPS is an acronym that stands for...I don't know...Measures of Academic Progress...or something."

"Well, whatever. What's MAPS?"

"It's a computer-based assessment. Kids take the tests on line and it generates some awesome data. It's totally connected to the state standards."

"Sounds interesting."

"It's amazing. More and more districts are using it. Poway has been using it for about four years."

"Poway? Those guys are getting results and I can never figure out why."

"This may explain it. I'll come by and show it to you."

"Sweet...But have I told you about our Blue Binders?"

"Yeah, you did. It's a great system. But your Blue Binders are only as good as the assessments you are using and you said your assessments suck."

"They do."

"Okay. Then I'll come by and you can check it out. You don't have to use it if you don't like it."

"I think we need to go to lunch."

So we went to lunch. And I learned about MAPS and I realized that it was a near-perfect fit for our system. In fact, it was the missing piece of a very complex puzzle.

I wondered how it is that Justin Cunningham continues to provide these puzzle pieces in my life. OMBAC easily beat a very tough New York rugby team suffering from jet lag. The sun shone brightly outside the shaded protection of a white-brimmed Hunter S. Thompson hat. That damned Justin Cunningham was right again. And the children of El Milagro are the indirect beneficiaries of a lifetime devoted to finding true north through good friends, rugby, and the allure of the surf.

MAPS

What the computer-based assessments of the MAPS system now provide us is real-time data at four strategic points of the school year. It quantifies where every child is performing relative to the California state standards. It tells us exactly what they know, what they are ready to learn next, and what they are not yet ready to tackle. It breaks it down student by student. We have nearly 1000 students who each have a unique academic profile generated by MAPS. We have not only pinpointed how far each student is from performing at grade level in math, for example, but we can also assess his or her precise skill set in the concept clusters that make up California's math curriculum: number sense, operations, algebra, statistics, probability, and geometry. We have the same detail for reading and language.

The MAPS test was developed by the Northwest Evaluation Association, also known as NWEA. We liked them from the beginning, because they are a nonprofit organization committed to research, not making money off of gullible or desperate school districts. They have developed an impressive array of test reports that any ninrod can print out, read, and decipher. The trends jump off the page.

The first trend to capture our teachers' attention was that in every classroom, at every grade level, the range of skills and abilities of children is unbelievably wide. Our students are all over the board in every subject area. We always knew that. In fact, teachers have always known some kids are further ahead than others...and that other kids just drag themselves to school and struggle every single day. But we continue to design our schools and our instruction as if they are all moving along at the exact same pace. If that were true, if every student learned the stuff we teach them at the same rate and had the same gaps and needs, then the "one-size-fits-all" approach would work. We could do whole-group instruction all day...every day.

But that is not how children learn and MAPS proves it.

Our MAPS data, which we now neatly tuck inside our Blue Binders along with all of the other indices of academic progress, serves as a kind of individualized prescription for every student. The data illuminated a path that was always there, even in the thickest and darkest clump of forest. For while whole-group instruction may be easier, and teachers everywhere practice—to some degree—the "one-size-fits-all" brand of pedagogy, the path to academic excellence is unique to every child

Thanks to NWEA, it is now easy to generate accurate formative data that describes exactly where each student is performing. Thanks to our Blue Binders, it is easy to organize the data into a tool that everyone can access and understand. Thanks to our calendar, it is easy to schedule periodic benchmarks to monitor children's growth. Thanks to the enthusiasm and expertise of our wide-eyed teachers, it is easy to discuss the results and trends and craft grade-level priorities.

We now had a compass pointing to our brightest stars in an otherwise darkened sky.

NFL GEEKS

One interesting feature of a live NFL game that you can't see from watching on television is that—along with the players and the referees and the coaches—there are literally hundreds of other people down on the field. There are cheerleaders, security guards, NFL back-up officials, photographers, grounds crews, VIP's, television crews, and technicians. You'd sort of expect to see them at such a huge event.

Then there are all of the people with field passes who got into the game for free to stand next to the team and perform a function that somehow blends into the fabric of the game: the electricians who operate the big fans on hot days, AT&T execs who answer the telephones from the coaches upstairs and hand them to the players, the

Sparkletts water specialist who keeps the water cups filled with plenty of Sparkletts water, the guy who hands the oxygen bottle to players who just made a long run. The list goes on. Hundreds of people—all of whom evidently wish that they had tried out for their high school football team or somehow morphed into a 325-pound NFL lineman.

Then there are the computer geeks. Right behind the team bench you can see them working as industriously as any other "official" experts plying their trade on the sideline of a professional football game. The computer geeks never take a break. And their work is telling. It has a potentially greater impact on the outcome of the game than all of the other experts combined! Because virtually every formation for every play on the football field is being photographed from above. The down and distance are being recorded. The gains and losses are measured. The penalties, the first downs, the big pass completions, the sacks, and the fumbles and the interceptions—all recorded. The tendencies and patterns of the opposition are recorded too. And so is the placement of the ball on the hash mark, and the position of the sun, and time of the game, and tilt of the world on its axis. All digitally recorded and printed out...nonstop...play after play after play.

And after each play there is a printout that records the data on a single page. The page is then placed in a plastic sheet protector and collected in—of course, a Blue Binder. As the defense comes off the field, one of the computer geeks provides the finishing touches on the Blue Binder and hustles it over to an assistant to the assistant of the defensive coordinator. After players have accepted water cups from the Sparkletts water cup specialist, then cooled off by the fan operated by the fan technician, and grabbed a fresh towel from the laundry director...they are ready to process the data from the Blue Binders.

NFL coaches are experts at processing data. And they do it quickly because their jobs depend on it. NFL coaches read the trends, teach their players, make midcourse adjustments and then send the guys back out onto the field with a plan that may be on different by degrees from the one they agreed to just moments ago. All before the next commercial time out or interception or three-down series—whichever comes first.

Teams that consistently win in the NFL are not just the ones that have the best players or the coolest uniforms. They are the ones that pay attention to the details—one play at a time—and make the right midcourse adjustments. They may have drawn up a brilliant game plan that they have practiced all week and even sold to the national media. But in the ferocious pace of an NFL game, when the facts and data and trends demand a new course of action, you change or you blow up right there on national television.

The skill set that separates the guy tinkering with the dials on the big electric fan and the coach who lines up his players to win is merely this: one toils in anonymity, aiming a household appliance so that it can blow relief across the smoking skulls of giant NFL linemen. The other reads the data and creates expansive change that is measured in the over-under line in Las Vegas.

LITTLE EYES

Likewise, we create change.

When the wisdom of the numbers from MAPS and our Blue Binders was revealed, our teachers immediately moved toward three very predictable conclusions:

- First, some groups of students were not being very well served through our present methodologies. Our English-language learners and our third-graders, for example, were falling behind every year relative to other students in the school;
- Second, we had to become experts at making midcourse adjustments; and
- Finally, our teachers had to improve their skills in differentiated instruction.

As we tracked our data trends, we quickly recognized that our parallel objectives of student achievement and academic excellence may simply come down to our teachers' capacity for *differentiating instruction*. We agreed unanimously that we had to teach individual students as individuals and get out of the traditional, whole-group/ whole-class context.

As this new reality set in during the first year of utilizing MAPS data, our teachers learned a lot about differentiating instruction. They learned, for example, that:

- There is no one right way to differentiate instruction in the classroom;
- Differentiated instruction is as different from learner to learner within a classroom as it is between classrooms;
- Differentiation requires an attitude of high expectations and high standards;
- Individually, students can be motivated to think and work

harder than they meant to—and simultaneously achieve more than they ever thought they could;

- Students who are challenged individually soon discover that learning involves risk, effort, and personal triumph;
- All learners are different and unique in terms of skills, ability, readiness, motivation, interests, experience, background, knowledge, styles of thinking and learning, intelligence, talent, aptitude; and
- Differentiation promotes a deep respect for the identity of the individual.

They also learned that they were already pretty skilled at differentiating instruction. Perhaps the terminology and sudden sense of urgency caused them to hesitate until they recognized their current practices that indeed promote individualized learning.

One Friday afternoon when our teachers were buried under their Blue Binders and we saw their little eyes peering out through the cracks and the pages, we said:

"Hey...come out of there. You are on the right path. Today I saw teachers who were engaging and challenging their students through varying modalities. I saw you modify your teaching according to your students and their interests, their rates of learning, the complexity of material, and the overall levels of effort from your classes."

"I saw teachers and students working together in a whole variety of different ways:

"Materials, pacing, large groups, small groups, different assignments, different group leaders...that's all part of *differentiation*!!!"

So our teachers cautiously pushed their Blue Binders to the side and sat up straighter in the meeting.

"Okay...try this. At your tables, brainstorm the methods that you used this week that you believe helped you individualize learning for your students."

So they did. And they wrote their strategies on chart paper and then shared their charts with the whole group. Every strategy written down, at every table, was in fact a strong method for differentiation. There were lots of strategies repeated on all the different charts. But taken together, they included:

Student growth plans
Learning centers

Interest centers

Student projects

Writing across topics, genre, publishing formats, and rubrics

Cooperative learning (including jigsaw, value lines, and triads)

Graphic organizers

Multimedia

Computer-assisted activities

Theme-based; integrated instruction

Self-selected (student choice) projects/assignments/homework

Flexible grouping

Learning environment

Bloom's taxonomy

Multiple intelligences

Learning styles

Scaffolding

Modifying content by pace, complexity, volume and breadth

When our teachers left the room that day, I knew they felt better about their expertise and that we had merely connected them to their own instincts. I was proud of them, as I almost always am. They never fail to amaze me with their devotion to the mission, with their creativity, and with the deep complexity of their collective intellect.

SHAKE ON IT

At El Milagro, our teachers care deeply about the academic results of their students. But if they do not get the results they are looking for, if they fall short, we do not accept excuses. They don't help anyway. We already know the excuses. We've heard them all already.

We have children who are absolutely overwhelmed by life circumstances that too often make learning extremely difficult. We could be overwhelmed by those circumstances too, like so many other schools are...or, we could devise a way for teachers to literally overcome the effects of poverty, high mobility, and low parent education levels. And so that's what we did.

While integrating the STAR system with the formative assessments developed by NWEA, Mueller Charter School continued to developed a program model that promotes resiliency and emotional health in our students: the Resiliency Quadrants System. This system prevents our children from becoming lost in deciles and stanines and national percentile rankings against norm groups that look nothing like them. It also prevents our teachers from becoming overwhelmed by the insidious life circumstances that are doing their best to rob our students of the opportunities they so richly deserve.

It is the *balance* that is otherwise missing in the STAR system and all the state and federal mandates, and it truly personalizes our work. Through the amazingly effective Quadrant System, we can recognize academic growth but also measure and celebrate resiliency, and character, and the wonder of human learning.

Ultimately, it is not just data and systems that make our student-centered accountability model so effective. It's the fact that we put the whole assessment game in perspective. It's our attitude. We thought it through. We aligned it with our values and core beliefs. Though we never really shook on it, we adopted it as a collective philosophy that is embodied in the hopeful song of El Milagro.

FINISH LINE

Kids aren't dropped on their heads at the moment of their birth. It happens later in the long journey from kindergarten to twelfth grade. They arrive at our schools wide-eyed and ready to learn. Even the poorest child with his or her borrowed lunch bucket in a half-day kindergarten dares us to teach them something they can learn.

But then there are critical and defining events along the way.

The K-12 journey is like a long race where there are thousands of runners stacked and stretching from the front of the starting line clear back for several city blocks. To get a place right up on the starting line these days it seems like you must come from Ozzie and Harriet's house. You must be white. You must have two parents. You must be affluent. You must speak English...and your parents must speak English. Some adult must be in the home when school lets out in the afternoon. You must have a home library filled with hundreds of book titles and computer connected like a tendon to the thin and invisible skin that envelops the globe like a worldwide web. You must take family vacations, and during dinner each night, you must have sustained and frequent conversations about interesting things.

The further away from this profile you are...the further away from the starting line you will be.

And, if during the race some of these variables become altered... (say, by experiencing the loss of a sibling, or parents' divorce, or abuse), you can find yourself knocked off the entire racecourse while the field rushes by and you try to catch your breath. The stronger your health, the more resilient you are prior to a life crisis, the quicker you get back on the track and the quicker you can make up for lost time.

Of course, for those who started the race three blocks behind already, whose capacity (and motivation) for overcoming adversity is strained every minute of the race...it must seem like a futile task. They will never catch up to Ozzie and Harriet's kids. At best, they will get to the middle of the pack. From there, they can never hope to win. They just hope to finish—limping, crawling, throwing up....or sprinting. By any means necessary.

After a while, nobody even pays attention to the runners in the back of the pack. They could fall down on the racecourse in a full epileptic seizure and no one would notice. Except maybe their moms. Everybody else is fixated on the runners in the front. "Wow...look at 'em go! They are so fast! They are so strong! No one's gonna can catch 'em!"

And, of course, no one will.

So at Mueller Charter School we decided that it would be our mission to challenge our children and our families and our communities and ourselves. So no matter where you stood at the start of the race, no matter how many miles back from the front of the pack, and no matter what happens along the way...we expect you to finish up front with the race leaders. There is room for you there. You have to run harder, you have to run farther, and you have to overcome obstacles that the runners in the front could never understand...much less endure.

But you will endure. You will compete. And the children of El Milagro are expected to win!

"Ladies and gentlemen, the runners are coming into view...we are about to see the winners of this prestigious and life-altering race pass right by us. And here they come...there are your leaders...just like we expected...just like we wanted...just like we fixed it...but wait! What's this? There seems to be a whole pack of kids we weren't expecting. What's that on their shirts? Looks...like...'Mueller...Mustangs....'

"Mueller Mustangs? Who are the Mueller Mustangs? And where the hell did they come from? Didn't they start about twenty-two city blocks to the rear of the pack? My goodness. They must have been flying. They must have been absolutely scorching this race course!"

"Or maybe they cheated. Could someone run back the video? I'll bet they cheated."

"But here they come anyway. We can't stop 'em now. They are crossing the finish line in the front of the pack! Look at them all. Why... it must be the whole freakin' school! I've never seen anything like it.

Not in a race like this. They just keep coming, and coming. Every one of them with a look of pride and determination. Defiant! Resilient! Every one of them, looking like they could run ten more miles or ten more years. Like they could run over, under, or around any obstacle thrown out on the racecourse to slow them down. Wave after wave...boys and girls...how did they do it?"

"My, my. We are witnessing something very special today, ladies and gentlemen. This is an astonishing group of children. But at the same time, they look so...ordinary. This is just incredible. It is...well...a miracle...."

EVERY DAY IN AMERICA

The celebrated No Child Left Behind federal law cannot unilaterally reform the public school system because the education of children is profoundly influenced by so many other sociocultural systems and conditions: like health care and law enforcement, employment opportunities, community economics, and social services. All of these systems are dysfunctional by degrees too. They are each limited by internal crises and shortcomings. The May 2007 data from the Children's Defense Fund (the organization from which, ironically, President George W. Bush lifted the name "No Child Left Behind") continues to remind us that:

...Each Day in America
- 1 mother dies in childbirth.
- 4 children are killed by abuse or neglect.
- 5 children or teens commit suicide.
- 8 children or teens are killed by firearms.
- 33 children or teens die from accidents.
- 77 babies die before their first birthdays.
- 192 children are arrested for violent crimes.
- 383 children are arrested for drug abuse.
- 906 babies are born at low birth weight.
- 1,153 babies are born to teen mothers.
- 1,672 public school students are corporally punished.
- 1,839 babies are born without health insurance.
- 2,261 high school students drop out.
- 2,383 children are confirmed as abused or neglected.
- 2,411 babies are born into poverty.
- 2,494 babies are born to mothers who are not high school graduates.

- 4,017 babies are born to unmarried mothers.
- 4,302 children are arrested.
- 17,132 public school students are suspended.

So if schools like El Milagro are successful, it is *in spite of* the paralyzingly myopic reach of NCLB. But I'm pretty sure there are plenty of people who don't really want the success they claim to want in schools like El Milagro anyway. What would America do if charter schools in Chula Vista started to crank out waves of Stanford-bound Latinos prepared to compete with Ozzie and Harriet's kids for jobs? It is easier to confine them to the fringes of society, to hire them as laborers, and then question their immigration status.

At El Milagro we push to help large numbers of children reach their academic potential because it is the right thing to do. Neither sanctions, nor rewards, nor name-calling, nor NCLB, nor President George W. Bush can intensify the intrinsic drive we feel to help our students succeed while all of those other social systems remain unchanged.

But what do I know? I'm just a principal who has been on the front lines of public school transformation efforts for thirty years.

I am just the general on the ground in Iraq warning the president that we need more troops and the proper body armor.

I am just the civic leader standing on the rooftops of New Orleans warning FEMA that a flood is coming and they better build an ark.

I am just the labor leader and child advocate and public health expert standing shoulder to shoulder in hopes of seeing a solution for a health care system that is so flawed that old people and children and veterans and the working poor become marginalized simply for becoming sick.

I am just the Nobel Prize-winning scientists and scholars warning of a cataclysmic climate change...one that cannot be stopped through piecemeal efforts—because we all function as organic systems within organic systems.

And what does expertise have to do with presidential legacies anyway?

HEAD COLD

The defining ethos of the Powerful Teaching model of El Milagro is that we treat every *individual child* as an *individual child*. We compile the clues from both summative and formative data and we chart a course that is only the course for now. We'll get new data soon and the course may change. Besides, formative and summative data still only reveal a partial picture.

Our children cannot be defined solely by numbers and statistical trends so we identify the life circumstances that affect their learning too. In the diagnostic medical model there is both a metaphor and a method for placing the learning needs of each child in a multi-dimensional context.

When you take your child to the doctor, it is to treat the unique symptoms that are manifesting themselves in the moment. They are *your* child's symptoms. You may not like them, but they are uniquely hers. The doctor walks into the room with your child's medical history in hand. You consult about your child's health. The doctor compiles all available clues: the symptoms, the medical chart, anecdotal behavior patterns, your child's age and general health history. Then, through a lens of training, research, and experience seeing a million children with similar patterns, the doctor can make an informed evaluation of what the condition is and how to treat it. It's a plan rooted in science. It is what, in the doctor's best professional judgment, your child needs to get better. And because it is a personalized, individualized, custom-designed medical plan, your child stands a very good chance to get better.

It's what we expect from our pediatrician. It is the standard of care.

If you take your child to the doctor with flu symptoms and she comes home with a cast on her arm, you need a new doctor!

"Well, she's got a fever and she's throwing up. She probably has the flu like everybody else. But you know what I am good at? Putting casts on broken elbows! And in fact...I just went to a big conference this past week and I learned about how to put really cool casts on kids! I couldn't wait to get back to the office and try it out. So here goes..."

"Wait a freakin' minute here, Dr. Strangelove. I thought you said she had the flu!"

"She does. But I'm no good at the flu. I'm good at doing casts. I like doing casts."

"But my kid doesn't need a cast. She needs a doctor who will treat her for what she needs!"

Obviously. So how is teaching any different? When a parent takes her child to school, shouldn't she expect that her unique needs as a learner will be addressed? Is it one-size-fits-all? Would you stand for that at the pediatrician's office?

Modern medicine could not tolerate doctors making a diagnosis with a dartboard. That's called medical malpractice. In education, however, one-size-fits-all *is* the accepted standard of care.

Not at Mueller Charter School.

We cannot get our students to grade level if every child is presented with the same curriculum, in the same sequence, through the same instructional strategies. Learners are too unique for that. It doesn't work. It has never worked. So teaching has to be differentiated and each child's learning goals must be different too...even if only by degrees.

The deepest meaning, however, does not come from achievement data at all, but rather from a process created at Mueller Charter School for knowing who our children are. *Really* knowing—if you have the stomach for it. It is called the *Resiliency Quadrant System* and through its full implementation we are able to name the life circumstances and conditions that too often interfere with learning: poverty, family crisis, socio-economic hardship, and the alluring influence from our community's darkest forces.

MAPS TO THE HOLY GRAIL

The teachers of El Milagro are not perfect. And they are not finished. But they are complete in their collective understanding and conviction. We have learned some things about assessment and data and the politics of school revolutions:

- The mission is still to get 90% of our children to grade level;
- The instructional strategies that we have used so far are not sufficient to get them there;
- To arrive at the journey's end will require MAPS and a willingness to change our course according to its clues; and that at this point...
- Nobody knows the secret path to the Holy Grail. Nobody.

CHAPTER TWELVE

Hope For Cristina

The world breaks everyone...and afterward many are stronger at the broken places.

— Ernest Hemmingway, *"Farewell to Arms"*

THE SIXTH SYSTEM

We created a way to identify student risk factors, coordinate support services, monitor their well-being, and foster resilient behaviors in virtually every child in the school...at the same time!

CRISTINA

On rare and wondrous occasions, there is a light. We are illuminated. We are shown the way.

On an otherwise typical Tuesday afternoon a few years ago, I visited Cristina in Children's Hospital. And there was a light.

Cristina had suffered two broken legs as a result of a drunk driver plowing into her, her older sister, and her mother in a crosswalk in Chula Vista. It was after school, and they were heading *homeward*. Cristina and her family are always headed homeward, because like many victims of the unforgiving California economy, they have no house. There is no home.

Her mom is deaf and speaks only Spanish. She is a member of the growing body of working poor, earning some $250 a month from her job at Burger King and providing for two school-aged girls. "Give us your poor...your huddled masses..."

Cristina was just one of nearly 1000 students at Mueller Charter School, and until she was nearly killed in crosswalk we were not aware of her family's circumstances. Perhaps I was preoccupied with the ocean of data my state and school district have provided me. Perhaps her teacher was preoccupied with the often-futile task of inspiring wonder in a room full of children who were enduring their own various life crises; children of the poor, all on their own journeys homeward. All of whom, like Cristina, speak to us like a blinding light.

Until then, I had reluctantly embraced California's system of accountability with its stealth principles of standards and data and contrived calculations. I had become a community resource quick to share my expertise on normal curve equivalents, percentile rankings, and the Academic Performance Index. I could weigh in on the parallel debates about retention and promotion and high school exit exams. I could create school board presentations with the best of them. I could cheerlead exhausted children and their teachers as they prepared for yet another season of tests that somehow standardize us all. And I could spin statistical trends with the data sent six months later to protect or promote even those who are woefully under-equipped to move on to their next grade level.

I had led this charter school, as if swept down a rushing river, toward a new status quo...a new paradigm with the catch-all label of accountability. And now, with new momentum inspired by a vision of No Child Left Behind, there was an even more intensive effort to define what it means to be performing at grade level. There is an ever more desperate effort to invest in standards-based texts and materials and programs and to create new systems to measure and report the outcomes.

But in consoling Cristina, in signing her casts and fighting back my own tears and emotion as her mama wept in the corner in the arms of her oldest daughter, I think I must have had my epiphany.

Cristina spoke very little. In her dark eyes, there was a sadness—a despair so deep, I felt as though I was looking into the very soul of our nation. A child of eleven should not have to leave a hospital bed and return to the uncertainty of the streets.

A child of eleven should not have to be nearly killed in a crosswalk to point out the obvious: that our children seem to always shoulder the burden of unemployment, homelessness, insufficient health care, family dysfunction, and the daily struggle of our working poor.

A child like Cristina should not have to wait for her adult caretakers to discover, by divine providence, the scope of risk factors that are interfering with her learning. Risk factors that *we know* have an absolute effect on a child's ability to attend school and successfully participate, let alone excel academically.

THE LIGHTS OF EL MILAGRO

And it shouldn't have taken a child of eleven for me to see that the state's accountability system with its imperfect assessments and perplexing statistical calculations do not delineate what our students really need.

We may be the richest nation on earth. We may have more millionaires and billionaires than all other twenty-five industrialized nations combined. We may be first in GNP, defense spending, and lots of other categories that celebrate affluence. But we are twenty-second among twenty-five countries in lifting children like Cristina out of poverty. You can be sure, without urgent care, she will be left behind, too. Who is accountable for that?

It seems like we have again come full circle. Twenty-five years ago the American public was advised in *"A Nation At Risk"* that "if another nation did to our children, what we do to our own children in schools, we would declare it an act of war". Strong language from a federal study that failed to look in the mirror for the root cause of Cristina's misery.

If only we had declared war on poverty instead of Iraq, and poured those billions of dollars into developing our own cities instead of destroying theirs.

Thus irony of our national preoccupation with standards and accountability is that ultimately public schools and the children in them suffer the consequences for our government's misguided political priorities. The conditions which we work feverishly to overcome to ensure that every child is learning, are conditions that our own political leaders have either intentionally created or, at the every least—allows to exist.

Under these circumstances, if Mueller Charter School were hit by a missile fired by a US jet fighter, we would be sanctioned by the principles of NCLB for not making sufficient progress in administering to the casualties. If El Milagro, like the city of New Orleans, had to claw our way up through thick mud created by governmental indifference, inaction, and ineptitude; we would be judged by how swiftly we swim through the debris.

Risk factors such as those experienced by children like Cristina are real. They grow from the seeds of failed public policy that make victims of the most innocent children.

Poverty, homelessness, and the despair of a childhood lost...has a face. It is, in spite of her sorrow, one of radiant beauty. For me, it is Cristina's. She did not intend to teach us and is no doubt unaware even of this book, but she has shown us a very bright light, and perhaps inspired a new pathway, created to save and stabilize our children. She reminds us still to focus—not on raising test scores—but on raising our children!

THE FOUR HORSEMEN

In a perfect world, all children would be protected and nurtured like children ought to be. In a perfect world, every child would come to school daily, well rested and well fed. Children would have resources and experiences at home that lead to a broad foundation of knowledge and experience. They would have attentive parents like Ozzie and Harriet and the Huxtables. The family's income would be well above any national mean. Siblings would all be successful. Children would never be exposed to over-sexed advertising or violence or drugs. They would not be treated as commodities. They would attend the same school from start to finish. Teachers would speak their language. And families would have complete access to health care.

In such a perfect world, teaching and learning would still be extremely difficult, but in the end, every child would learn. No one would be left behind.

But, of course, this is not a perfect world. Our children do not all come rested, prepared, healthy, and ready to learn. And it isn't always their fault.

And maybe it's nobody's fault.

Poverty, family dysfunction, high mobility, and the challenges of learning English as a second language continue to represent the most debilitating factors associated with learning in America. For all the technology of school reform, these conditions are consistently among the very root causes for an achievement gap that persists along socioeconomic lines and, too often, racial and ethnic lines as well. They are the four horsemen of the apocalypse.

Somehow children who live in poverty have fewer books to read in their homes. They don't seem to travel as much—at least not for pleasure or curiosity. They talk less at the dinner table with highly educated adults about topics that enrich their learning. They are not afforded the luxury of regular dental checkups. They rarely see an optometrist. Children who live in poverty simply do not begin school from the same starting point as children from more affluent homes.

No matter how many state and federal laws are passed mandating an end to the gap, no matter how many accountability systems are created to monitor student progress, no matter how many sanctions or rewards are conceived of to compel good people to comply...the presence of poverty will always influence school readiness and thus always produce limited academic results.

Forty-some years ago the Coleman Report issued findings that tied socio-economic status to learning. Using data from over 600,000 students and teachers across the country, researchers led by the sociologist James Coleman found that academic achievement was less related to the quality of a student's school, and more related to the social composition of the school, the student's sense of control of his or her environment and future, the verbal skills of teachers, and the student's family background.

Coleman essentially established a social context for public education. His report was regarded as one of the most significant education studies of the twentieth century and it ignited a movement that led to the acceleration of desegregated schools by way of busing. It was also the first significant effort to link academic results, in the form of test scores, to the notion of equity.

Looking at test results in California, and all across the country, it is easy to see trends emerge that echo Dr. Coleman's conclusions:

- Schools with high poverty and high numbers of English-language learners are consistently outperformed by schools in more affluent communities where there are fewer children struggling to assimilate and to learn English;
- Children who live in poverty are exposed to far more significant risk factors than children from more affluent homes; and
- These risk factors associated with poverty can significantly inhibit academic growth and achievement.

Perhaps until now.

At El Milagro, we recognize the trends. We accept that Coleman led a long line of well-intentioned sociologists who provide for all of us the perfect excuse: "It is not our fault that our students perform at lower levels...they are a product of their environment."

We could pick our horse from that apocalyptic barn and race it into absolute mediocrity and underachievement...and we would be absolved for our lack of results. "After all," the absolution would read, "at least we tried."

Instead, we decided to prove Coleman wrong.

We decided to address the risk factors that are produced from within the social context of children's families, community or peers, and at the very least, neutralize them.

We decided to grow our children's "assets" and foster their capacity to be resilient. We decided to beat the odds; to teach children to rise above even the worst of circumstances.

Developing resilient children is fundamental to our mission. It separates Mueller Charter School from El Milagro.

CRISTINA'S GIFT

On the Monday morning after visiting Cristina at Children's Hospital, I invited Greg Valero, Ryan Santos, and the Wizard to meet me in my office. I drew a square on the whiteboard and divided it into four equal quadrants. And then I labeled the quadrants: Q4, Q3, Q2, Q1.

"I was just thinking…" I said out loud.

"Uh-oh," said Greg Valero. "When you start thinking, it means a lot more work for us."

"Maybe. But I have an idea on how we can keep track of kids like Cristina so they don't end up getting run over in a crosswalk before we know they need our help."

"You must have created another system, " said the Wizard in partial amusement.

"Yeah…but this one could be awesome. Now check this out. Our kids come to us from all kinds of life circumstances—some are good… some are not so good. Would you agree?"

They agreed.

"Ok then," I said. "Think about our students in four separate categories that represents their academic, social and emotional needs: they are either at or above grade level, approaching grade level and doing ok, below grade level because of the crap in their lives that they can't control, or they are in need of intensive care. If we can identify who is who as it relates to those descriptions, we will be able to harness all of our systems and resources and provide children services in a more strategic and proactive way."

Greg Valero, Ryan Santos, and the Wizard were still listening. So I continued.

"Look…these four squares, these quadrants, represent those four descriptions. If you had a class of twenty or thirty students, which box would you put each of your students in? If they are at grade level and doing okay, we would list their name in QUADRANT 4."

"That's about 25% of our students, school-wide," calculated the Wizard. "So…215 kids would be in that tiny little square."

"Well it's just their name. We don't really put *them* in the square."

"Really? I wouldn't have known that." The Wizard is also a smart-ass.

"Next, place all of your students who are below grade level—but making progress, in QUADRANT 3. These are kids that will likely get to grade level at the end of the year, if they work hard and we do our job as teachers."

Ryan Santos leaned forward in his chair and squinted at my squares and brightly colored quadrant labels. "OK," he said, "QUADRANT 4 kids are *at* grade level. QUADRANT 3 kids are *below* grade level but making progress. Where is Cristina?"

"Hold on," I said. "She's not here yet. QUADRANT 2 contains all of our students who are below grade level—*Far Below Basic, Below Basic*, or even *Basic* kids—who are not making academic progress due to external conditions that are beyond their control. Like their parents are going through a divorce...or..."

"Their dad is in jail..." said Greg Valero.

"Or they have a family member smokin' crack in the garage..." said Ryan Santos.

"Or they have a medical condition that hasn't been treated..." continued Ryan Santos.

"Or they have been to 106 schools before they came to us..." said Greg Valero.

"Or they came right to us from a school in Tijuana where the teacher showed up whenever it was convenient..." said Ryan Santos as we all simultaneously began to see the same picture emerge.

"Or their mother has a terminal illness..." said the Wizard, because he would know.

And Greg Valero and Ryan Santos and the Wizard continued on describing the kaleidoscope of crappy conditions and circumstances that too many of our kids live in.

"Wow...that's a depressing QUADRANT," said Greg Valero.

"What if it doesn't have to be though?" I asked. "If we know who is in QUADRANT 2, and why they are there, we can align our resources. We can prioritize our services. We can create an individualized plan to assist and monitor each child—one by one! We go on the offensive. Proactive. No more victims! I know this, I'll feel like we are doing a hell of a lot more for kids than just cranking up their test scores in math."

And in that moment Greg Valero and Ryan Santo and the Wizard stared quietly at four squares on the whiteboard. And for the first time those squares represented *possibility*.

Ryan Santos looked for Cristina in the concept. He is not one to be distracted by systems or by whiteboards that dehumanize our children. He will not abide a discussion that fails to make our students real. Their lives are not hypothetical. Their pain is not to be taken for granted.

"So is this where Cristina goes? She would be in QUADRANT 2?" he asked.

"No. Cristina goes in QUADRANT 1," I said. "QUADRANT 1 represents children who are literally in need of intensive care. This is a school's equivalent to ICU. Their very lives are in the balance. Literally. They are hospitalized like Cristina. Or they have just lost their parents. Or they are being exposed to extreme violence or abuse."

"We're gonna need lots of help for QUADRANT 1 kids," said Greg Valero to no one in particular.

"That's the whole point. These kids need a thick, thick web of support. We bring every social agency to bear. We weave in the entire community for support."

"Wow. You're on to something here, Kevin. Did you come up with this over the weekend?" asked Ryan Santos.

The answer to Ryan Santos' question stuck in my throat. Ideas come to me like poems. Sometimes I have only a fragment of an idea, sometimes, a whole verse. Sometimes I can imagine a completed project but I struggle for the details that will get me there.

And sometimes ideas, like poems, come to me in their entirety. They are intact, word for word, with their near-perfect rhythm and metrical magic already aligned. It is hard to take credit for them because they arrive like a postcard and I merely write them down. They come as a gift. I unwrap them and give thanks to the poet of the universe who whispers in the ears of those who will listen.

"I don't really know where it came from," I said in response to Ryan Santos' question.

"I do," said the Wizard. "It came from Cristina. It was her gift to us"

And, of course, the Wizard was right.

Over the past few years, the Quadrant System has done exactly what it was intended to do: it has resulted in tremendous movement of children along the achievement continuum, it has become a highly effective system for coordinating services to children and families, it has improved our communication immeasurably, and—most impressive of all—it has, more than once, saved the very lives of children!

On that Monday morning on which I shared my Quadrant idea, Cristina experienced the normal discomfort associated with broken limbs adjusting inside the suffocating confines of plaster casts. She rolled over and fell briefly asleep. Each time she woke up she saw the dark and tear-swollen eyes of her mother looking on...lovingly, patiently. And in the warmth of that love, she knew that at least for the moment, she was safe. And so she slept again.

THE QUADRANT SYSTEM

The rest of our dialogue about children in our various quadrants has lasted seven years. We can't seem to close the discussion. It takes us down different paths. It generates different conclusions. And it has led to some highly effective programs and services.

We know that every child is unique. But at the same time, our students, like children everywhere, have common needs. Some are more intense than others. Some more urgent.

We created The Resiliency Quadrant System in an effort to nurture resiliency in children, to stimulate their desire to excel in school, and to help them overcome even the worst of life circumstances to compete every day in school. This integrated *system* aligns our services and programs, resources, timelines, schedules, processes, and personnel; it enables us to focus intense support for children who need it the most.

The Quadrant System has become part of the culture of our daily work. Each year we initiate our new teachers into its subtleties and retrain our veteran teachers. There are essential steps and phases to the system that we constantly revise and improve.

When teachers first report back to school in late July the process begins.

From their first day back they immediately begin to learn about the students in their new class. They not only review assessment data, they also review their school history, check the cumulative records and conference with the child's previous teachers. Then they meet with each child's parents. Most of the meetings are home visits and are organized at the convenience of our parents' schedules. By Labor Day, when most other children are only just returning to school, El Milagro has been under way for more than a month and our teachers know their students intimately.

They are now equipped to determine which quadrant description is appropriate for each one of their students. So we distribute the "Quadrant Worksheet," a single page divided into four sections (quadrants). Teachers are asked to consider everything they know about the students in their classes and tentatively place every child's name, one by one, in one of the four quadrants, according to the guidelines:

QUADRANT 4: Children who are at or above grade level in *both* language arts and mathematics as measured by their performance on the California Standards Test in the previous spring.

QUADRANT 3: Children who are approaching grade level and who can reasonably be expected to achieve a performance level of *Proficient* or *Advanced* on the CST as a result of their learning experiences and classroom-based interventions this year.

QUADRANT 2: Children who are below and/or far below grade level. These are students who are experiencing life circumstances that make high academic achievement difficult and unlikely for this school year. It also would include students who have been consistently *Far Below Basic* for multiple years.

QUADRANT 1: Children who are experiencing profound and immediate life crisis (homelessness, a death in the family, extreme family dysfunction, trauma, etc.).

In effect, by placing each student's name in the appropriate quadrant, we can begin to accurately diagnose their individual learning needs on an academic, social, and emotional level and ultimately prioritize the services they may require.

Sometimes our teachers just don't know which is the best quadrant for their students so we developed another tool for teachers called *personas*. The concept was borrowed from Intuit, the developers of tax and personal income software. The company's "usability" experts struggled to enlighten their engineers and give them an intimate understanding of how people actually use their software in their homes or businesses. So they completed exhaustive profiles on their diverse customer base, and from those, they were able to pinpoint some common characteristics. By creating personas—composite profiles of Intuit customers—they were able to put a face to the product and make the task of engineering software a more human endeavor.

We knew we could lose ourselves in the risk factors and quadrant descriptions and our new glossary of made-up words...so we created personas, too. We described a hypothetical student that represented the features one could expect to find in the children listed in that quadrant. When teachers struggle with the quadrant designation for an individual student, they can review the personas and determine the best match.

The personas prevent the Resiliency Quadrant System from being just one more way to label kids. We make sure that every child in every quadrant maintains his or her identity. We emphasize that the quadrant placement is both an approximate and a temporary one. The Wizard has inserted each child's picture into a FileMaker Pro database so whether we are working on a Risk Inventory, a Growth Plan, or a Retention Plan...we always have that child's picture present; a reminder that while the personas are hypothetical, our students are not.

Our children are deeply mysterious. Enigmatic. They are like holiday gifts. So we open each present, one by one. We first tear through the colorful- but illusionary—exterior ribbons and wrapping, then ever so gently peel back the soft material that folds over them like delicate tissue paper. And having thus unwrapped the layers that hide our students from the light, we can at least initiate the extraordinarily complex task of teaching.

Each quadrant provides its own direction. Not a detailed roadmap. But at least a compass. So now we have a plan for how we serve the students in each of the four quadrants:

For children in Quadrant 4: *enrich and extend* their learning!

Children in QUADRANT 4 (Q4) are already at grade level and they are generally demonstrating continuous academic growth. Nevertheless, they must be challenged every day to extend their learning, to go in greater depth and breadth, and always to accelerate and stretch their competency within the grade-level standards. Their classroom teachers are their primary support providers at school. Through differentiated instruction and an emphasis on the multiple intelligences, Q4 students can be served in the context of any classroom, while their natural talents and interests are continuously stimulated.

We want Q4 children moving forward. They cannot afford to lose ground. We will not let them.

For children in Quadrant 3: *accelerate* their academic growth!

QUADRANT 3 (Q3) students have different needs than those who are in the other quadrants. They are the largest group of students and represent nearly 50% of our total school enrollment. Many are on the bubble, having barely missed scoring at the proficient level the previous year. Some literally missed scoring at grade level by one or two questions on the California Standards Test. These are the children who many schools pour their time and resources into because 1) there are a lot of them, 2) they are the easiest to move into Q4 because they are so close, 3) the movement of Q3's into Q4 will yield impressive school-wide results, and 4) they will give the API a big one-year boost!

We want our Q3 students to move into Q4, but not just to bump up our Academic Performance Index. Many of these students have overcome the same risk factors that proved debilitating for the children in Q2. They demonstrate resiliency in many ways that we need to replicate with Q2 and Q1 students. If we capitalize on their resilient nature, we can accelerate their academic growth and get them to grade level. We can literally teach them to perform to their full potential for the remainder of their school career and beyond.

To accelerate these Q3 students, we utilize four strategies:

- We create individualized learning plans that are based on a thorough diagnostic analysis of each student's unique academic strengths and needs. The main source of our data is both classroom work and quarterly results from MAPS;
- We provide opportunities for intensive after-school tutoring as well as technology-based skill building using *SuccessMaker* and *Read Naturally*;
- We organize students according to their RIT scores so they know exactly where they are academically and what they must learn to move up; and
- Each grade level holds monthly Academic Growth Conferences to collaborate and discuss trends in students' writing.

Our teachers will address any curriculum area they choose during the Academic Growth Conferences but writing is a top priority because it requires improvement in reading, language mechanics and English fluency. It also requires critical and creative thinking. It teaches process and discipline. It requires cooperative structures in peer editing. And it awakens children to a powerful voice that they all have within them. Our teachers like that.

I have a bias toward writing, too. I saw the magic in the Hispanic Reading Pilot back in the mid-1980s at Muirlands Junior High School. I have read the research that clearly showed huge academic gains in students who were desperately in need of huge academic gains, owed in large part to the multidisciplinary nature of the writing process. So we developed Academic Growth Conferences mostly around a coordinated, school-wide approach to teaching writing.

The Academic Growth Conferences are conducted with Q3 students in mind, but all children's work is included. The process is effective because, along with differentiated instruction and after-school support, it tightens teachers' focus and creates a cohesive approach to instructional improvement.

And then come the children in Quadrant 2.

For students in Quadrant 2: *create an intensive network* **of communication and support!**

Unlike our Q3 students, children in QUADRANT 2 tend to be more fragile and unlikely to make the necessary strides required to perform at grade level on the California Standards Test. Most have risk factors that are compromising their academic progress. Schools have historically resigned themselves to the notion that these risk factors are beyond anyone's control, and that Q2 students just need to work harder. They definitely need to work hard, but through the alignment of our resources we can also provide a network of significant support that helps many Q2 children overcome their adverse external circumstances so that they can concentrate on their responsibilities as students.

The work around Q2 students begins early in September when teachers identify the students who are serious need of our support. At that point we convene our Student Support Team, which includes the principal, assistant principal, school psychologist, head counselor, student advocate, nurse, literacy coach, speech therapist and resource specialist. Together we focus on the risk factors and life circumstances of virtually every single child identified in Quadrant 2. But the real distinguishing feature of the Quadrant System is our ability to design an individualized support plan for every student.

The Student Support Team meets with all forty teachers during this process and then collapses to the ground under the weight of heavy hearts and sheer exhaustion. For nearly two weeks, they listen to the stories:

- Of the five siblings who were each independently placed in Q2 by five separate teachers. Mom, who speaks only Spanish, is the sole provider—but she is suffering from an advanced stage of cancer.
- Or the child who tearfully stares out the classroom window whenever anyone walks by because his grandmother was kidnapped by drug runners in Tijuana in exchange for an unpaid debt, and he doesn't know where she is.
- The family whose father dies of a heart attack after being told he would have to return to jail. In his attempt to participate

in his son's education, he attended the Halloween carnival the night before. His son woke up, saw his father in full cardiac arrest on the front lawn and hurried on to school so he would still qualify for perfect attendance.

- The quiet fifth-grader who visits his father in Donovan state prison every weekend.
- Or our new fourth-grader whose family is on the run. His father was just murdered in Tijuana. Then the police investigator who was assisting the family was assassinated and Mom got the message: "You're next." They come to El Milagro in hopes that at least the children will be invisible. They flee a force more evil and more pervasive than they can imagine, much less control.

And there were the many stories of our students raised by grandparents:

- Like the child whose mom is a crack addict. Since there is no father, grandma and step- grandpa take care of three kids. The stress is literally killing Grandma who just suffered her second stroke.
- Or the nine-year-old child who knows that her Abuelita has terminal cancer but is not permitted to talk about it because even Abuelita doesn't know! She carries her heavy burden like a backpack filled with thick mud and fears that she might explode if she can't hug Abuelita soon and tell her that she loves her and doesn't want to lose her.
- Or the cousins all crammed together in a tiny green trailer on Broadway; a living space so small that their grandmother sleeps outside in hopes that the children will carve out space enough to do their homework.

And there are our low-income families struggling to get by while one or both parents serve in the military. El Milagro is surrounded by low-rent apartments, and after the Navy transfers young family to San Diego, it is often the only affordable housing other than Navy Housing:

- We hear about children who have no idea where their mother has been deployed to—only that she is out to sea. Perhaps ignorance is bliss. There is a difference between sitting on

board a ship off the coast of Oregon versus somewhere near the Strait of Hormuz or the Mediterranean Sea.
- Then there are the children waiting every day for their dad to return from Iraq. When he finally comes home, like the answer to a prayer, Dad is different. There are psychological and emotional issues too deep for anyone, much less young children, to ever understand.
- And there are children who have learned, as I learned as a Navy child, that nothing is permanent for a vagabond. They don't bother to unpack. They try not to get too attached. New orders are always coming.

This is childhood for our students we consider to be in Quadrant 2.

The risk factors that are present for these children are largely conditions that we cannot change. They are a brutal reality. But we do not have to be overwhelmed by them either. In fact, after this stage of the process, we cease to dwell on the potential impacts of risk factors at all, and instead concentrate on the process of asset development and creating resiliency in children. Thus the name: *"Resiliency* Quadrants."

Children, after all, have little control over many of the crummy circumstances that happen in their lives—whether it is the unemployment of a parent, an acrimonious divorce, delinquent siblings or homelessness, or family mobility, adult substance abuse, or exposure to violence. The one thing they *can* control, however, is *their response* to those circumstances. Just as we work to teach children to read, to compute abstract operations, to learn the periodic table of elements or the function of the governments...we can also teach children to enlarge their capacity to face personal adversity and rise above it.

Sometimes we see trends in our Q2 students and recognize that groups of students could benefit from the same support services. Since we are a charter school, and we have our own budget, and we are expected to be creative, and we are expected to make stuff up as we go along...we make up stuff as we go along:

- We created a program that enables children to continue in a second year of kindergarten without the stigma associated with retention. Ours is a half day kindergarten anyway, so for some children, we provide the second half before sending them to first grade.
- We created a Newcomers program to help support and enculturate children who transfer midyear from Mexico.

These children have virtually no English and no concept of school in America.

- We created the Breakfast Club for the children being dropped off at 6:00 in the morning. After we opened this program, all children were expected to report to the Performing Arts Center and read quietly until breakfast is served at 7:15.
- We created extended learning opportunities after-school and Saturdays for children to invest more sustained time on SuccessMaker.
- We created a series of parent outreach programs and seminars on parenting.
- We partnered with the YMCA to provide targeted support and counseling services to children who had one or both parents in prison.
- We partnered with the Lion's Club to provide glasses for our students who needed one or more pair of glasses at school.
- We created our own seventh and eighth grade middle school as a Leadership Academy, so we could continue to foster resiliency in our older students and provide them opportunities to lead and model for younger children.

The work we do with Quadrant 2 students is extensive. We invest tremendous time and resources into their development. This is our choice. Our commitment. We could focus our resources and energy and attention on the Q3 students and likely create greater school-wide gains on the Academic Performance Index. After all, the Q3 students are the ones on the cusp. They are the ones who can cross over into the promised land of academic proficiency with a little more sustained attention and push. But we feel we achieve that through the efficacy of our teachers themselves. Q2 students remind us that we must keep our children whole. Build resiliency and get back in the game.

Our Q2 students can be heartbreaking to work with. But then there are children for whom this chapter of El Milagro has been written. Quadrant 1.

For Students in Quadrant 1: Provide *Intensive Care.*

QUADRANT 1 (Q1) students are experiencing catastrophic life crisis. They need focused, intense attention and we now have the capacity and system to provide it. They are temporarily homeless, or they have just lost a parent, or they are experiencing a life-threatening illness. Or worse. They come to us like Samantha did.

One quiet afternoon last year an elderly volunteer from Midway Baptist attempted to register Samantha in our school. She came to the counter without any paperwork: no birth certificate, shot records, school history, or report cards. She could not even produce basic information like where Samantha's mother was or Samantha's last name. So naturally, red flags went up.

"Well, she dropped her off at the church and said she would be back in an hour and we haven't seen her since," said the elderly woman."

"How long ago was that?" I asked.

"Two weeks ago."

"Where is mom now?"

"She lives with Samantha's younger brothers and sisters in Tijuana."

"Why did she bring Samantha to you?"

"I don't know. They just showed up. Her mom said that they just needed to get Samantha out of Tijuana as fast as she could."

"Where's her father?"

"Oh I believe he's in jail. Isn't he dear?" The elderly woman appealed to this child's memory of a father she has never met. So she didn't respond. "Yea I think that is what her mother told me."

"How old did you say Samantha was?"

"She just turned twelve."

There is no way that Samantha is younger than fourteen. I've seen those eyes before. I worked in the Juvenile Court Schools for five years. I saw thousands of Samanthas. Maybe she was twelve. Maybe fourteen going on twenty-six. There is the sweetness of childhood somehow encased in the shell of street toughness—hard as iron.

"Ma'am, do you know why Samantha's mom did not come back in an hour like she promised?"

"No. Maybe she lost her directions. Or maybe she is still searching for Samantha's birth certificate. Or maybe her other children are sick. Or maybe her mother is sick…I just want to get Samantha in school."

"Well, we want to get her in school too. But we have to have a birth certificate. We have to have her shot records. What school is she coming from?"

"She went to school in Tijuana up until this year."

"And where has she been this year…where has she been since September?"

"She was enrolled at Memorial Junior High."

"In the San Diego School District?"

"Yes. So how come they enrolled her without a birth certificate and you people won't? I just want to get her in school. Call Memorial and get the birth certificate from them."

"Well, actually, we called over there and they didn't have a birth certificate on record for her. Did you personally enroll her there, ma'am, or did her mom?"

"No, her uncle did."

"Her uncle? Where does he live?"

And for the first time Samantha lifts her head to look at me right in the eyes. So I asked again.

"Do you know her uncle's name or where he lives?"

"Well, it's not really an uncle; it's just this man that was caring for her..."

"Excuse me...?"

"Some man. There seem to be a number of men and..."

"Ma'am...can we step into my office for a few minutes?"

And that is how it is for some of our Quadrant 1 children. Their mothers abandon them for weeks at a time, or even longer. Samantha was transported to the Polinsky Children's Center within the hour as Ryan Santos and an officer from the Chula Vista Police Department and I tried to piece together the sordid details of this sweet child's awful life. At Polinsky, there are far more skilled social workers who can assess the needs of neglected, abandoned, and abused children.

Sometimes the violence and lawlessness and childhood prostitution rings that have gripped Tijuana spill over into America. They spill over like the thousands of souls fleeing generations of poverty and corruption and squalor for a brief glimpse of downtown Los Angeles. Cibola. The Seven Cities of Gold.

The old lady from Midway Baptist wept for fear that she had made a huge mistake by bringing Samantha to Mueller Charter School. "Can't you just put her in your school? She is happy with me. She is doing fine. Please don't take her away. Please don't take her."

"Ma'am. Listen. You did not make a huge mistake. There is a high likelihood that you have saved this child's life today."

"No she was fine with me."

"Are you a trained counselor or medical care provider, ma'am?"

"No, but she doesn't need counseling or medical care."

"Are you qualified to assess the degree of trauma that is associated with a child who has been abandoned? Her mother said she would be back in an hour. She has had no contact for two weeks. Can you see how that could be traumatic for any child?"

But the old lady only wailed through a strange, tearless, and almost feigned grief.

"Ma'am, can you tell us the extent to which Samantha may have been the victim of sexual abuse?

"Oh, there was no sexual abuse. She just said that one night she woke up and some man was on top of her and..."

End of discussion. Samantha was under the immediate protection of the State of California. And this is El Milagro too. On the very, very good days when we stop to ask questions and actually *listen* for the answers, we literally save lives.

Which brings us back to Cristina. Quadrant 1. The original charter member of a very, very bad group to be in if you are only a child.

SANTOS, SANTOS

Ryan Santos is officially our head counselor but we call him our Student Advocate. He is as strong as he is gentle. He speaks softly, even when he roars. He protects children as if God sent him here to protect the weakest and the most fragile. And, of course, He did.

I sometimes think Ryan Santos has so much spiritual wisdom that I search in his eyes for meaning even beyond that which he provides for shattered children. I am not alone. Our teachers quietly seek him out and I suspect they don't always know why. But even in fleeting conversations there is a sense of healing and meaning. And advocacy. There is in this gentle and extraordinary man at least one principle that remains absolutely inviolate: on this planet, at this time, NOBODY messes with our kids! Nobody.

Ryan Santos is the primary case carrier for the handful of children who are placed in Q1 and he will get them what they need. While their teachers are encouraged to sustain their focus on the academic progress of these most fragile young lives, they entrust Ryan Santos to weave his magic. No matter how horrific or tragic their lives, we know that daily school participation contributes to a child's sense of stability. There is something ironic and absurd about teaching Samantha how to diagram sentences or convert mixed fractions to whole numbers while she is being treated as a commodity in the evil market of childhood prostitution. But there is normalcy in those lessons. What is left of her childhood may be found there. She will find deliverance and reconciliation and hope in the healing power of resiliency. It will be because one school and the people in it cared more for her than they do for themselves.

It will be because of Ryan Santos, who is one of the many faces of El Milagro.

CHILDREN RISING

Ultimately, the Resiliency Quadrant System is designed to engender academic success for every student. For some children, their life circumstances will interfere with what otherwise would have been normal academic growth and progress. They may experience that growth later. Our system ensures that we are organizing all of our resources to give every student an opportunity to reach his or her full academic potential...even if it does not occur until middle school, high school, or even later in life. It is no quick fix.

Neither NCLB nor California's STAR accountability system take these factors into account. Nor should they. All schools have children who come to them with difficult personal and life circumstances. At Mueller Charter School, we do not make excuses about our students, but we cannot afford to treat them all the same...as if they all come from idyllic, suburban homes.

Still, as a result of the Resiliency Quadrant System, we have seen some promising developments that support higher academic gains:

- Our overall school attendance improved from 94% in 2004 to 96% in 2007.
- We have seen our mobility rate stabilizing from 34% in 1999 to 19% in 2007.
- We have provided medical insurance referrals for over 245 families, with 90% of those families gaining health care coverage.

There are lots of other developments too:

- Our teachers know their students intimately. They know their academic needs, their families, and the unjust life circumstances that too often interfere with being a kid.
- 98% of our parents participate in quarterly conferences with their child's teacher.
- 75% of the parent conferences that we hold in August are *home visits!*
- Our teachers remain focused on the root causes for why students are currently performing lower than we want...and how to mitigate those effects.

- In conjunction with the individualized Student Growth Plans...the members of the Student Support Team have completed literally hundreds and hundreds of effective interventions including family counseling, parent education, school attendance reviews, student counseling, play therapy, change in classroom placements, medical insurance, dentist and optometrist referrals, after-school program referrals, etc.
- Teachers are moving children from Q2 to Q3 in greater numbers.
- Teachers are no longer relying on Special Education as a quick fix. They are much less likely to give up responsibility for goals of the Student Growth Plans and much less likely to refer kids for testing as an intervention.

We should not have to wait until we get a call from the police department or the hospital to discover that we have a student in life crisis. We should not have to scramble to piece together the life history of a child whose family moves from school to school with alarming regularity. We should not have to ignore the effects of poverty, or pretend that learning English is easy to do. We should not forget that improving the school's API may not be a high priority for a child settling in to his tenth new foster home.

It is the business of raising children.

Through the MCS Resiliency Quadrant System every child has a name. There are no excuses. There are no easy solutions. But there is a reliable network of support that lifts children and their teachers and gives them the tools to battle together. This is how we build relationships that lead to learning. This is how we engender achievement. This is how we foster hope.

BENDICIONES

Every child must have a name and a face within our schools and communities. I am deeply pained for Cristina, but she cannot survive on our sympathy alone. She has enlightened me and I have promised her in thought and word...and even in the silence of my prayers, that I will lead a revolution on her behalf and create a school that is responsive to her needs. There will be one charter school that stands for children. There will be at least one institution that is worthy of its angels.

Gracias Cristina. Ten esperanza. La luz, tu luz, ha creado un cambio en este mundo. Que Dios te acompañe a donde vayas.

CHAPTER THIRTEEN

La Casa de Leon

When people care for you and cry for you, they can straighten out your soul.

—Langston Hughes

THE SEVENTH SYSTEM

We learned to accept our parents as they are; to engage them as they are equipped to be engaged, to grow their capacity to influence their children's learning, to cultivate relationships, and to meet them in their own homes.

VICTORIA DE LEON

In the moment, Victoria De Leon is real to me.

If you scan our school rosters from the previous ten years you will find thousands of children with similar surnames, but you will not find Victoria De Leon. She is a composite of multiple home visits over time; a composite of all of the pets and hospitality and poignant conversations that have framed our visits. As a staff we have done thousands of home visits and so we have a thousand stories. I've tried to capture them here—embodied in a single child named Victoria De Leon and her dog La Paz.

There is however, nothing fictitious about home visits. In fact, they may represent the most authentic activity we do together as a school.

LA PAZ

I circled the apartment complex five times, and as far as I could tell, I hadn't moved at all. I was navigating by building numbers but they all looked the same. So I just circled as if circling would provide some requisite level of familiarity and out of the monotonously consistent buildings, apartment C-108 would reveal itself.

The apartment buildings are spread out over several city blocks just north of Mueller Charter School. We are separated by a mobile home park that is even older than Mueller. Then there is the trolley station. And H Street. Conceived no doubt to be a major freeway exit into Chula Vista, traffic now speeds and grinds with an unrelenting pace that the city founders could never hope to manage. In Old Man Mueller's bucolic vision of rural Chula Vista, H Street would have been little more than an extra lane to handle milk deliveries. Side roads branch like the thick pepper trees that provide their cover. Many of them have been removed too. They were a good idea once, until they grew, like Chula Vista grew, into massive shadows. Their roots lifted sidewalks and invaded the plumbing. They've mostly been replaced along H Street now, by gas stations and taco stands and cash express windows. H Street has been replaced too. No longer just an entryway into sleepy Chula Vista, it is a major thoroughfare connecting east and west, old an new, rural and suburban, the "haves" and the "ain't got muches."

The Chula Vista Shopping Center is a neighbor too. It has stood since the '60s as that one-stop shopping solution that malls were supposed to be until the property owners realized that—other than at Christmastime—the mall and all its stores were virtually empty. They realized that they better create new malls that inspired more than just shopping for stuff. So like all modern shopping centers competing for constant customers, it now features Starbucks and Jamba Juice and a gazillion-theater multiplex where the popcorn lasts longer than the movies do. The bones of the original mall are there though. If you squint you can see the old Broadway sign on the side of the main building.

When I was in high school, we didn't have to squint. We shopped at Broadway for Christmas presents and then ignored the place for the rest of the year.

I passed all of these on my way to visit the De Leon family in apartment C-108. I passed Pep Boys and a line of restaurants built to last a hundred years. I passed a few banks that were built to last even longer. But when ATM's evolved their fate was sealed. Their deep vaults and teller windows have long since been replaced and the buildings converted to carpet stores. Someday we may purchase our thick-fiber carpets out of ATM machines and the buildings will evolve still again.

The De Leon family moved into C-108 about the same time that the finishing touches were being completed inside the multiplex at the Chula Vista Shopping Center. Just when they were plugging in the new high speed movie reels and finishing their debate on why we should still use film and not digital image projectors.

Like old H Street, this giant apartment complex swallows each address and demands you navigate by GPS. Someone might have thought to give them some distinctive color. But they are all army-barracks-grayish-brown, all stubborn in their drab resistance to any hue that might distinguish one from the next.

Nevertheless, after circling the area like a police helicopter, I finally broke the code and located building C. I parked down the street and walked back through the complex.

The greenbelts and common areas seemed remarkably well kept, and in windowsills I saw the hallmarks of childhood: Sponge Bob figurines, race cars, an AYSO soccer trophy, a stack of Kennedy fifty-cent pieces...

As I wound through the apartment complex, familiar students ran outside to greet me. "Dr. Riley!? Dr. Riley?!" It was more of a question than an exclamation. They were surprised to see the principal walking by their home. I was surprised to see them too.

From my car circling I had only the aerial view. There was no sound, no life, no bustle. Only row on row of indistinctive barracks-buildings laid out to test visitors' resolve.

From the ground, though—from inside the complex itself—the world changed. The volume was turned up as if the projectionist at the multiplex just discovered the surround-sound switch. I could hear televisions and babies crying. Kids were chasing through apartments and teenage boys made their incessant skateboard racket—skipping off of curbs and spinning their boards before they landed. With mind-numbing repetition they perform one failed "Ollie" after another.

Occasionally one of them falls and lands on his hip. The skateboard shoots out across the sidewalk and into the street. Defiant.

Apartment C-108 finally reveals itself. No wonder I couldn't find it. C-108 could just as easily have been B-303 or N-20-something. History will remember the Golden State for its remarkably creative films and billionaires and innovative technologies. But it will also note the ubiquitous strip mall, the rolling roads lined in pepper trees and duplex houses...and the apartment complexes built in forgotten corners of neighborhoods for three hundred families who send their children to Mueller Charter School.

The screen door of C-108 is bent at the bottom and nearly ajar. I look inside the apartment through the dusty screen. It is hard to see. So I touch the doorbell and ignite the De Leons in an explosion of activity:

La Paz, the family Chihuahua, starts yapping like a guard dog. The kids come running from every direction in the complex, just for a quick look at the visitor ringing the door bell at C-108. Inside, Grandma looks up from the couch where she is watching the afternoon *novelas*. And finally, Ms. De Leon comes into the living room light. Drying her hands in the apron tied to her waist, she smiles, and greets her child's principal who is standing at the door.

"Oh, hello, Dr. Riley. Come on in. ¡La Paz...cállate!

"I'm sorry...he thinks he is a pit bull. Victoria, hold La Paz until Dr. Riley can sit down."

I noticed Victoria standing shyly at a distance. She is a third-grader at Mueller Charter School. At this moment, there is nothing more compelling to her than her principal sitting down next to her Abuelita on their living room couch.

"Hi, Victoria. How are you?" I asked.

"I'm fine. I did my homework already."

"Good for you. What did you have for homework tonight?"

"I had to write a descriptive paragraph about my house. Wanna read it?"

"Of course. I'd love to read it."

So Victoria disappears into the back of their apartment. She takes longer than she should to retrieve a paragraph freshly written. In the meantime, her mom and I begin to talk.

"So, no problem finding our house?"

"No, I came right to it. I've been here before so I am kind of familiar with how they number the buildings." I figured there was no point in telling Ms. De Leon the truth about how hard it is to distinguish C-108 from the endless blocks and rows of look-alike apartments.

"I love that you guys do home visits," she said "Victoria's teachers have come every year. Last week Ms. Orenstein came. It really helps me to know what she is going to be doing in school this year."

"We like home visits, too," I said. "We love to see the children in their own homes, and meet the people that are so important in their lives. Meet the pets. Like La Paz. Where did he get his name, by the way?"

"It is because of his white feet. It looks like he is wearing socks so we started calling him La Paz...you know like La Paws!"

"Oh, yeah...got it. Well it's a cute name."

"Do you have pets? You have children, don't you?"

"Yes, I do. Two children. A boy and a girl. And we have two cats and two dogs. My daughter has a Chihuahua too. He looks very similar to La Paz."

Victoria finally returns from her bedroom with her paragraph. She hands it to me and then sits down next to me. As children do, she watches my eyes as I read. Perhaps the eyes will be the first clue that their work is valued. Perhaps it is in the eyes of adults that they can gauge whether words and feelings are aligned. Victoria wants to be a good writer and she demands honest feedback.

Her paragraph says:

My hous is warm. I have a Chawawa named La Paz and he keeps Abuelita compny all day. I likes the smells in my house cuz my mom cooks good. I like my room. My brother has a room to. There is always lite.

As a first draft, Victoria's paragraph was lovely. She captured the essence of her house—La Paz and her grandma; her mom's cooking and her older brother who was out on the sidewalk practicing Ollies with his friends and landing on his elbow.

And the light.

It is not the scarcity of furniture that attracts my attention. Nor the meticulously clean apartment, nor the pictures on the walls and tables of little league and field trips and birthday parties; it is not the fifty-inch big screen TV seemingly out of place in the otherwise modestly suited living space; it is not the American flag folded into a triangular memento, like a giant paper football. (It is folded like my father's flag. It can only mean one thing, and so I do not ask about it.)

It's not even the thick and familiar smells of Mexican food that roll in from the kitchen like jalapeño cotton. I smell the soft corn tortillas, the freshly grilled nopales. I smell onions and red peppers marinating in a pan. I smell the full pot of handmade tamales, wrapped in light husks.

But what captivates my attention more than anything is the light.

If I had not read Victoria's paragraph, sitting in her house bathed in the aroma of her mom's nopales; if I had not met her Abuelita and shared half glances at *La Bella Mas Fea* on the melodramatic afternoon novella; if I had not seen the flag folded in pristine dignity and encased in glass—I would not have understood her imagery. I would not have seen the light to which she so elegantly referred. But I get it.

"There is always lite."

Ms. De Leon smiled as I read her daughter's work.

"Victoria wants to be a writer. She wants to write novellas," she says with a wink.

"Esta bien, Abuelita?" she asks, engaging Abuelita for the first time. Abuelita smiles. She has few teeth. I realize that Abuelita is really Ms. De Leon's grandmother or great grandmother. She is everyone's Abuelita. There are multiple generations here that reach back to old Mexico and more stories and histories than any of us could comprehend. She doesn't understand any English...or so we are all led to believe. But even the ancient Abuelita, sitting on the couch in C-108 a few blocks from Mueller Charter School, can fully appreciate what it means for Victoria to grow up writing screenplays.

America is like that. There is hope. And hope burns like a bright light.

NOPALES

"Would you like a homemade tamale, Dr. Riley? Or some nopales?"

Before I could answer Ms. De Leon had risen and started for the kitchen. She is a working mom. She is younger than me by twenty years. She could have been a former student.

In the half light shining through the kitchen window, her countenance glows. I wondered: where do young single moms learn to be moms? Where do they learn to raise their babies, go to work, put food on the table...let alone cook the traditional foods of Old Mexico and the recipes passed on through generations like some genetic breath.

Ms. De Leon lives here with her children, her mom, and her grandmother. And for this brief moment in time, I live here too. I breathe in their light. And I am not about to refuse her homemade tamales, even though I just had lunch a little while ago. I am not hungry.

"Dr. Riley...when Ms. Orenstein came last week, she went over the work that Victoria would be doing this year. Man, those standards for third grade are hard!"

"They are. School gets a little more challenging each year. That's why we really emphasize getting kids to grade level each year. One step at a time. They don't want to play catch-up every year."

"That's what happened to my brother Niko. He could never seem to catch up. He struggled every year and my parents couldn't figure out how to help him. When he was in elementary school they didn't do home visits."

"Did Niko go to Mueller Charter School?"

"No, he went to school in San Diego. He rode the bus all the way to La Jolla because my mom thought that the school there was so much better."

"Really? Did he go to Muirlands Junior High?"

"Yes, he did. I didn't want to go there so I stayed at Gompers."

"I used to teach at Muirlands! I wonder if he was there when I taught there. When did he graduate from high school?"

"He didn't. He went into the army and that's where he finished his GED. He would have graduated in 1988."

"That's amazing. What a small world. My writing class was for kids who were bussed from areas outside of La Jolla."

"You might have had him in your class then. Niko loved writing and he seemed to really take an interest in it while he was there. We think that's why Victoria enjoys it so much. She is inspired by her Tio. He wrote beautiful poetry."

"Why didn't he stay in school? Why didn't he keep up with his writing?"

"I don't remember except I know my parents were really frustrated with his high school. The teachers kept putting him in low classes and bilingual classes where they just did grammar stuff. He spoke perfect English. He barely even knew Spanish! He could never find another class that inspired him to write."

This was such a familiar story. Somehow I thought I knew how it was going to end but Ms. De Leon continued.

"His teachers didn't take the time to know him. Not like you guys. They even accused him of being a gang member once. They had a big meeting with my parents and warned them that he was showing all the signs. You know...he was carrying a bandana and wearing Oakland Raiders clothes. One night we were all eating dinner and laughing about how the high school counselors and teachers all thought Niko was this big, bad vato. But I guess, looking back, it wasn't very funny. He was no gang member. Do you know why he wore Raiders hats and shirts all the time?" she asks rhetorically. "Because he liked the Oakland Raiders! The school wanted it to be more complicated than that. He was a gifted writer. But they couldn't see it. That brought so much pain to my family, Dr. Riley, you will never know how it hurt my parents."

"Where is Niko now?" I asked. I felt compelled to. I suppose I already knew.

"He joined the army and fought in Desert Storm...you know, the first Iraq war. He was a proud soldier but my mom suffered every single day he was there. She said the rosary twenty times a day. My dad couldn't concentrate on his work. He was a welder at NASCO and it was dangerous for him to be so distracted. So he retired. He just sat at the kitchen table and looked out the window like any day Niko would come home. He did okay there. Eventually he came back. But a few months later he was killed while he was on leave. He was visiting some buddies that he had met in the army. Guys he went through Desert Storm with. They lived in LA. In Boyle Heights...kind of a bad area. I guess they were having a barbecue in the park when he was just shot. Out of nowhere. Nobody knows why. Nobody even knew who did it. He survived a war in Iraq. But not the war in the barrios. And I guess that was my parents' premonition."

"I'm so sorry, Ms. De Leon."

She has told this story many times before. Perhaps the tears no longer come. Abuelita has heard it many times too—recited in both English and Spanish. Niko was her favorite. While she watched her novella, seemingly entranced in the horrible story plot and second-rate acting...tears streamed down her cheeks. They found their way along familiar wrinkles and folds...like a river carving its path through ancient canyons. For as long as Abuelita lives, and no matter the language that the story is told in, the death of her Niko will bring tears that bead and swell from some infinite source.

"That's his flag there. It's kind of a memorial. Not to his death, though. To his life and his energy. His poetry. Wanna read one of his poems?"

"I'd love to," I responded out of respect and courtesy. But I was deeply moved. Niko was one of ours and I was teaching at the time that he was in school. I couldn't help but feel that we had all failed him and that as an educator, I was complicit in that. I even wondered if Niko had been my student in the Hispanic Reading Pilot at Muirlands Junior High School. I wondered if I had been his writing teacher. I wondered who had awakened the voice that was his—that gave some meaning to school and meaning to his life.

Ms. De Leon handed me a poem called "Gustavo". I read it to myself several times. The imagery and choppy cadence were captivating. I wanted to read it out loud to hear Niko's voice but it seemed like that would be intrusive. So I just read it quietly, fixed on the eloquence and the anger:

> *San Ysidro's streets are paved*
> *with human pain machines,*
> *and the oven won't relinquish...*
> *For here the sun comes angry*
> *to test the best the immigrant dreams;*

and the heat will not relinquish...
But burns the Barrios' darkness

Until the blood and asphalt boils,
and the man in violence
Steams.

...And so on.

"Wow. What an amazing poem. Who is about?"

"Gustavo was an extended family member whose story always fascinated Niko. He was kind of an OG from the '60s. A war veteran. Niko had researched his life for a high school English project and that's when he wrote this poem. Kind of ironic, huh? It's probably why he joined the army. In fact, that is how we found out about Mueller Charter School. All of Gustavo's kids went there back in the late '60s and early '70s."

I searched the verse for something I might recognize, but so many years, so many students, so many poems have passed by. The imagery was unmistakable though. I had been greatly influenced by Gary Soto when I took a writing class from him as an undergraduate student back at San Diego State.

"Use imagery that appeals to the senses," said teacher/poet/award-winning author Gary Soto. "Hard images engage the reader. Rock and bone."

So that's what I told my students in the Hispanic Reading Pilot at Muirlands Junior High School. That's how I told them that they would find their voice, even if no one else wants to help them.

"Even if they stick you in bilingual classes or special education classes or remedial classes..." I told them. "...You will always have your voice. Use it. Scream. Write your asses off. Speak to the world so no one will ever forget your writing, and so that they will always know you are in the room."

In the end, I couldn't decide what made this poem seem so familiar.

"You can keep that copy. We have more," said Ms. De Leon. "We have all of Niko's poems."

I didn't recognize Niko, even when I saw his picture. He was extraordinarily handsome in his army uniform. The American flag was strategically posed behind him as if to say "this soldier, Corporal Nicolas

De Leon, willingly joined the army to serve his country because he was called to do so."

But that is not the case. Niko could have graduated from high school and gone to college. He could have majored in English with an emphasis in creative writing. He could have written books. He could have been Victoria's writing coach. He could have been a teacher. He could have been the principal of El Milagro if they hadn't pushed him out into the street with nothing but his poetry to show for his efforts.

USC

Ms. De Leon invited Victoria to come and sit with us for a few minutes so we could talk about the school year and the future.

"What college do you think you want to go to Victoria?" I asked.

"I'm not sure what happens in college but my teacher wears her USC sweatshirt on Fridays and I think I will go there."

"USC, huh? That's a very good school. And it is such a pretty campus. You could definitely go there if you wanted to. It's a great school for writers, and you seem to be a very good writer."

"I love writing. So when can I go to USC?"

"Well, you have to finish third grade, then elementary and middle school, then high school," I said. Victoria feigned disappointment. College seemed a long way off.

"What about the middle school at Mueller?" asks Ms. De Leon. "It's new, isn't it?"

"It is. We opened it in 2007 so we could keep our seventh and eighth-graders."

"I read that you call it a leadership academy? What does that mean?"

"It is one of our themes. We want to inspire leadership in our students. We work hard to give them the basic skills to be at grade level, but we are all realistic enough to know that that is not enough. Children need to be able to develop their talents in lots of ways. They need to develop an appreciation for community service, become more aware of others, and influence the world around them. We call that civic literacy."

"I agree. Now, will Victoria be eligible for the middle school—for the Leadership Academy?"

"Of course. She would be a perfect candidate for it. The time flies by quickly so it is never too early to think about her staying at Mueller. There are only sixty students selected out of 120 or so sixth-graders, so the sooner you commit to it the better."

"How are they selected? Do you take the best students? Victoria is at grade level."

"We actually invite the students to select themselves. They need to be honor students. They need to be disciplined and willing to work. We let everybody know that the program is very rigorous and that we want to prepare students for the Advanced Placement courses at the high school. And we prepare them for college. Every year the seventh-graders tour all of the local universities in San Diego. So Victoria would visit USD and San Diego State and several other schools. Then in eighth grade, we take them to LA to visit some of the schools there. And one of those schools is USC."

Victoria's eyes light up.

"I want to show you something!" She jumps up off the couch and runs down the hall to her bedroom.

"You know that park I mentioned that Niko was killed in?" asks Ms. De Leon while Victoria is still gone.

"Yes," I replied.

"They said it was within a few miles of USC." Ms. De Leon must have felt her life was coming full circle every day. Her eyes trailed off, imagining this place that she has never seen. For a moment though, it is holy ground, linking the horror of that Sunday barbecue with the hopes of her youngest child.

Victoria returned to the living room holding a red and gold pennant from the University of Southern California.

"This is my teacher's school," she said. "She gave every student in the class one of these USC flags. Someday it's gonna be my school."

"Well, start planning today, Victoria. You can go to any college you want to go to."

"That's right, mi hija," said Ms. De Leon. You pick the school, I will get you there. We will find a way. We will get you to USC."

Victoria took her first steps toward attending USC the day her teacher gave each student in the class a small red and gold pennant. I don't know what other students did with their flags, but Victoria came home and put hers up on her bedroom wall.

STORE BOUGHT

"I want to thank you for visiting us today, Dr. Riley. It was really an honor. You must be so busy."

"It is my honor. I have enjoyed meeting you and your Abuelita. And your tamales are awesome."

"Okay...I have to be honest," said Ms. De Leon looking down at her apron. "They aren't really handmade. At least not by me."

She laughs and so do I.

"Are you kidding me?" she said. "I work so many different shifts at the hospital there is no way I have time for that kind of cooking. My mom cooks though. You just missed her. She had to go out to the store."

"Well, whoever made them, they were very good."

"So you don't visit everybody in the school, do you? I know the teachers go to all of their students..."

"No, we have nearly a thousand students now so I can't make it to everyone's home. But all the teachers do. They go to every home of every student in their class at the beginning of the school year. We have been doing them for the past six years now."

"Don't all schools do home visits?"

"Oh, no. In fact, very few do. It takes a lot of time. A lot of the teacher's personal time. They have to be willing to do it. When I first brought it up there were some senior teachers who didn't want anything to do with the idea. They talked about how dangerous it was and how unpredictable it was to go into people's homes. That said a lot to me about how they felt about our kids. I even asked them: What do you think is going on in our community that is so dangerous? And if it is that dangerous, don't you want to know what is happening in your students' lives?"

"What did they say to that?"

"Not much they could say. They went out and did them and were blown away by how much they learned. It has completely changed the way our teachers see our students. It's been transforming."

"Well, I can see why. It is transforming for parents too. Although when I first heard about it I was suspicious. Like, are you coming to check up on us or to see if we really live where we say we live? Or are you coming to check on our immigration status?"

At that phrase, I saw Abuelita's eyebrow arch as she snatched a quick glance at me. Even La Paz snarled.

"Then I worried that our house was not going to be clean enough or that you guys were going to judge what kind of mother I was by looking around. For the past four years, I have had all of Victoria's teachers come and do a home visit. Last year it was Ms. Jones, before that Mr. Knox. I look forward to it now. We all do. They are always so kind, so patient. I know they have twenty other homes to go to and that they are doing it on their own time, but they never seem to be in a hurry. To tell you the truth, now it's like sitting on the couch talking to a friend. Ms. Orenstein was fantastic. She was so helpful. She gave Victoria some really good ideas on reading projects...right while she was sitting here."

"That's great feedback, Ms. De Leon. Our teachers are quite amazing."

"Yes, they are."

"Every year when we talk about doing the home visits, it's just understood that it is going to happen. In fact, when our teachers leave and go to other schools, they continue to do them."

"Well, look at this," said Ms. De Leon as she produced a small keepsake box. "As if our teachers aren't already sweet enough, they sometimes bring a gift when they come. They always have the standards and parent compact and all of those business kinds of things. But one year her teacher brought this little book to Victoria. The next year it was this really sweet picture of children listening to their teacher read. And Ms. Orenstein brought these little *aretas* for Victoria. She loves them. And she loves her teacher. You know, Dr. Riley, sometimes it's hard to pay the rent here. We have family in Las Vegas and we know it is a lot cheaper to pay rent and live there. But I can't leave. Not now. It would break Victoria's heart. I don't think that there is any school in America where she would be happier."

Ms. De Leon stood and held out her arms to hug me.

I had done a lot of home visits. I had done several today. There are times when my heart is heavy for our students. There are times when I go home and hug my children and my wife and thank them all for being a part of my life. When that happens they know I've been doing home visits.

"Uh-oh, Dad's getting all sentimental on us. Been doing home visits today?"

They know.

Perhaps this was just the end of a very long day and a long week, but in the moment of Ms. De Leon's genuine embrace, I was moved. I felt such a strong spiritual presence that was a part of Victoria, and her mom, and her Abuelita, and La Paz. And, of course, her Tio Niko. It was an extraordinary gift. A home visit. An opportunity to see our children and the lives that they leave in suspended animation for the few hours that they spend at Mueller Charter School.

No parent survey could have provided such clarity for me. No coffee club, no PTA meeting, no Kiwanis Club breakfast, no impromptu visit on the playground. We learn things in home visits that make us better teachers. We build relationships.

In these silent, poignant moments when our lives cross with our students, and perhaps even former students, there is nothing but raw honesty and appreciation. You can neither measure nor define nor fully describe those things.

So we simply acknowledge it as their *light*.

MONDAY MORNING

On Monday mornings we all return from our lives to Mueller Charter School. Sometimes it's hard to get started. You have to want to come back. It is hard for teachers and it is hard for students. But we are on the long journey to that moment of truth in May when we discover whether our efforts have inspired the depth of learning that we all hope will take place. Along that journey, Mondays happen.

The weekends are harder on some than others. The weekends, away from their teachers, are sometimes a reminder that growing up in the lower-income areas of Chula Vista create hardships and life experiences that kids should not have to endure. But sometimes, it is no one's fault. So they show up when the bell rings and we pick up where we left off the week before.

We leave nothing to chance. So each week, without exception and without fail, we convene in the Performing Arts Center for the Monday Morning Assembly. During the assembly we celebrate the upcoming birthdays for the week. We have a class do a demonstration of something they are learning or a performance that they want to share. We announce the honor students. We highlight one of the multiple intelligences that is being featured during that particular month. We award a pizza party to the class with the best attendance.

And we cheerlead.

It's a pep rally and parents are full participants. They didn't seem to notice the Monday assemblies a few years ago. Now it is part of our culture. Parents know they are invited and sometimes I see Ms. De Leon there. I often remind our parents that there is nothing more important as a community than celebrating the accomplishments of our children.

Some parents are regulars. They don't just come when their own child is getting an award. They represent the community and their presence brings so much more authenticity to our work. It's a sacrifice for our parents to take time off from work for their children, even though state law permits them to do so. Still, they come with their cameras and the flash goes off in assembly after assembly.

When we celebrate our monthly honor students, children are invited to the stage by their teachers and they receive a certificate. It is a classy piece of paper designed by the wizard. Many of our students collect them. Since we started doing these assemblies and certificates seven years ago, there are students who have collected dozens and dozens of them. Parents say they frame them and put them on walls or in scrap books. Siblings compete for wall space. Some parents and grandparents have described entire hallways and room additions covered with Honor Student Certificates from Mueller Charter School.

We once got some plastic license plate frames that congratulated our Honor Students: "My child is an honor student at Mueller Charter School." Like the bumper stickers you can see on cars in any community of America. They seemed so trite and tacky that they are still in boxes and stuffed in storage.

Monday Morning Assemblies are so much a part of our routine that no one ever asks if we are having an assembly today. If it is Monday, the answer is "yes." They are never cancelled.

Like many things at Mueller Charter School, our assemblies are somewhat of a victim of their own success. So many parents routinely come to our Monday Morning Assembly that we had to make more room for them. We hold them in the Performing Arts Center, which no doubt evokes the image of a 1,500-seat theater. It's not, however, a 1,500-seat theater. It is a converted cafeteria with carpeted floors that the students sit on. We set chairs up for parents. At best, we can squeeze about 300 people into the space.

We used to have to have two separate assemblies to accommodate all of the students in the school. Then we went to three assemblies so parents had more room. Then we created a fourth and separate assembly for the kindergarteners because fifty to seventy-five parents were showing up every week. And now, because of our middle school, we added still another.

Visitors can come to any assembly they want. It's like church on Sunday. Pick a mass at a time that is convenient for you. Same program. Same sermon. Same message of salvation through hard work and caring about one another.

3,000 PHOTOGRAPHS

Our Monday Morning Assemblies are choreographed to last twenty minutes. They are fast paced. We use lots of music and visuals and technological effects. The Wizard controls all of those. We know with whom we compete when it comes to entertaining our students and that we often have to entertain them to inspire them. In that sense, they are not unlike adults.

Monday Morning Assemblies also regularly feature photographs of our students. The photographs tell the story of school life and capture the spirit of Mueller Charter School. They are laughing, playing, hugging, posing, sleeping, eating, reading. Taking good photographs at Mueller Charter School is easy to do. Our children are extraordinarily photogenic. You just aim the camera and shoot and the accidental image often takes your breath away.

We have thousands and thousands of photographs. We continue to find new places and new ways to display them. They are in our trophy case and message board. They are in the office and the lounge. A computer displays them on a flat screen for visitors in our office. We have over 3,000 photographs in the office exhibit and parents will stand for hours waiting to see if their child's image emerges from the endless sequence of angelic faces. The image fades in, stays for three seconds, and is then replaced by the next photo. To parents, it is worth the wait.

The photos go on. Past and present. There are faces of children who are long gone now. We knew them on their journey. We loved them in the moment. Their pictures outlast the manila folder that contains their academic records—forwarded now to a new school staff.

As our children shine, day after day, we record their presence here in 3,000 photographs. One day they will tell our history.

CHORIZO

Watching Ms. De Leon working in the kitchen to prepare store-bought tamales after working a full shift at Sharp Hospital reminded me of something: being a parent is a full-time commitment. In the quiet evening moments when she should have collapsed on the couch with her Abuelita and sweet daughter, Victoria, Ms. De Leon could have been secure in the cocoon and apartment space she calls her home. But today, she had to entertain the principal who was making a random home visit.

"How did you choose to visit us, anyway?" asks Ms. De Leon somewhat facetiously. "Did we win a lottery or something?"

"No I see our kids every day in their classrooms, or at lunch, or out on the playground. Victoria always hugs me when she sees me. Last week she told me about her teacher doing a home visit and asked me why I have never visited her house. And actually, I try to do as many home visits as the teachers do every year, so it seemed like an invitation."

"Well, we are very honored, Dr. Riley."

The honor was mine.

As I quietly observed Ms. De Leon in full command of her kitchen and her home, I wondered: where would most schools rate her on the "Parent Involvement" scale?

- We rarely see her on campus.
- We occasionally see her at a Monday Morning Assembly when Victoria is being honored.
- She is not active in the Parent Teacher Organization.
- I don't see her standing on the playground socializing with other parents in the morning or after school.
- In fact, even when she has been on campus for an event, I see her only at a distance.

But these are not the only activities that define parents' *involvement* in the lives of their children. Ms. De Leon is raising her children. And raising children is all-consuming.

As I drove back to Mueller Charter School after my home visit, I had a renewed sense of admiration for Victoria and her family. I had a renewed sense of responsibility. I was an otherwise "perfect stranger," welcomed into their home on a school night. Ms. De Leon seemed to speak for so many parents—not just at Mueller Charter School—but parents at schools all across America. In those tender and intensely private moments, she had unwrapped her life like the corn husks that envelop Costco's discount tamales. And I realized some things about parent involvement:

For as long as I could remember, educators have talked about the role of parents in educating children. As we often do, we paint "parent involvement" with a very large and ambiguous brush. And according to our terms.

Yet it seems to me now that we have to take our parents as they come—some are involved, but all are committed. Like eating eggs and chorizo. When the relative contribution of the chicken and the pig are considered...the chicken is *involved*...but the pig is *committed*. Or so the metaphor goes.

Ms. De Leon is involved in Victoria's education. She is engaged. And she is deeply committed.

RIDE ALONG

The Provider.
The Cheerleader.

The Advocate.
The Volunteer.
The Decision Maker.

This is who our parents are and the many shades of their "involvement" at Mueller Charter School. During the hundreds of home visits that we conduct, we come to know them and to redefine their level of involvement with their children.

You would come to know them too, if you could only ride along as we visit house to house.

You would meet "The Provider," for example.

When it comes to participating in their child's education, parents' most significant contribution is not volunteering to coordinate the holiday fundraiser. It's being a care provider. It means fulfilling their duty as parents to provide basic food, clothing, and shelter; and provide for medical, vision and dental care.

The Gonzalez family over on G Street lives a block away from El Patio Restaurant. Sometimes the smells of authentic Mexican food blow through the back apartment window on an afternoon breeze. They get by on a daily prayer. But they ensure that their children are safe and cared for. They offer them full-time supervision at home and in the community.

If this is all parents can do by way of their child's school...it is a lot! We'll take it. So we recognize their involvement and thank them for it.

Victoria's mom, on the other hand, is "The Cheerleader."

We see many single parents raising their babies like Ms. De Leon. There are intergenerational households. There are multiple family dwellings. There are frantic efforts to stay ahead of the accelerating cost of living in Southern California. There are committed parents doing all they can to get by and they are counting on their children's teachers to forgive them if they cannot be room parent this year.

We may not often see them at school, but we see the effects of their work. We don't see them at school because, like Ms. De Leon, they are stretched thin running to the dentist or coaching the Little League team or scheduling dance lessons or shopping at Von's, or building the backyard wooden play structure that they financed at Home Depot or serving as an usher at the 8:00 a.m. mass...or just loving their kids. It's what good parents do and it provides children the context they need to focus on school and find success where they can in their educational journey. They are their children's biggest cheerleaders. They provide motivation and support. They inspire their children to reach their full potential. They create opportunities to extend learning experiences at home. And they provide their children with a vision of themselves in a bright future.

"That's right, mi hija," said Ms. De Leon. "You pick the school, I will get you there. We will find a way. We will get you to USC."

The Cheerleader.

This is parent commitment. No matter what level of education an adult may have attained, no matter how stressed out they may be at their work...they serve their children when they reach back to the school.

Or ride along on our home visit to the Bowens' house on Oaklawn Avenue.

Their street borders El Milagro to the east and runs the full length of Chula Vista. Many of our families live in homes on Oaklawn. In the morning, when Oscar Bowen comes out to retrieve the morning paper, he can look up and see what is being advertised to the million or so motorists on Interstate 5 today. The billboards frame the campus. At the moment the one off J Street and Oaklawn advertises Budweiser in Spanish...";El Sabor!" A block to the north, there is another ad for Indian gaming and the Barona Casino.

Mr. Bowen probably wonders, as I do: "Even though the ads are for freeway motorists, what effect does it have on our children to look up every day at fake poker chips the size of Volkswagens or giant models in bathing suits drinking beer on the beach?"

Mr. Bowen is "The Advocate."

Ask him how he remains involved in his children's school and he will tell you that he and his wife maintain constant communication with school staff. They learn the grade-level standards and what it takes to master them and how to monitor their children's academic progress at home. They make a point to know and follow school policies and expectations. They participate in school-based conferences, activities, and events. They look forward to home visits.

We realized a while ago that if our parents consistently do the things that these families do, we will achieve the mission of our charter. Just these things. So we commit our energy and resources to helping parents get better at doing them.

Ms. Tapia lives in Imperial Beach, which is a long way away from Mueller Charter School, but that doesn't stop her teachers from making their home visits anyway. That's how we do it. Just tell us where your home is...we'll make the visit. Ride along.

Ms. Tapia makes the commute every day, on time, with her three El Milagro-aged children. They once lived in the same apartment complex as the De Leons. Then they had to move out of the entire school district. They kept the children at Mueller Charter School because their children would have it no other way. And as a charter school, Mueller has no official boundaries. Ms. Tapia figures that after getting three kids ready for school, fighting the morning traffic rush up Interstate 5 past all its billboards, she might just as well stay and volunteer. And so she does. She is "The Volunteer."

School volunteerism is an authentic way for parents like Ms. Tapia to become even more immersed in their child's progress. We want you to come if you choose to. Get your fingerprints and your TB shots and we will put you to work...somewhere. I don't know *how* some of our volunteers find the time to be at school. But I know *why* they do. They get to be with their children. Learning. In school. And El Milagro is a place where the learning is as thick as the marine layer blowing in off the bay shore. It is an intoxicating mist.

"The Volunteers" are in the classrooms, on the playground, in the lunch pavilion, and ever present at school events. They go along on field trips. They share their knowledge or expertise or experience. They even share their travel photos.

We appreciate our Volunteers but no more and no less than we appreciate the Providers and the Cheerleaders and the Advocates.

And the "Decision Makers."

The authors of charter law envisioned that parents would be deeply involved in governance at their charter school. Some parents do play a major role in serving on the governing boards of their charters. Some have served in such roles at Mueller Charter School. They are Decision Makers.

They are leaders in the Parent Teacher Organization; they are on ad hoc curriculum adoption committees or hiring panels; they work on the six charter committees. Sometimes, if they are really dedicated, they become voting members of the Leadership Council.

Parent involvement and parent *engagement* is as diverse and varied as our parents. Some parents are "Providers," some are "Cheerleaders," some are "Advocates" or "Volunteers." Some are the "Decision Makers." The one common, universal commitment that doesn't change much is that they serve their children.

But don't take my word for it. Do your own home visit. Or ride along with us.

THE LION

Ms. De Leon does not have time to serve on a curriculum committee, though she is certainly welcome. In her absence, we figure we know a little about curriculum and about how our students learn, and so we feel comfortable making those decisions. As long as Ms. De Leon masters her other responsibilities along the Parent Engagement continuum, Victoria will excel at Mueller Charter School, and so will we.

A lot of parents haven't quite understood this model or why it is important to their children. Some of our parents are barely keeping their head above water. Some work long hard hours and some hold down multiple jobs. Some barely stay out of jail. Some can't stay sober. This is what poverty can do to adults. That's why we created the Resiliency Quadrants—so we can monitor their children and keep them whole when the rest of their lives seem to be crumbling.

Children like Victoria De Leon, however, will go to USC because she has a mother who is committed to her success. And she will go because she had teachers who loved her and treated her as if she was their own. And she will go because she has writing in her blood. And she will go because she has the soul of a warrior. The heart of a lion.

Like Ponce de Leon.

CHAPTER FOURTEEN

The Soul of El Milagro

Our deepest fear is not that we are inadequate, Our deepest fear is that we are powerful beyond measure. It is our light, not our darkness that frightens us.

—Nelson Mandela

THE CENTER

This book has described the deep and transforming change that has taken place at one charter school in the western-most corner of Chula Vista, California. It has happened in layers: first, the *Foundation* changes altered polices and routines and everyday operations. Then our evolving *Systems* created the momentum and structure we needed to channel those change efforts into coherent, interdependent units that burn like rocket fuel. But there is still one more layer. It is called the organizational *Culture*.

And after traversing through Foundations and complex Systems change, you might arrive there: at the cellular wall...the life-altering chromosomes that determine whether an organism is going to be a giraffe, a cactus flower, or a concert pianist. It is an elusive substance. In the subatomic world of organizational cells...it determines whether its host will be an Enron or El Milagro.

Organizational culture influences how people at every level think TOGETHER, behave TOGETHER, interact TOGETHER, communicate TOGETHER, celebrate TOGETHER, pray TOGETHER...win and lose TOGETHER.

Touch the culture and you have reached the soul of your organization. You can't get there no matter how many times you move the salad bar or reorganize the principal's advisory committee. It is not a logo or a vision statement.

It lies beneath the Foundation: beneath mission, programs and services, resources, policies and guidelines, people's attitudes and expectations. It lies even beneath the systems. You can't alter the culture simply by trying to alter the culture. You have to drill deeper. And so we did.

We had to sit quietly in the silence of our ambitions, and presume that we could communicate with the very spirit of Colonel Robert L Mueller and his Sunday fried chicken stand.

STONEHENGE

Borders has hundreds of books on organizational development, all authored by the masters of the trade: Jack Welch, Tom Peters, Jim Collins, Peter Senge, Malcolm Baldrige, and W. Edwards Deming. And there are many more.

Their books teach us how to be better organizations, how to be better managers and more effective leaders. They remind us that effective organizations have a common mission, visionary planning, high-functioning teams, and an appreciation for change.

But I would suggest there is still another element at the core of organizational excellence that even the giants rarely address. It is—for lack of a more precise description—the presence of a *spiritual* force. Successful teams somehow create harmony. In their passionate pursuit of a mission that is pure, their energy creates an invisible, combustible power. They don't need to pray together, to define the force, to convert others, to launch a crusade, to build an alter, or even to whisper about it. But it is there nonetheless, and it has more to do with their success than almost any other factor.

Successful human enterprises have a spiritual core. They share a common faith, a common belief. It is deep. It is impossibly complex.

By the lights of El Milagro, you will feel that incredible spiritual force. We often hear visitors say, "You can sense an energy here," or "Boy, the staff is really together."

Even our visitors search for meaning.

It so obvious that you can't even see it. Like England's ancient stones piled with a purpose and pointing to heaven...the energy of El Milagro originates neither in our intellects, nor our busy hands, but rather, in a mystery as old as Stonehenge.

MORONI

If you drive about twenty miles north of Mueller Charter School along Interstate 5, there is an enormous Mormon church that sits among shopping and business centers as you approach San Diego's "Golden Triangle" district. It is bright white and sparkles in the Southern California sun. Like other temples built by the Latter Day Saints, access is restricted to all but the faithful. Moroni stands on top, cast in gold, his trumpet so large you can almost hear him serenade the city. If nothing else, he has a spectacular view, over his shoulder, of the Pacific and the wet-black backs of the California gray whales migrating to Scammons Lagoon for their winter mating ritual.

Not being Mormon, I could never fully appreciate the opulence so prominently displayed along one of California's most heavily traveled corridors. Now I think I get it. Every culture, down through generations, have built their churches, or mosques, or temples or synagogues as an offering to their God. But they also build them as a metaphor for the human organization that they perceive to be "the church".

Moroni stands every day scouting the surf in solid gold sunblock, calling to the *people*. Not the bricks. Jesus said to Peter, "You are a rock, and upon this rock I will build my church." You can hold the Sunday service in a multigazillion-dollar, bright white, limited-access palace along a Southern California freeway...or you can hold it in a tattered circus tent.

Or you can hold mass in an obscure and ancient village of Old Mexico, where the old women crawl up the aisle on their knees, pounding their chests and their rosaries in deep prayer to the blessed mother..."Madre Maria, por favor, bendiga a mis hijos y mis nietos...all lost somewhere in America." — In this tiny old building the size of a shoe store, where mud walls and borrowed materials are all slapped together without regard to earthquake code...God is alive.

It is a long way from Mormon excess. But I suspect it doesn't much matter to God. The building is not the church. The people are.

And just as the building stands as a meeting place and metaphor for the faith and unity of its collective congregation, so too does the metaphor of *church* provide an illustrative image of organizations in which the people rise to a still higher level of productivity and purpose and service. They become a "community of believers" for whom even miracles are possible.

HARMONY

Leaders avoid discussions about spirituality in secular organizations.

It is too personal. Too controversial. Maybe even too manipulative. When an organization, like a school achieves any level of "spiritual intelligence," it calls it something else: "unity of purpose," or "getting on the same page," or "synergy." Perhaps that is as it should be. It is enough to know that when all employees strive together to achieve more noble values like equity or service...then their sacrifice becomes all the more meaningful.

Perhaps there is an even stronger motive to ignore the spiritual aspect of organizational development altogether. The call to greatness is a heavy burden. But it is hard to envision that when we strive for justice and democracy for others, our God would not be present.

El Milagro is, in the end, a search for harmony. Where there is no struggle for power or control; where there is no infighting, backstabbing, or one-upmanship. No treachery. No hierarchy of authority. Where the rewards of the journey are abundant...and there is plenty for everyone.

And most importantly, where our work is defined by what we do for others and how we serve children.

We learned that as we strike our arc across the skyline, we leave an unintentional spiritual trail that both lights and compels us. The more our voices rise in unison on behalf of children, on behalf of *El Milagro*, the more we call upon the infinite power of the universe to lead us to some yet-undiscovered treasure that is the "way."

Some people don't bother to pray, and that is fine. We have never started a staff meeting with a group prayer. However, there are times when our collective energy—spiritual or otherwise—feels like prayer. It feels like the common force of our intentions, our dreams, our admiration for our students, our deep, deep passions—somehow begin to synergize. As if our work is bundled into hymns and sacrifices and laid—in all humility—at the feet of the Almighty:

We are the cloistered Buddhist monks somewhere choking on incense and impossibly pure mountain air in Tibet.

We are the Gregorian Brothers singing chants that are at least as good as the ones you can buy on iTunes.

We are little old Irish ladies, breathlessly mumbling the rosary in the dark.

We are the pilgrims at the Wailing Wall, bobbing in supplication.

We are family, at the foot of a hospital bed, whispering a desperate novena to the rhythm of machines...and a loved one's final hour.

We are Friday-night football. Young men kneeling in a quiet invocation, saying the *Our Father* before going out to perform under the glaring lights of their high school, and their community, and their fleeting youth. Catching in a Crowd.

We are grace before supper.

We are a fisherman's creed.

We are a nation on a day of rest, ringing one bell for the name of each fallen hero.

We are Islam and Hindu, and Jew, and Jesus.

We are "the gleaners, paused to pray...in the sillion and the soil... carved by Millet..."

We are every religious faith and doctrine.

And we are no organized religion at all.

And we know there is no "one right way."

We do not invoke God's name. We simply call upon Him by way of our work. And our work is our gift to Him. Blessed are the children.

Don't bother us now. We are deep in prayer.

THE GRAND OLE OPRY

If you listen closely you can hear the bulldozers coming. It won't be long now. Gaylord Entertainment from Nashville, Tennessee, promised to build a convention center on the bay front that will completely transform this area of Chula Vista. There will be hotels and high-rises and condos and restaurants and retail businesses and multimillion dollar homes. It's what they do. They have built resort hotels all over America. They are big business. They even own the Grand Ole Opry, for God's sake.

The vast 550 acres across the freeway from El Milagro currently house a few small businesses, an RV park, a controversial power plant, and the marina. But it is mostly ghosts. It is empty. There are only the skeletal remains of the Convair plant that once provided jobs to former residents of Chula Vista. They built Cold War rockets and strategically aimed them to detonate over Moscow. But they never got to launch one. If they had, there might be a whole lot more than just the old Convair rocket factory sitting in spooky desolation.

And since the end of the Cold War meant less demand for rockets to detonate over Moscow, Convair was a goner. When the aerospace industries moved away, so did the engineers—and the first major demographic shift in western Chula Vista was on.

So this morning the wind howls through abandoned buildings. Litter and sagebrush are blown up against the fences. There is an emptiness. Silence.

But this is not some isolated desert. This is a bay front in one of America's most rapidly growing cities. Whether Gaylord or Donald Trump or Disneyland send their bulldozers, it is only a matter of time. We can hear them now. They will dig up the foundations and raze what is left of the buildings. They will excavate the remains of a lost industry. They will haul away soil tainted by atomic fuel and the bad karma associated with a project whose sole purpose was to kill hundreds of thousands of people. They'll build new fences. There will be no litter or sagebrush in what promises to be one of the largest waterfront development projects on the entire West Coast.

Gaylord and the Chula Vista City Council will have to solve their philosophical differences on who will provide the labor for their 8th Wonder of the World. They will also have to solve the traffic problem on Interstate 5. We can't help them with that. They may not drive cars to the Grand Ole Opry back in Tennessee, but we get into our cars to drive to the corner ATM. Gaylord's project could bring over 2,000 jobs to the area and the increased demand on infrastructure will rise proportionately.

But to tell you the truth, I don't give a shit about the Grand Ole Opry or Gaylord or their high-rise hotels. I don't even listen to country music.

I am more concerned with looking westward over the freeway sound wall and seeing a 10,000-story convention center black out the sunset. I wonder...if they build it:

- What kind of jobs will there be on the other side of our freeway sound wall?
- What will happen to property values in this poor area of Chula Vista?
- What will happen to our families?
- How will the infrastructure and the traffic and the people and the immense success of a luxury resort change the face of El Milagro?
- Where will our children go?
- What will become of the De Leons and their far-flung apartment complex and the many other low-end homes and trailers that our children currently live in?

There is an even greater sense of urgency in our work now. The business executives of Gaylord Entertainment in Nashville, Tennessee, have never even heard of El Milagro. They have no idea that we would exist, as neighbors, separated by only a freeway sound wall and eight lanes of breathless traffic running in opposite directions every minute of every day.

At Mueller Charter School we are about change. So we are not afraid. But don't count on our students to grow up to be your hotel's hired help. Victoria De Leon is coming. Her potential will be infinite. She will lead from the executive offices—someone else can pour the coffee and mow the lawn.

In Nashville, tourists come to the city and are drawn to the Grand Ole Opry to see their favorite country music legends. They will no doubt come to Chula Vista too. But they needn't draw all their inspiration from the sunsets over the San Diego Bay. Look out the other way, across the parking lot, due east, and past the freeway to the schoolyard and El Milagro. If you listen, you can hear the sound of children playing. You can navigate by their sweet music.

PUERTO NUEVO

The oncoming 2007 school year chased off the summer weeks before we could comfortably blink. Our staff reported back on July 26 and our kids came in the following Monday. Short summer breaks are expected at El Milagro. Three or four weeks. Or was it three or four minutes?

Parents would have it no other way. This summer, nearly a thousand children registered for Mueller Charter School and they were anxious to get started.

The first day back for the staff is always a professional development day. It is hard to come back mid-summer. Teachers fly in from all parts of the country just days before and are suddenly thrust back into the march. So we take some time to re-connect, build team momentum and rededicate ourselves to the mission.

This year we loaded 80 staff members on two buses and headed south to Puerto Nuevo, Mexico for the day. We don't bring in guest speakers or teambuilding facilitators or outside experts to pump up the troops. We are the troops. And we are all we got. So we light the fire from the source of our own collective energy.

One of the activities we all participated in is called "The Well". It is a simulation in which 15 teammates collaborate to draw water from the ocean in small cups, pass them up the line that runs up the side of a small cliff, and fill an entire bucket within a prescribed time limit. Only one person can draw water up from the ocean at a time, and only one person can empty their cup into the well at a time. Other than that, there are no guidelines, so teams try to rise to the challenge through trial and error. To complicate matters, many of the cups have holes in them and are either too small to transport water or too weak to hold it. The furious pace of their efforts sends cups and quarts and gallon-loads of otherwise perfectly salted ocean water into the breeze. The faster they go, the more water they lose. Hope becomes mist.

The Well reminds us of the folly of doing the same stuff over and over again when you are getting the same unsatisfactory results every time. It also reminds us that no matter how committed, no matter how skilled or passionate or optimistic, we still too often fall short of our own expectations. And that in those disappointing moments we cannot quit.

Puerto Nuevo attracts thousands of American tourists every year to their lobster restaurants. The food and the view and the margaritas are worth the drive — through lawless street traffic, third world poverty, and the promise of another larger-than-life hotel built for *gringos* by Donald Trump.

And at the end of a long day of planning and playing and preparing for the school year that will begin in just a few days…after simulation activities and deep reflection, we all sat down for lobster at Angel Del Mar Restaurant, overlooking the Pacific Ocean. We were 80 educators starting a new year. At one point, I looked at the youthful faces that lined the long table. Their energy and optimism released into the air like caged birds discovering a new window. They laughed, tossed back shots of Cuervo and danced to the mariachis. They shared summer stories. They shared their hopes and dreams.

And I felt that presence again.

"I wonder when our test results will come back," one teacher said. "I can't wait to see how we did."

"A toast…to a new school year! Imagine…90%!!!!"

And they cheered.

The next day we were back in the familiar air of Mueller Charter School. While our teachers busily met and planned and debriefed what they had learned from our off-site in Mexico, I received an e-mail saying that our test results for 2006 had just come in. I immediately went and retrieved our box of student scores from the district office…but I could not bring myself to look at them. Not there. Not just yet.

Opening these boxes of student test scores represent our moment of truth. Game 7 of the World Series. Two outs. Bottom of the ninth. "May I have the envelope please?"

I can't bring myself to just crack open the box and look at them. There has to be some ceremony—some spontaneous and weird integration of prayer and intellectual anticipation, and of course, my inclination toward superstition. As an athlete, I learned to control the variables I could control. Preparation and prayer covered most of them. The rest I managed by wearing the same baseball uniform every day until we lost. Or getting dressed at the exact same time and in the exact same sequence. Or carrying two and a half pieces of beef jerky and 19 sunflower seeds (my jersey number) in my back pocket until the end of the game. Or driving around the morning of a game until I saw exactly two stray barking dogs. Or sacrificing live chickens or chanting voodoo psalms. I swore by my superstitions. But you would never know it because I was convinced it was bad luck to tell somebody else about my superstitions.

Nevertheless, each year I improvise and ceremoniously open up our box of test scores.

One year I slowly unfolded them while sitting in the first pew at St. Rose of Lima Church where we had celebrated my father's funeral mass. That didn't work—we improved on the year before but failed to get 90% of our students to grade level. The next year I drove around the neighborhood looking at the homes from which our children come— then pulled over and took out all the test scores under a pepper tree. One year I tore them open on the freeway, hoping that if I drove fast enough and looked at them—kinda squinting out of the corner of one eye—perhaps the numbers would run together and create the outcome that we so desperately wanted for our kids. That one didn't produce our miracle either.

But this time, I was sure we were going to get it right.

In part because the fresh Baja air and Dos Equis were still steering me to the sea, I opened our boxes in a quiet park that overlooks San Diego Bay. As always, my heart pounded. I mumbled a disjointed prayer...like someone who was incredibly distracted by the contents of a cardboard box.

And then I opened the cardboard box.

I lifted out stacks of familiar reports. Fresh paper, cool to the touch. I organized them into a neat pile on my lap...separated by grade level. Stacked in sequence.

I searched quickly for the numbers that mattered most: *the percentage of children who scored at the **Proficient** or **Advanced** level.* These are the metrics that determine the percentage of students who had risen above the odds and performed at grade level. These numbers, typed by a computer on green-trimmed paper and sent from Sacramento to thousands of schools—justify a year's worth of work. High stakes.

I suddenly have the strangest feeling that the eyes of our teachers and our students and our parents are on me all at once now. The quiet drum roll.

"Did we make it? Did we get to grade level this year?"

In those final moments of adrenaline and anticipation, an extemporaneous prayer in faith gives way to one final appeal. Under breath I mumble:

Heavenly Father...please bless these results...

I finally find the displays that will soon appear in the San Diego Union Tribune and the Internet and a thousand different district-generated graphs and comparisons...

OK Lord—if we can't pull off the full 90% this year...I'll settle for 85%... or even 75%—that would be pretty remarkable, too. 65%! Come on God. We worked our asses off. You saw us. Our children deserve some sign that all of their effort is paying off. Just one big bump. Please. Give us...one...big...

...damn.

Another year. Another extraordinary effort on the part of our children and their teachers and parents. And yet another heartbreaking reminder that the excellence we so deeply desire for our students and ourselves is as elusive as Puerto Nuevo.

I have gotten skilled at quick calculations so I can estimate a net increase of 20 points on the API. A 20-point increase may be higher than a lot of other schools, but it is well below the 70-point gain we were shooting for. We didn't get to 801. Imagine. And though our 7th graders have outperformed the 7th graders in the entire high school district that they would have otherwise attended, there are too many other grade levels standing still.

Hope...becomes mist. Modest gains, troubling trends and yet another academic year in which we failed to get 90% of our students to grade level.

But we swore to *The Well* that we would not quit. And so we won't.

Epilogue

The dream was always running ahead of me. To catch up, to live for a moment in unison with it, that was the miracle.

—Anais Nin

GUACAMOLE

This morning I stood out on the playground just beyond my office door. It is week one of the 2007-08 school year. Our journey continues.

A line of third-graders has just filed past—each one "high-fiving" me, each one reaching out to me on their way by. I wonder if, as they grow older, they will remember me as I will remember them.

The last student in line turned to look at me before his class disappeared around the corner. His image is like a photograph now, downloaded, but perhaps not printed. His smile is angelic. His eyes reflect some sweet combination of faith and confidence. My name tumbles from his tongue with the unmistakable innocence of a child who is unafraid to experiment with the nuances of his new second language: "Hello Meester-Doctor Reeely!"

You have to feel that moment to know the deep and utter joy of this place. You build your relationships one child at a time. You capture their hearts in these unplanned and unexpected moments. And of course, they capture yours.

A school is transformed when it becomes—at some point—worthy of its children. There is no other more authentic measure. That is the miracle of Mueller Charter School.

I have a habit of going in and washing my hands after greeting these long lines of third-graders. They are little kids and you don't know where those hands have been. Sometimes I look down after so many high-fives and it looks like I have been holding a fistful of snails or guacamole.

"My Lord," I wonder. "Where the hell did *that* come from?"
Nectar of the Gods.
These are our babies. They are our hope. El futuro.
The lights of El Milagro.